BUSINESS OWNER'S
TOOLKIT
Total Know-How For Small Business

BUSINESS PLANS THAT WORK

FOR YOUR SMALL BUSINESS

Third Edition

A *Business Owner's Toolkit*™ Publication

from the editors of Toolkit Media Group

Wolters Kluwer

WITHDRAWN

Cover designed by Tim Kaage, Laurel Graphx, Inc.

Books may be purchased at quantity discounts for educational, business or sales promotion use. For more information please contact:

Toolkit Media Group
Wolters Kluwer
2700 Lake Cook Road
Riverwoods, Illinois 60015

ISBN 978-0-8080-1793-6

Printed in the United States of America

THE BUSINESS OWNER'S TOOLKIT TEAM

Troy Janisch, Publisher, Toolkit Media Group (*troy.janisch@wolterskluwer.com*) has more than 20 years of experience as a journalist, journalism instructor and entrepreneur. Troy holds a master's degree from the University of Wisconsin-Madison School of Journalism and Mass Communications and a BS in journalism from the University of Wisconsin-Oshkosh.

John L. Duoba, Managing Editor, Toolkit Media Group (*john.duoba@wolterskluwer.com*) has more than 20 years of small business experience in book, magazine and web publishing, fulfilling various roles in editorial and production management. John holds a degree from Northwestern University's Medill School of Journalism and is currently pursuing his Master's in Business Administration.

Joel Handelsman (*joel.handelsman@wolterskluwer.com*) has almost 25 years of experience writing about business, tax, and financial topics. He has been involved in multiple new product and business ventures in the publishing industry, and has held a variety of management positions. Joel holds degrees from Northwestern University's Medill School of Journalism and DePaul University College of Law.

Alice H. Magos (*alice.magos@wolterskluwer.com*) has over 35 years of experience running the operations of numerous small businesses. She is the author of the *Business Owner's Toolkit*™ online advice column "Ask Alice." Alice is a popular instructor at small business seminars on accounting, financial planning, and using the Internet; is an accountant, a Certified Financial Planner and a Certified Fraud Examiner; and holds degrees from Washington University in St. Louis and Northwestern University.

Catherine Gordon (*catherine.gordon@wolterskluwer.com*) has over 15 years of experience in the tax, business, and financial publishing field and has worked as a tax consultant providing services to individuals as well as large and small companies. Catherine holds a juris doctorate degree from the State University of New York at Buffalo School of Law and a BA in sociology from the State University of New York at Stony Brook.

FOREWORD

There are dozens of articles and books being written about business plans today. Many provide very good, thorough advice about the process of writing a planning document and, incidentally, how to run your business effectively.

Yet knowing what a real business plan looks like is *exactly* the information that you need most, in order to write your first plan. In fact, what you really need to see are different types of plans for different types of businesses and their business owners – plans that have helped the owner obtain needed financing, get a new business started, or embark on an expansion or change in direction. We have included samples of these situations.

Business Plans that Work for Small Business, third edition, will help you understand the elements that must be included in a planning document, and the information you need to gather to create your own plan. You'll see that creating a business plan need not be difficult, and the time you spend planning will save you many, many hours of time you'd otherwise spend dealing with major problems in the future.

Why should you turn to us? Wolters Kluwer is a leading provider of information and software to the business and professional community. More than four generations of business advisors have trusted our products, and now you can too.

A caution and an invitation—the discussions and plans contained in this book are current as of the date of publication. But remember, things change. To keep abreast of the latest news affecting your business, visit *Business Owner's Toolkit* on the Internet (www.toolkit.com).

While you're there, take a look at the other interactive information and tools we offer to assist you in running your business. You can also ask follow-up questions of our team of small business experts. We welcome and look forward to your questions and comments.

Troy Janisch

Publisher, Toolkit Media Group

Table of Contents

Table of Contents

Creating A Business Plan That Works

Coming up with a great idea for a new business, or for a way to turn around or expand an existing business, can be a tremendous challenge in itself. While there's never a shortage of raw ideas, finding one that's solid enough to support a successful company for an extended period of time takes a great deal of investigation and research, good judgment, timing, and even luck.

But coming up with a great idea, difficult as it may be, is not enough. Countless businesses have started out well, sailed through the first few months or even years, and then foundered as soon as the first real problems cropped up.

How can you make sure this won't happen to you? You can't, of course. But you can greatly improve your chances by taking the time to thoroughly research your business idea before plunging into it. Then you can take the most important step: using what you've learned to create a detailed plan that plots out your objectives, your marketing strategy, operations procedures, and the right combination of expertise, equipment, location, and sheer capital that will be required to convert your ideas into reality.

Creating a business plan need not be difficult. However, it does require a step-by-step approach, and a willingness to persist in digging for information and thinking through all the essential factors that will contribute to your operation. You'll find that the time you spend creating your plan will be some of the most valuable hours in your entrepreneurial career. By creating a business plan, you'll know exactly what pieces must come together at the right time, place, and amount to make your project a success. What's more, you'll be able to explain your idea to others whom you must convince to write a loan, invest in your business, or join you as a partner or co-owner.

While the planning document itself can be important, particularly if you're going to use it to obtain necessary capital, the planning process is even more important. It's during the process of creating the plan that you round out your knowledge base by gathering information, consider numerous alternatives, and make dozens, if not hundreds, of decisions about how to proceed.

Where available, you can and should enlist the help of others (e.g., your accountant, lawyer, consultant, or even a professional business plan developer) to help you pull together the physical document. A review of the financial section by an accountant can be particularly helpful. But *you* must ultimately do the essential thinking and decisionmaking yourself. Your plan must reflect your own individual strengths, personality, and intentions for your business, and no one knows them as well as you.

In Part I, we'll describe the process of creating a plan, and the important elements you need to include in the formal document. We'll also describe some ways that you can use your plan in the future to manage your business more effectively.

Chapter 1: Preparing to Put Your Plan Together shows how to shape your plan to match your reason for creating it, and the audience to whom your plan is directed.

Chapter 2: Format and Introductory Elements presents an overview of your written plan, discusses format and presentation issues, and describes the executive summary, table of contents, and appendix portions of the plan.

Chapter 3: The Company Summary discusses the parts of your plan that will describe the ownership, mission, objectives, and keys to success of your company. Where appropriate, it may include descriptions of your facilities and your company history.

Chapter 4: Market Analysis explains the portions of your plan that describe your industry, your target market, and your competition. We suggest you include a Strengths, Weaknesses, Opportunities, and Threats (SWOT) Analysis and a Needs Analysis.

Chapter 5: Product or Service Description discusses the part of your plan that provides a detailed description of what your company's offerings are or will be.

Chapter 6: Marketing and Sales Plans explains how to present your marketing strategy and plans for implementing that strategy.

Chapter 7: Operations and Management Plans discusses the portions of the plan that address your management team and employees, important processes, and other operations issues that are important to your business.

Chapter 8: Financial Plans, discusses the financial statements that must be included, as well as the assumptions and projections you must make in order to complete them.

Chapter 9: Using the Completed Plan explains how a business plan can become an important tool for keeping your business on track, long after the plan is completed.

Chapter 1

Preparing To Put Your Plan Together

Before you sit down to write your business plan, it's important to think about your reasons for doing it, and what you hope to get out of the process and the plan itself.

Remember that no two business plans will look alike. There are a number of key considerations that will play an important role in shaping the scope and contents of your particular plan. What's more, your plan should reflect your personality and your management style. You'll want the readers to feel as if they know you, and have a good handle on what your business is all about.

Work Smart

Try to avoid the cookie-cutter template effect that you can get by using some business planning software. Software can be a tremendous time-saver, certainly, but some business owners are tempted to just "fill in the blanks" without attempting to consider whether another organization or style might be more appropriate for their business.

This can be a serious error if you're applying for a loan, and your banker has read dozens of plans using the same software (and boilerplate language) already. Resist the temptation — make sure that your plan expresses your creativity and individuality.

Obviously, your business's position in its life cycle will have a significant impact on the type of planning that's needed. A startup may need extensive planning of all its aspects, while an ongoing business might require a plan that relates primarily to a new market that it wants to enter, or a new product that it wants to introduce.

The most important consideration will be the uses to which you expect to put your plan, and the audience who will read it. Will people outside the business see your plan? Will you be seeking outside financing, and if so, from whom? The type of lender or investor you're pursuing will dictate the type of information and details you need to include. On the other hand, if the plan is to be used primarily as a management tool for yourself and/or other owners or key employees, you can be more flexible about the length and contents of the plan.

A Plan for an Outside Audience

Just as a person seeking a job prepares a resume that outlines qualifications, experience, and other relevant information, a business that is seeking debt financing or an infusion of capital from an outside investor will benefit from having a "resume" of its own.

You can think of your business plan as a rather lengthy resume. To the extent that it reflects the reasonable plans of a good manager, it gives your audience a positive image of what your business is and what it can be expected to do.

For Lenders and Investors

Starting a new business, or expanding an existing one, may require more money than you can get together on your own. This means turning to an outside source for financing. While you might consider taking on a partner or finding an investor, you also might go to a bank to apply for a loan.

If you're just starting out, you obviously won't have a history of profitable operations to indicate that you can function successfully enough to make all your loan payments. In the past, this lack of a history made most banks extremely hesitant to lend money to new, unproven businesses. However, there are indications that bankers are becoming somewhat more open to financing startup operations.

Nevertheless, with the majority of conventional lenders, a workable business plan is essential to getting startup financing. It is one of the first things that a potential lender will want to examine (along with a list of your *personal* assets).

If you've been in business for a while and you need financing to expand or introduce a new product or service, your lender might not require you to submit a full-fledged business plan. However, a solid plan that illustrates a successful track record can provide strong support for your loan request, and should increase your chances of getting the amount and type of loan you want.

Venture capitalists, prospective partners or shareholders, and even relatives who might loan money or invest in your business will want some assurances that they have used their money wisely. A business plan demonstrates how their money will be used and what they, and the business, can expect in return.

Finally, if you expect an ongoing need for funding, showing that the business is meeting or exceeding planned goals can help you build a history that might let you borrow under more desirable rates and conditions in the future.

For Prospective Employees

In some cases, portions of a business plan can serve to introduce prospective employees to your business. Particularly if you intend to hire long-term or high-level employees, you'll want to present a fair picture of what your business is and what types of work need to be performed. You can also establish expectations regarding income and growth opportunities based on the plan's projections.

Shaping the Plan for an External Audience

If you are writing a plan primarily to be shown to an external audience, you'll want to pay close attention to the established conventions of business plan documents. There are certain elements and types of information that your lender or potential investors will expect to see, and it doesn't pay to disappoint them. Similarly, a business plan is expected to have a "professional" appearance, which means that it must look somewhat like every other business plan.

For any outside lender or investor, the executive summary is the most important part of your plan. Venture capitalists, in particular, typically receive hundreds of plans and don't have time to read them all cover to cover. If your summary doesn't capture their attention, they won't go any farther.

A plan destined to be shown to a banker must include a financing proposal or statement that succinctly describes the type of loan(s) you are seeking, the purposes to which the funds will be put, and how you will pay the money back. In the lender's view, this is the most important part of the plan, so place it up front, in the executive summary or immediately afterward.

Any plan for an outside investor will have to emphasize the financial side of your business. The section that includes your financial statements is often the second section a banker will turn to, so make sure that it is complete, accurate, and reasonable in its assumptions.

Venture capitalists and outside investors will want all the financial information that a banker would need, plus a good deal of marketing, operational, and personnel information. These types of investors view themselves as owners, so they tend to want a lot of detail. They also need to get a strong sense of your vision, experience, and commitment to the company.

Venture capitalists tend to be short-term investors, and it's important that you include an exit plan if you are seeking VC backing. You'll need to show that you have a workable plan for cashing out the investor, generally by selling stock to the public or by selling the business to a larger company. There may be some other options, depending on the particular investor, but you should at least consider the possibility that your own involvement in the company's management will be greatly reduced within the foreseeable future.

However, with any plan for an outside audience, keep the reader's attention span in mind. If the plan is too short, it won't provide all the answers that the reader is looking for; if it is too long, the reader may give up before coming to the conclusion. Somewhere around 20 to 30 pages should be the right length for most small businesses.

THE BUSINESS PLAN AS A MANAGEMENT TOOL

An extremely important, but too-often overlooked, reason for creating a business plan is to help you manage vital business activities better.

If you're just starting out in business, the time it takes to create your first plan will be more than repaid by the insight you gain. If you're in business already but have never created a business plan, you'll be in a much better position to assess opportunities and risks that accompany the various changes you may be considering.

You should consider creating a business plan if:

- You want to open a new business.

- Your business has grown significantly since you last did any significant planning.

- You want to introduce a new product.

- You want to enter a new market.

- You want to acquire a new business or a franchise.

A Business Plan for a New Business

For most entrepreneurs, it's only when you take the time to create a written document that embodies your thoughts that you realize the scope and magnitude of what's involved in running a business. In your head, you've concentrated on the idea. In your plan, you can examine the nuts and bolts of running a business to exploit your idea.

Since you're considering a wholly new business, a big part of the planning process is going to involve developing an initial set of assumptions. You'll have to make assumptions regarding costs, labor, the number of potential customers, pricing, and many other factors.

Your business plan will also identify the essential events that must occur and actions that must be taken, and set forth a clear timetable for accomplishing them. You may want to show these important activities in a chart.

Perhaps the most important component of the business plan is your marketing plan, which identifies your target audience and explains how you will position your product or service to reach that audience. Your specific advertising and promotional activities will be linked to sales targets. Your operational plans will explain how your business will conduct its day-to-day activities. The timing of these activities in relation to marketing plans is crucial; for example, there is little point in running ads for a product that isn't available for sale.

A good business plan also includes a substantial amount of detail regarding cash flow projections that set forth the projected timing of revenues and expenses. These projections help establish whether and how the business will meet its obligations to vendors and others who provide the business with goods or services. Most of these projections are tied directly to planned operational results. For example, the sales projected to occur in one month are supposed to generate the income necessary to pay expenses that are due the following month.

Work Smart

If you work hard to create a business plan and your plan demonstrates that you can't profitably exploit your idea without making some pretty wild assumptions, you haven't lost anything. To the contrary, you've saved yourself the time, money, and heartache you would have expended on a hopeless cause. It is far better to realistically appraise your chance for success before you commit your time and money to a new enterprise.

In a well-crafted plan, the overall rhythm of the business will be realistically reflected. If some portion of the business is cyclical, as is often the case, the cycle will be identified and accounted for. For example, many retail outlets rely on the Thanksgiving-to-Christmas period for a substantial part of their annual sales volume. This cycle is reflected in the plan by, for example, increasing inventory as November approaches, planning for the addition of temporary workers to handle the expanded sales volume, and clumping expense payments directly following the busy season when cash is most available.

Business Expansion

If your business experiences gradual growth, at some point that expansion alone will make it worth your while to create a plan to explore the opportunities that growth might provide. For example, a production-based business might be able to acquire additional or better production equipment because the volume of business has reached a level that justifies the expense. Or, it might be time for a retail establishment to consider the costs, benefits, and risks of opening a second business location.

Planning for growth also can reveal some of the disadvantages of getting bigger. For example, as your sales volume increases, your need for working capital may increase correspondingly. Careful planning can help you to become aware of the magnitude of your future cash needs, and make arrangements to meet them. As another example, as your business expands you may need to hire more employees, or train your existing employees for expanded duties. By thinking through your needs ahead of time, you'll be able to make better hiring decisions.

Ideally, before launching a new product, moving into a new market, or developing a new distribution channel, you would revisit your existing business plan and integrate the new product or project into the overall plan. As an alternative, you might create a plan that is limited in scope to the impact that the change will have on your existing operations.

Acquisitions and Franchise Opportunities

If you're considering the purchase of an existing business, how do you know how much to pay? Will the business provide you with the income you need three years down the road? While there's no substitute for a thorough investigation, a business plan can be a useful tool to help you assess whether you should buy a business or let the opportunity go by. In fact, many sellers will create a selling memorandum, which is really a business plan in reverse, to fully acquaint prospective buyers with their business and convince them that the opportunity is a good one. You can use this as a starting point for creating your own plan for the future.

Similarly, deciding whether to purchase a franchise is a serious issue. By becoming a franchisee, you agree to conform to a wide variety of very specific requirements. A business plan provides the framework for considering whether the benefits of holding a franchise outweigh the associated costs and restrictions. The plan is the perfect tool for modeling how your business will perform as a member of the franchise. If you're already operating as an unaffiliated business, you can compare your current operations to the costs and opportunities presented by joining the franchisor.

Managing an Existing Business

Obviously, no one likes to take big risks to obtain a small return. A business plan can be used as a modeling tool to look at a variety of scenarios.

Suppose you decide to drop your prices, which generally means that you'll accept a somewhat lower gross margin in exchange for greater sales volume. How much will sales increase? Will you have enough production capacity? Will you need additional help, or storage space? Can your suppliers provide the raw materials you need? Will lower prices fit your mission and image? Answers to these questions are more readily available if your business plan is used as a baseline, so you can see what happens as you change some of the variables.

Tracking Your Progress

It probably comes as no surprise to you that, until recently, even some very large companies used a "cigar box" approach to tracking business results. That is, every dollar that comes in to the business goes *into* the cigar box. All the expenses are paid *from* the cigar box. As long as the box isn't empty and there's adequate money left over for the business owner, everything is just fine.

But there are better ways to stay on top of how your business is doing. A business plan can provide the foundation for a tracking system that lets you evaluate your business's progress. This tracking function gives you, as the business owner, real-time feedback regarding operations. Deviations between actual and planned results provide clues that you can use to tweak or fine-tune certain elements of the plan.

Shaping the Plan for an Internal Audience

If your primary reason for business planning is to use the planning process and the document itself as management tools, you can be quite flexible about the length, scope, and style of your plan.

While you'll want to include all the elements that are customarily found in a plan for an outside audience, you may choose to emphasize certain areas where you feel your business is weak. You may also decide to create a longer plan that provides more detail in terms of the specific tasks you want to undertake during the year. For example, you may want to use your cash-flow statement as the basis for a more detailed budget that you'll attempt to adhere to during the year.

You may also want to do more thinking about various contingencies that may occur during the year, and create a plan to deal with the most likely scenarios. For example, you may want to consider what you'll do if a major new competitor enters your market, if a key supplier goes out of business, or if a natural disaster forces you to close down for a while. The time to unearth all the potential pitfalls is in the planning stage, not later on when unexpected events tend to be unfavorable and costly.

There may be others within the business with whom you will share the business plan, or substantial pieces of it. Clearly, if you have partners, co-owners, or a Board of Directors, those individuals should see the plan after its completion. They may also be able to provide you with significant input into the plan as it's being developed.

If you have employees, many of the goals that you set for them will be derived from the plan. For example, your sales projections might translate directly into the level of sales your representatives must achieve. In general, your people will be able to do a better job if they see exactly where they fit in with your business objectives.

Example

Let's say that your business plan provides a detailed strategy for achieving a 50 percent increase in sales over the next 12 months. It would be a good idea to share the strategic analysis and your mission statement with your sales people. Your sales force will have a much better idea of what is expected of them, and they'll have a solid understanding of where they fit within your organization.

Obviously, there may be parts of the plan that you won't want to share with your employees. This is particularly true of portions that might reveal more than you want them to know about your personal finances. Similarly, you may not choose to share information regarding how the business finances its operations.

You'll have to use your judgment regarding the type and amount of detail that will be relevant to each of your employees. In many cases, you may want to share with them only your executive summary and the top-line goals for the year. In other cases, greater detail will be necessary and helpful in motivating key employees to "get with the plan."

HOW FAR OUT CAN YOU PLAN?

When you hear an extended weather report, you know that the predictions for today and tonight are more likely to be accurate than the five-day forecast. Similarly, many of the variables that can affect businesses in general or your business in particular aren't easily predicted. The value of the dollar compared to foreign currencies, interest rates, and many other factors that can affect a business's profitability change constantly. There are no guarantees. So how far out do you plan?

The answer is: *it depends*. For example, there were no doubt dozens of aspiring entrepreneurs in Salt Lake who figured out a way to profit from the Olympic Games held there in 2002. Some of these businesses came into being and shut down in less than a year, as one-time opportunities.

On the other hand, some businesses may spend months or years in a product development stage before any sales activities begin. A software business may expend tremendous amounts of money and time developing a product, with the expectation that the product will be sold, and upgraded, for a number of years to come. Obviously, the planning horizon for the software business would be far longer than a business designed around the Olympics.

As a general rule, for an "average" business, a three-year plan is a reasonable starting point. But that doesn't mean that you need to map out, month-by-month, or week-by-week, what is going to happen over the next 36 months. The level of detail will drop as your plan covers periods further into the future. The cash flows that are tracked monthly during the first year of operation may be projected by quarter or by year for the second and third years. Just how this transition from detail to the big picture is managed will depend on your specific situation.

Example

If your goal is to obtain a five-year term loan, you may want to project your plan out for five years to better convince your banker that the loan will be paid off on time.

Predicting your sales, costs of goods, or what the prevailing wage rates will be one, two or five years down the road is no easy matter. Obviously, the assumptions relating to the very near future are more likely to be accurate than those relating to periods further out. For example, if interest rates have held reasonably steady for the past year or so, assuming that the interest rate on a variable-rate loan won't increase by more than a point in the next six months is a fairly safe bet. But you would be much less certain where the rates might be in 12 or 24 months.

PLANNING FOR YOUR TYPE OF BUSINESS

Very few businesses deal exclusively in the provision of goods *or* in the performance of services. For planning purposes, however, it is useful to consider whether your business is primarily a service provider, a seller of goods, or both. Issues that might be extremely important to a product-based business, such as inventory, can have vastly less significance for a service provider.

Service Businesses

One of the first things the owner of a service business must consider will be the question of who, exactly, who will be providing the services that your business sells? Will you be the sole provider, or will you need to recruit other employees or independent contractors to serve your customers?

If someone other than yourself will be providing the services, you'll need to build in some procedures to ensure that the quality is up to your standards. This may involve screening prospective employees very carefully, providing special training to workers, and following up to check on their work.

Many personal service businesses require the owner to spend substantial time doing presentations, preparing bids or estimates, or doing other sales-related activities to acquire future business. To the extent that your time must be spent on sales activities, you can't devote time to actually providing the services. If performing services is what you do best (or even, what you *like* to do best), you may need to plan to hire a manager, or at least an administrative assistant, at some point down the road.

Another issue service providers face relates to billing and collections policies. When goods are sold, there is a clear event that triggers the need for payment. For some service providers, the event that should trigger payment might not be so clear. For example, a contractor may feel that payment should be made when he or she informs the homeowner that the job is complete. The homeowner, however, may feel that he or she has a right to have the work inspected before tendering payment.

One way to reduce the possibility of this type of problem is to include clauses in all your contracts for larger jobs stating that customers must make progress payments of a specific percentage of the total price as a job proceeds. Another is to establish credit terms and consider offering a discount to customers who pay earlier than required. Ultimately, you must plan your cash flow requirements realistically, allowing for the possibility that a certain portion of what you are owed might not be immediately forthcoming.

Product-Based Businesses

Retailers, wholesalers, and manufacturers can all be considered product-based businesses. In each case, the business plan will have to include some type of inventory planning. Even if you intend to carry little inventory but order it from suppliers as you make a sale, you'll need to state that fact in your business plan. In some cases, you'll have a lot of money tied up in inventory, and your financing needs may be more extensive.

Your needs for employees may also be an important issue that needs to be addressed in your business plan. Will you use part-timers or full-timers? How will you recruit and retain these workers? What pay and benefits will you need to offer, and what raises should you budget within the time frame that your plan will cover?

Businesses engaged in manufacturing typically need a good deal of equipment in order to operate. Leasing or buying, maintaining, repairing, and insuring your equipment must all be part of your plan. You'll also need to plan for the eventual replacement of obsolete equipment. Similarly, retailers and, to a lesser extent wholesalers, must plan for the shelving, counters, lighting, and other fixtures and decorating their particular business will need.

Since a retailer's business can sink or swim based on its location, a business plan for a retailer must place some importance on this issue. Your plan should explain what a "good" location means in your industry, and how the location you've chosen fits the bill.

Mixed Goods and Services

A business that provides its customers with both goods and services will probably have a somewhat more complicated business plan than a business that primarily provides either goods or services. There are many logistical considerations relating to managing the interaction between the delivery of goods and the performance of services.

Example

 Take the case of a restaurant, where customers expect to receive good food and to be served by an attentive wait staff. Everything has to come together for each customer in order to meet his or her expectations. This is no mean feat for the business owner.

Probably everyone has experienced an "almost good" meal, where one small aspect of the meal didn't go quite right. Perhaps the food was excellent but too long in coming, or maybe you had to ask for the check three times before you finally got it. Whatever the reason, it is clear that people expect both the product and the service to meet their standards. If either fails, customer satisfaction will suffer.

The financial aspects of a mixed goods and services business require careful scrutiny. The relative mix between goods and services must be managed to maintain a reasonable return on the entire enterprise. Pricing is more of an issue because you are trying to cover the wide variety of components that make up the entire package. The business planning process affords you with an opportunity to examine this and other relationships that can impact on the profitability of your business.

Chapter 2

Format and Introductory Elements

After you've considered the purpose of your plan and done some background preparation, it's time to consider the actual elements that you'll include in the written document, and the format your plan will take.

A business plan customarily has a number of major elements or sections. Each of these elements serves a particular purpose in the overall presentation of your plan. The following list identifies and briefly describes each of the documents or document categories that will make up your plan.

Components of a Written Business Plan

Cover page: *This page identifies you and your business, and dates the plan.*

Table of contents: *This element makes it easy for readers to find and examine particular documents.*

Executive summary: *This is arguably the most important single part of your document. It provides a high-level overview of the entire plan that emphasizes the factors that you believe will lead to success.*

Company summary: *This section provides company-specific information, describing the business organization, ownership, mission, objectives, and history. If location is important in your business, you can include a description of your business facilities here.*

Market analysis: *This section or sections presents an analysis of the industry, target market, and competition that the business faces.*

Product or service description: *This section describes exactly what your company will offer its customers.*

Marketing and sales plans: *These sections set forth the marketing strategy that the business will follow, and provide details of your marketing activities to support sales.*

Operations and management plans: *Depending on your type of business, your operations and management plans may include production and inventory plans, customer service and order fulfillment plans, facilities and equipment plans, management and personnel plans, expansion plans, and any other pertinent issues.*

Financial plans: *This section includes your projections (and historical financial information, if you have it) that demonstrate how the business can be expected to do financially if the business plan's assumptions are sound.*

Appendix: *This is the place to present supporting documents, statistical analysis, product marketing materials, resumes of key employees, etc.*

This is one way to present the items in the plan. But don't feel constrained to follow this exact format if another way makes more sense because of the nature of your business.

Work Smart

Remember that there is no requirement that these items be created in the order shown. In fact, conventional wisdom has it that the executive summary, which is preceded only by the cover sheet and table of contents, should be prepared after the rest of the plan is complete.

The relative mix of product and services to be offered will affect the content of a plan. For example, a business that relies on the services of many professional employees would provide substantial details about acquiring and retaining these vital workers. Issues relating to suppliers, production, inventory, etc., become more significant as the product/service mix moves toward a purely product-based business.

In any event, it pays to at least mention all the major issues discussed here, even the ones that are relatively less significant to your particular business. This is particularly true if you're developing a plan with the object of obtaining financing. Someone who's reading your plan will be more confident about your assessment of the situation if you identify such issues and resolve them, however quickly.

Example

If you plan to work alone and perform all services personally, you might note that you don't anticipate a need to hire employees or engage independent contractors if the business succeeds at the levels projected in the plan. You don't want to raise any questions in the mind of your audience that aren't resolved somewhere within the plan document.

FORMAT AND PRESENTATION ISSUES

First of all, remember that the business plan is a clearly recognizable type of document, and your audience will have some expectations with respect to style and contents. Just as your teachers in school expected you to conform to certain standards, the people who will look at your business plan will have certain expectations.

You want your plan to look professional and be a useful tool. There are a number of things you can do to ensure that is the case:

- Print the plan on a high-quality white or cream colored paper. Print on one side of the paper only.

- Incorporate a cover page that includes your logo, company motto, or other identifying information or graphic. Be sure to include an address and phone number for the business and to name the person who should be contacted about the plan.

- Use a typeface that is easy to read, and a font size that is large enough to prevent eyestrain. This may require financial projections to be spread over several pages in order to maintain readability.

- Maintain reasonable borders for your pages. Allowing one inch of white space all around is a good rule of thumb.

- If those in your business use specialized language or acronyms, use them sparingly and be sure to define any terms that someone outside your area of expertise wouldn't readily know.

- Number the pages, and be sure that the page numbers are accurately reflected in the table of contents.

- Keep the plan short and concise: 20 to 30 pages should be sufficient for most small businesses. You can always provide additional details in an appendix, if required.

- Be certain to carefully edit the document. Spelling and grammatical errors do not make a good impression.

- Don't go overboard on expensive binders, paper, printing, etc. Elevating the form of the plan over its substance can raise doubts among those reading the plan. If the plan is for an outside audience, a simple plastic spiral binding will allow your plan to lie flat while opened, without adding too much to the weight and bulk of the plan. If the plan is for internal use, you may want to use a three-ring binder so that you can insert additional materials as needed.

THE COVER PAGE

If you have spent any time and effort at all on a company logo, slogan, or other identifying graphic or text, the cover page is the place to highlight it.

If you haven't considered these basic marketing tools, we strongly suggest that you do so. Building an identity is vital if you want people to recognize and remember your business.

In addition, the cover sheet contains all the usual and appropriate identification information about the business. This includes business address, telephone numbers, facsimile numbers, etc.

The cover sheet should state the date that the plan was prepared. It should identify the person to contact regarding any questions about the plan (generally, you). If you have prepared multiple copies of your business plan, you might also put a copy number on the cover page to help you ensure that none go astray.

THE TABLE OF CONTENTS

The table of contents should clearly and simply lead a reader to each of the documents in the plan. Be sure that page numbers are accurately reflected. If the plan is long, consider dividing it up into subsections, if that will make it easier for readers to find specific documents. For shorter plans, just numbering the pages in sequence is fine.

If your table of contents is more than two pages long, reconsider the length of the section headings, the length of your plan, and the number of documents you've included.

THE EXECUTIVE SUMMARY

The executive summary is one of the most important sections of the business plan. Its purpose is to summarize the highlights of the plan and to provide a brief snapshot of the business. It must be concise, specific, and well-written.

The summary emphasizes those factors that will make the business a success. It must give the reader a fix on the size and type of company for which the plan is written, its management, and the types of products or services it offers. It should briefly present some basic information about the industry, the size of the target market, and company financial goals in terms of revenue and profits, and indicate any funding required.

For new businesses or businesses seeking funding, credibility and excitement are key elements of the executive summary. Venture capitalists receive hundreds of plans each month, and just a few are actually read from cover to cover. A quick 20-second scan of the executive summary is often the basis for determining whether the plan will be read and whether your company may be considered for investment. When the plan is the vehicle used to attract financing or investment, the executive summary should make it clear to the reader who is a potential source of funds why the company is a sound investment.

If your business plan is designed to help you get a loan, the executive summary should include some information on the amount and purpose of the funds you are seeking, and indicate how you intend to pay the money back. The more specific you can be about the type(s) of loan you are seeking (e.g., a term loan, a working capital line of credit, a mortgage on real estate), the more you will favorably impress the lender. Some business owners choose to highlight this information by placing it in a separate subsection, entitled "Financing Proposal" or something similar.

THE APPENDIX

The appendix is the repository for those items that aren't part of the plan itself but that are helpful or persuasive to someone reading the plan. While it will appear at the very end of your plan, we mention it here to remind you that you can add to it as you develop each section of your plan.

Your plan document is intended to present a concise summary of your business; in the process of creating it, you'll uncover a lot of interesting information that won't actually be included in the plan itself. If you think it is likely that a reader will seek further information regarding some portion of your plan, you can include the appropriate supporting material in the appendix.

The appendix may also house sample marketing materials such as brochures, ads, sales scripts, letters of reference from customers, and good product reviews. If you are just starting out, consider including resumes of key employees if you are relying on their skill and experience. Consider material for inclusion only if you believe that it adds to or clarifies the rest of the plan.

Chapter 3

The Company Summary

The company summary section of your business plan generally consists of four to six subsections that, when considered together, present information that gives a general overview of the nature, structure, and goals of your business.

For many businesses, the information that needs to be presented is your company's ownership and organization structure, a mission statement, and a list of your business objectives. Depending on your business, you may need to include a description of your location and facilities, your company's history, and/or startup information. For all businesses, we recommend that you include a listing of what you perceive to be the keys to your business's success. This will help you to prioritize your goals and your activities throughout the year.

Note that startup businesses face a special challenge when drafting the company summary. In the absence of an existing operation, the background will be couched in terms of what the business *will do*, not what it has done. This makes it even more important to have a clear picture in mind as to how your business will look and operate once it's up and running. When you have a track record, it's easy to point at the results you've achieved as an indication of your potential for success. Without any history, you'll have to work a little harder to make sure that you've developed, and presented, a realistic idea of what it will take to make your business work.

COMPANY OWNERSHIP

The company ownership portion of the plan provides information that describes the form of organization of your business — that is, whether it is a sole proprietorship, partnership, corporation, or limited liability company.

For a sole proprietorship, a simple one-line statement to that effect may be all you need. If the business has more than one owner, this subsection should list the owners and the percentage or number of shares that they own. If the owners are active in the business, you may want to briefly describe their role, although you should also include a lengthier description of each principal's responsibilities in the "management and employees" section of the plan.

If the structure of your business has changed over the years, you may want to include that information and a brief statement as to why you decided to make the change. For example, you might say that "in 2007 the business was incorporated to facilitate succession planning for the owner."

THE MISSION STATEMENT

A company mission statement can be a powerful force to clearly define your company's purpose for existence, and to determine the direction that all future activity should take.

Your mission statement will not necessarily describe what your business provides to customers, right now, but rather expresses your vision for the company. It should focus on the future and present an expansive view of what your company is all about.

The most successful company missions are measurable, definable, and actionable project statements, with emotional appeal, that everyone involved with the company knows and can act upon. For an example from corporate America, a mission to "to organize the world's information and make it universally accessible and useful" for Google sounds good. But a simple mission statement from Walt Disney — "To make people happy" — is better because it's a project statement that can be measured every day by every employee.

Case Study — Creating a Company Mission Statement

As an example of how a company mission statement can serve as a focus for improvement in your business's performance, consider the case of Fred's Grocery, a small one-store business, which suffered sales declines when a large chain supermarket opened in the neighborhood.

Fred initially considered lowering prices and adding many new items to compete, at great expense and lower margins. However, a family discussion about the "mission" of Fred's Grocery caused Fred to respond in a less direct, less costly, and less risky manner.

Fred and his family realized that their mission was to serve the convenience needs of local, upscale neighborhood shoppers for specialty items and "fill-in" grocery items that they needed.

The majority of Fred's shoppers spent an average of only $40 per visit, considerably less than at the larger chain store. Fred and his family decided they would offer more services and specialty items than the larger chain store. Their array of specialty goods, prices, and services also separated them from convenience store chains like 7-Eleven.

Fred's carried all groceries to the shoppers' cars and apartments and delivered gift baskets/flowers, at no extra charge within a five-block radius of the store. They also added specialty items to their store, putting in an espresso coffee bar, wine kiosk, and food/flower gift assortments. They upgraded and limited the amount of fruits and fresh vegetable selections and added fresh, warm breads and cookies.

After one year, Fred's Grocery realized its best year ever and increased both shopper traffic and average sale by 100 percent to an average of over $80 per shopper. Fred felt the new chain store was the best thing that ever happened to his business, thanks to the time he took to discuss and refine his mission statement!

YOUR COMPANY OBJECTIVES

The statement of objectives in your business plan is basically your short list of goals for the year, or for the time period covered by the plan. In order to be meaningful, an objective should meet three standards.

First, it must be *specific*, not vague or general. For instance, "grow the business" is vague, while "increase sales" is specific. Second, the objective must be *quantified*. As an example, "increase sales significantly" is not quantified, while "increase sales by 10 percent" is quantified. Finally, an objective must be *time-limited*. "Increase sales by 10 percent in record time" is not time-limited, but "increase sales by 10 percent in 2004 over 2003" is time-limited, and meets all three of the standards.

Most business owners find it helpful to set a number of annual financial goals. For example, you may set goals of hitting a certain volume of sales in dollars or units, maintaining a certain percentage of gross margin, achieving a certain inventory turnover rate, or increasing your market share to a certain percentage. For a startup business, one of your goals may simply be to become profitable within a certain number of months (or years) after you open for business.

You may also have some non-financial goals, such as opening a new location, establishing a training program for employees, reducing customer complaints to a certain number per month, introducing a certain number of new products, or modifying your customer base (for example, transforming a 50/50 split between retail and wholesale, to a 35/65 split in favor of wholesale).

It's important to keep your goals realistic and limited in number. If outsiders are reading your plan, they will generally expect to see at least three financial goals, and they will expect you to set goals that are reasonably achievable.

But even if you are writing a plan that no one but yourself will see, your goals should be set high enough to motivate you into action, but not so high that you'll give up in disgust after three or four months.

Work Smart

One of the most difficult parts of running a small business can be prioritizing your time. Particularly if you're just starting out, it can be tempting to get caught up in the thousands of details that go into the business's operation, and to feel overwhelmed by all the decisions you need to make. It can be extremely helpful to keep your goals in sight at all time, to remind yourself of what's really important, and to stay focused on relentlessly pursuing those tasks that will help you reach your goals.

KEYS TO SUCCESS

While not absolutely essential to every plan, we believe that an effective business plan should list, early on, the most important of the actions that you must take to reach your goals.

Identifying these key activities can itself be an art, not a science, and the keys to success portion of your plan will illustrate your style as a manager as much as it will tell the reader about your business. You may find it useful to hold off on writing the keys to success until you have completed the rest of your plan. When you know how all the pieces of the plan fit together, you can identify those tasks that are most crucial.

One important point: your keys to success should be things that you can control.

Example

As a very simple example, a snow removal company may know that it will have more work if there is a heavier than normal amount of snowfall this year, but there's obviously nothing the business owner can do to control the weather! There's little point in listing, as a key to success, "snow on at least 40 days this winter."

In this instance, the key to success might be to increase the percentage of sales made to customers who are willing to pay a monthly charge for snow removal, regardless of the number of times that the plowing must actually be done. That way, the uncontrollable but important factor can be effectively neutralized.

COMPANY LOCATION AND FACILITIES

The company summary section of your business plan may include information about your business's location and facilities (e.g., your retail store, manufacturing plant, etc.), although you may need to devote a separate section to this subject if your facilities are very important to your business.

At a minimum, the facilities description should list the type, address, and size of each business location you own or rent. It should also briefly describe the surrounding area (i.e., is your store located in a commercial strip mall with off-street parking, or are you located on the second floor of an indoor shopping galleria). Is the area zoned residential, commercial, or light industrial? Is it convenient to major transportation routes? Is there adequate parking? What are your hours of operation?

You may want to describe your most immediate neighbors, if relevant. For example, if you have a small retail store, the presence of a major department or food store in the vicinity may be an important source of walk-in business, and a major advantage to your company.

COMPANY BACKGROUND AND CURRENT STATUS

For a business that has been in operation for a while, you need to set the stage for the business plan with a narrative that explains how your company came into being and what were the major milestones you've passed along the way.

This will give the reader a sense of why you chose the business you're in, where you currently stand in the business lifecycle, and a general overview of your major strengths and weaknesses.

This section of the business plan need not be lengthy and filled with facts and figures — those will have their place later on, in the marketing, operations, and financial sections. The emphasis here should be on conveying the broad outlines, in a way that presents a very positive image of your company. It's a good opportunity for you to express your personal style.

STARTUP SUMMARY

If your business is in the startup phase, you should include a section that provides detailed information about the costs you expect to incur in starting your business. The chart that follows can be used as a starting point to determine your business startup costs.

Initial Cash Requirements for the New Business
One-Time Startup Expenses

Startup Expenses	Amount	Description
Advertising		Promotion for opening the business.
Building/Remodeling		The amount per contractor bid, materials, etc.
Decorating		Estimate based on bid if appropriate.
Deposits		Check with the utility companies.
Equipment Lease Payments		The amount to be paid before opening.
Insurance		Bid from insurance agent.
Licenses and Permits		Check with city or state offices.
Miscellaneous		All other.
Professional Fees		Include CPA, attorney, engineer, etc.
Rent		The amount to be paid before opening.
Services		Cleaning, accounting, etc.
Signs		Use contractor bids.
Supplies		Office, cleaning, etc. supplies.
Unanticipated Expenses		Include an amount for the unexpected.
Total Startup Expenses		Total amount of expenses before opening.
Cash		Requirements for the first 90 days.
Beginning Inventory		The amount of inventory needed to open.
Other Short-Term Assets		
Total Short-Term Assets		
Building		Use the actual price of the property you want.
Fixtures and Equipment		Use actual bids.
Installation of Fixtures and Equipment		Use actual bids.
Other Long-Term Assets		
Total Long-Term Assets		
Total Startup Expenses		Total expenses and assets before opening.
Left to Finance		Amount of financing still needed.

You'll also need to explain how you expect to finance these costs. If you are seeking a short-term line of credit, equipment financing, a mortgage, or other type of loan, this should be explained in your startup summary. If the initial costs will be borne by yourself and any other owners, be sure to state that fact.

The amount that you've invested in the business will be a point of interest to any prospective lenders, since owners with significant personal investment are considered to be much stronger credit risks. This information may also be presented in the form of a "sources and uses of funds" statement that you include in the financial statement section of the plan.

Funding Plan for the New Business
One-Time Startup Expenses

Funding Source	Amount	Description
Investment		
Investment from Owner A	_____	Investment by individual owner, if appropriate.
Investment from Owner B	_____	Use if necessary.
Investment from Owner C	_____	Use if necessary.
Total Investment	_____	Total investment by business owners.
Short-Term Borrowing		
Unsecured Short-Term Loans	_____	Often, credit cards are used for fill-in cash.
Line of credit	_____	
Other Short-Term Loans	_____	
Total Short-Term Borrowing		
Long-Term Borrowing		
Mortgage	_____	On business property or on your home.
Equipment Loans	_____	
Other Long-Term Loans	_____	
Total Long-Term Loans	_____	
Total Borrowing	_____	Total amount of short and long-term loans.
Loss at Startup	( )	Total amount of startup expenses (not assets)
Total Equity		Total investment
Total Debt and Equity		Add your total investment to total borrowing.

Chapter 4

Market Analysis

A business plan is the blueprint for taking an idea for a product or service and turning it into a commercially viable reality. The Market Analysis section provides the evidence that there is a niche in the market that your company can exploit. It consists of:

- an industry analysis, which assesses the general industry environment in which you compete

- a target market analysis, which identifies and quantifies the customers that you will be targeting for sales

- a competitive analysis, which identifies your competitors and analyzes their strengths and weaknesses

- a SWOT and/or needs analysis may be included to further describe the Strengths and Weaknesses of your business and the market Opportunities and Threats you face (SWOT), or the met and unmet needs that you perceive in the marketplace

The precise way in which you choose to organize this information is up to you. As long as you include all the basic facts, there are a number of outline forms that can work well. Just keep the purpose of your plan in mind, and highlight or expand the sections that have the greatest application to what you're trying to accomplish.

It's also important to realize that as you go about planning a business startup or expansion, you should be doing a lot of research and learning an enormous amount about its marketing environment. Your business plan is not intended to include everything you've learned. It will just summarize the highlights, in a way that shows the reader that you understand your industry, market, and individual business.

THE INDUSTRY

The industry analysis is the section of your business plan in which you demonstrate your knowledge about the general characteristics of the type of business you're in. You should be able to present some statistics about the size of the industry (e.g., total U.S. sales in the last year) and its growth rate over the last few years. Is the industry expanding, contracting, or holding steady? Why?

Who are the major industry participants? While you might not compete directly against these companies (they are likely to be large national or international corporations), it's important that you can identify them, and have a good understanding of their market share and why they are or aren't successful.

You should also be able to discuss the important trends that may affect your industry. For example, significant changes in the target market, in technology, or in other related industries may affect the market's perception of your product or your profitability.

This kind of information is often available for free from the following sources:

- trade association data

- industry publications and databases

- government databases (e.g., Census Bureau, state trade measurements)

- data and analysts' opinions about the largest players in the industry (e.g., Standard & Poor's reports, quotes from reputable news sources)

Of course, online research can get you much of the information you need, via Google or other search engines. The American Marketing Association (the "other" AMA) may be able to help you as well. You can reach it by phone at 1-800-AMA-1150, or on the Internet at http://www.marketingpower.com.

THE TARGET MARKET

How do you determine if there are enough people in your market who are willing to purchase what you have to offer, at the price you need to charge to make a profit? The best way is to conduct a methodical analysis of the market you plan to reach.

You need to know precisely who your customers are, or will be. If you've been in business for a while, you may know many of them by name, but do you really know what type of people or businesses they are?

For example, if you sell to consumers, do you have demographic information (e.g., what are their average income ranges, education, typical occupations, geographic location, family makeup, etc.) that identifies your target buyers? What about lifestyle information (e.g., hobbies, interests, recreational/entertainment activities, political beliefs, cultural practices, etc.) on your target buyers?

You may very well sell to several types of customers — for example, you may sell at both retail and wholesale, and you may have some government or nonprofit customers as well. If so, you'll want to describe the most important characteristics of each group separately.

Directly surveying your current customers can be expensive. For planning purposes, it's acceptable to substitute published industry-wide information; for example, "the average U.S. household computer owner is between the ages of 31 and 42, has graduated from college, and earns $40,000 to $60,000 per year."

Once obtained, this type of information can help you in two very important ways. It can help you develop or make changes to your product or service itself, to better match what your customers are likely to want. It can also tell you how to reach your customers through advertising, promotions, etc.

Example

A company that sells athletic shoes may know that its typical customer is also a sports fan. Thus, if it can build shoes good enough to be worn by professional athletes, it will have a convincing story about quality to tell. It can also benefit by using well-known athletes as spokespersons in its advertising, and by placing advertisements in sports magazines where its customers are likely to see them.

It is also important to be able to estimate the size of your target market, particularly if you're thinking about a new venture, so that you can tell if the customer base is large enough to support your business or new product idea. Remember that it's not enough that people like your business concept. There must be enough target buyers on a frequent enough basis to sustain your company revenues and profits from year to year. Small businesses have a strong advantage here, in that they can often be profitable while serving a relatively small niche

— one that a Fortune 500 company would consider too small to pursue.

Niche Marketing

Most marketers know that "20 percent of buyers consume 80 percent of product volume." If you could identify that key 20 percent and find others like them, you could sell much more product with much less effort.

The heaviest users of your product or service can be thought of as a market "niche" that you should attempt to dominate. The driving force behind niche marketing is the need to satisfy and retain those consumers who really love your products or services. It is much more efficient to continue selling to the same customers, than it is to continually go out and find new ones.

Therefore, in your target market analysis, you'll want to identify your ideal customer niche as narrowly as possible, keeping in mind that your niche must be large enough to profitably support your company.

Influences on Consumer Behavior

If your customers are primarily the ultimate consumers or end users of your product or service, identification of your target market is generally done in terms of demographic and lifestyle factors.

Demographics are tangible, measurable facts that distinguish one group of people from another, whereas lifestyle analysis is more concerned with the intangibles.

Demographic Factors

- *ethnic background*
- *age*
- *income*
- *education*
- *sex*
- *location*
- *occupation*
- *number of people in family*
- *children's ages*

Lifestyle Factors

- *cultural background*
- *religious beliefs*
- *political beliefs*
- *music preferences*
- *literature preferences*
- *food or menu preferences*

- *value systems*
- *recreation and hobbies*
- *social interaction patterns*

- *entertainment preferences*
- *travel preferences*
- *media habits*

For example, heavy coffee, liquor, and tobacco users are not easily identified with demographic information. They may be found in any age group or socio-economic category. However, lifestyle analysis shows high correlation with certain characteristics, including media habits, recreational pursuits, social interaction patterns, music, and other attributes.

Influences on Channel Buyers

If you sell to other businesses that turn around and resell your products and services, your buyers are predominantly channel buyers. Examples of channel buyers from the grocery and drug industry are:

- national master distributors

- local/regional distributors

- chain store wholesaler buyers

- individual retail store buyers

Influences on channel buyers may include things that have little to do with what you consider the key benefits of your products.

Influences on Channel Buyer Decisions

- ***Profitability of the item*** — *the higher the margin and dollar profit per item as compared to competitive category products, the more likely the trade will accept it, regardless of product quality.*

- ***Availability of discount deals*** — *they can increase margin, volume, and velocity of the item. For example, 10 percent to 25 percent off invoice for all purchases during a quarter is a typical discount range for grocery and drug retailers.*

- ***Advertising and promotion support programs*** — *multi-media TV, radio, print, and PR support, plus heavy consumer couponing, sweepstakes, or contests are typical consumer packaged goods programs that may be run one to four times per year.*

- ***Other cash deals*** — *for example, new item "slotting fees" are the subject of controversy and frustration for many manufacturers supplying grocery, drug, and mass merchandiser retailers. Slotting fees are cash payments and/or free goods that are not refundable, even if the products are dropped after six months by the retailer. Slotting fees range from a few hundred dollars to over $25,000 per item in some chains.*

- ***Availability of free goods*** — *for example, one free case per store is common for new grocery item distribution.*

- ***Personal buyer/seller relationships*** — *there will always be personal relationships influencing buying decisions as long as there are people selling to people. That's why you hire good salespeople!*

- ***Sales incentive programs*** — *these programs may spur salespeople on to greater productivity and sales of a particular item or offering.*

THE COMPETITION

Once you've identified what's unique about your business and who your target buyers are, you need to take a good, long look at your competition.

In the industry overview section of your business plan, you may have identified the largest players in your industry. Not all of these businesses will be directly competing with you, however. Some may be located in geographically distant locations, and others may have pricing or distribution systems that are very different from those of a small business.

Therefore, in your competition analysis, you'll focus on those businesses that directly compete with you for sales.

Levels of Competition

It may help to think of your competitors as a series of levels, ranging from your most direct competitors to those who are more remote.

- **First level** — the specific companies or brands that are direct competitors to your product or service, in your geographic locality. In many cases, these competitors offer a product or service that is interchangeable with yours in the eyes of the consumer (although, of course, you hope you hold the advantage with better quality, more convenient distribution, and other special features). For example, if you operate a local garden center, you may compete against the other garden centers within a 10-mile radius.

- **Second level** — competitors who offer similar products in a different business category or who are more geographically remote. Using the example of the garden center, a discount chain that sells garden supplies and plants in season is also your competitor, as is a landscaping contractor who will provide and install the plants, and a mail-order house who sells garden tools and plants in seed or bulb form. None of these competitors provides exactly the same mix of products and services as you, but they may be picking off the most lucrative parts of your business.

- **Third level** — competitors who compete for the "same-occasion" dollars. Inasmuch as gardening is a hobby, third-level competitors might be companies that provide other types of entertainment or hobby equipment; inasmuch as gardening is a type of home-improvement, competitors might be providers of other home-improvement supplies and services.

The point of this analysis is to consider carefully, from the buyer's point of view, all the alternatives that there are to purchasing from you. Knowing that, you can attempt to make sure that your business provides advantages over your competitors, beginning with those who are the most directly similar to you. In fact, you can even borrow ideas from second- or third-level competitors in order to compete more effectively against your first-tier competitors.

Competitors' Strengths and Weaknesses

It's to your advantage to know as much as you reasonably can about the identity of your competitors, and the details of your competitors' businesses. Study their ads, brochures, and promotional materials. Drive past their location (and if it's a retail business, make some purchases there, incognito if necessary). Talk to their customers and examine their pricing. What are they doing well that you can copy, and what are they doing poorly that you can capitalize on?

Secondary data, as well as information from your sales force or other contacts among your suppliers and customers, can provide rich information about competitors' strengths and weaknesses. Basic information every company should know about their competitors includes:

- each competitor's size and market share, as compared to your own

- how target buyers perceive or judge your competitors' products and services

- your competitors' financial strength, which affects their ability to spend money on advertising and promotions, among other things

- each competitor's ability and speed of innovation for new products and services

There may be a wealth of other facts that you need to know, depending on the type of business you have. For example, if you're in catalog sales, you'll want to know how fast your competitors can fulfill a typical customer's order, what they charge for shipping and handling, etc.

Even for new businesses, company data from competitors may be available by interviewing competitor company executives, attending industry trade shows, and asking the right questions from industry "experts." They may be unaffordable as consultants but willing to direct you to free databases that you would not ordinarily know of or have access to. And don't overlook your competitor's suppliers. They can be excellent sources of information to aid your research.

Future Competition

Along with your current competitors, your business plan should give some consideration to the possibility that other competition will arise in the near future.

So, you should discuss the barriers to entry for a new business in your industry and market. Is it relatively easy, or relatively difficult, to join the fray in terms of capital, staffing, inventory, distribution control, workforce, relationships with suppliers, etc.?

If your business is new, you'll have to show how you can overcome these hurdles yourself.

What other types of businesses (or other entities) are most likely to be able to overcome these hurdles? What is the likelihood of new entrants to the market in the next few years? Remember that, with the increasing influence of the Internet and catalog merchants, companies that are geographically remote from you may already be selling directly to your customers.

(SWOT) ANALYSIS

One useful way to organize information about your company and its marketing environment is to do a Strengths, Weaknesses, Opportunities, and Threats (SWOT) analysis. While this section is not mandatory for all business plans, it can help you to think more creatively about the factors that will affect your business.

Strength and weakness analysis is an internal company exercise to gauge your ability to compete effectively. Opportunity and threat analysis is an external exercise centered on competitors and the external environment that affect your company's ability to compete. Almost every business can come up with a list of at least five or six items, for each of these four categories. Some key questions are:

Strengths and weaknesses:

- What are your company's greatest strengths in terms of product or service, name recognition and reputation, production processes, workforce, location, distribution channels, favorable supplier relationships, management knowledge and experience, and creativity?

- What are your greatest weaknesses in these areas?

- Are some or all of the items you sell subject to varying product life cycles? How do your products compare to competitors' product life cycles?

Opportunities and threats:

- How does the overall economic outlook, and the economic outlook in your geographical area, affect you? Is the local population growing? Is the job market growing? Are income levels increasing?

- How big are your competitors, and what are their financial resources? Is your competition actively seeking to grow through new product or service introductions, new outlets, new distribution channels, or acquisitions?

- Are competitors' market shares growing, or are they loosing their grip on your target buyers? What types of competitive spending, promotions, advertising, and field sales response will your business encounter?

You may need to network with potential customers, industry associations, suppliers, and competitors to answer these questions.

In the case of weaknesses and threats, you should give a considerable amount of thought to how you'll go about compensating for (or better yet, eliminating) the problem, and discuss that in your plan. In the case of positive factors, you may want to give some thought to how you'll preserve your edge.

For an example of how SWOT analysis might be conducted for a small service company, consider the following case study.

Case Study — Life Designs Architecture

 An independent architect who specializes in designing residential homes, Life Designs, has a strengths, weaknesses, opportunities, and threats (SWOT) list that includes:

Strengths:

- *ability to respond quickly to customer demands and changes*
- *ability to make acceptable margins on small jobs, with low overhead*
- *high quality of work and experience*
- *reputation for being affable, honest, and easy to work with*
- *reputation for good value of services and prices*
- *appeal to customers of working directly with the architect/principal*

Weaknesses

- *very limited financial, personnel, and time resources*
- *a limit of three to four projects at any given time*
- *inability to sell and work on a project at the same time*
- *not having a personal relationship with influential local business leaders*
- *being known for a limited number of architectural design "styles"*

Opportunities

- *a growing market for new homes and more upscale homeowners moving to the area, fostered by a growing local economy*
- *a chance to contract with a local developer for an exclusive agreement*
- *a chance to work with the university architectural design department as a visiting lecturer*
- *a chance to relocate his office from his home to a co-op business office center, with shared secretaries, receptionist, conference rooms, and computers*
- *the availability of hiring independent sales reps to work with residential owners, real estate firms, and contractors*

Threats

- *a growing amount of advertising and business inroads by outside regional and national firms in the local area*

- *new local zoning codes and state/federal legislation increasing the cost of new home and remodeling/addition work*

- *Increasing costs of building materials*

- *a possible shortage of skilled building trade people in the area*

- *a new competitor in the area specializing in residential home design, especially in his known "style" of design*

NEEDS ANALYSIS

While not absolutely essential for all business plans, a needs analysis can help you to further refine your expectations for the success of your business.

Particularly for new business owners, it's important to remember that, while you may be drawn to a particular type of business because of your knowledge of its operations or your affinity with the type of product or service you're planning to offer, ultimately your success will depend on how well you satisfy your customers' needs.

Example

A small business that operates an auto repair shop must remember that customers patronize the shop because they need reliable transportation. Everything that the shop does must come together to serve that need.

By focusing on the customer's need, the shop owner can devise ways to improve service in the eyes of the customer, such as by offering loaner cars, providing free rides to the customer's workplace, or guaranteeing the service performed for a specified period. The typical auto shop customer is less likely to be concerned about the decor of the shop or about bargain-basement prices, since those don't immediately impact on the need for transportation.

Once you've come up with what you believe to be the customer's most important needs in relation to your products or service, and to your category of business in general, you can divide your list into two parts: needs that are already being successfully met in the marketplace, and needs that remain unfilled. You can then describe how your business will fill these gaps in the marketplace.

You need to be aware of the needs that are already being filled, so that you can avoid being simply a "me-too" business with little chance of breaking down your customers' already established loyalty to another provider. Particularly if the competition is well-established with a substantial market share, it will be difficult to break in unless you do a noticeably better job of meeting more of your customers' needs.

On the other hand, there are few customer needs that go unnoticed and unserved for long. If you believe that you've discovered a huge, gaping hole in the marketplace, chances are that either (a) the need isn't as large as it appears, (b) the need can't be profitably satisfied, or (c) your competitors are already making plans to move into the market.

Although there are a few exceptions, particularly where new technology is being employed, most small businesses can thrive by becoming more closely attuned to their customers' needs, and offering a product or service combination that meets those needs in a significantly superior way.

Warning

You may discover that virtually all of the customer's needs are already being filled. If so, you'll have to reexamine the situation a bit. Either you must dig deeper to uncover more unmet needs, or rethink your business plan more dramatically. Perhaps going into a slightly different type of business would allow you to function in a marketplace that's not quite as saturated.

Chapter 5

Product or Service Description

If you've reached the point where you are trying to write a description of what it is that your business actually does or sells, you've probably been thinking about your product or service for quite some time. Now is the time to take a step back and reflect.

What's the view from 40,000 feet? What's the big picture overview of your product lines or the services you offer? How would you categorize them and describe them for a reader who's unfamiliar with the terrain?

Remember that the product or service idea you have hasn't been kicking around for months in the heads of the people who might read your plan. You may have to set the stage a little bit to make sure that a reader understands exactly what your product or service is. On the other hand, don't go overboard with detail. For example, you won't need to list every single product that will be carried in a retail store, or every item that will be on the menu for a restaurant.

The starting point is a clear statement of what the product is or what service your business will provide. Focus on those factors that make your offering unique and desirable to customers. Explain what it does, how it works, how long it lasts, what options are available, etc. Especially if your plan is being written for an external audience, be sure that you explain any special terms with which people outside your industry might be unfamiliar.

If you're a service provider, what categories of services do you offer, and approximately how long does it take to provide each unit of service? Are packages available?

Explain whether you are selling a standalone product (e.g., lunch) or a product that must be used with other products (e.g., computer software or peripheral devices). Be sure to describe the requirements for any associated products (especially vital for software). And, if there are special requirements for successful sales, say so.

Another issue to consider is whether you hope to sell items on a one-time or infrequent basis, or whether repeat sales are the goal. If you're opening a bakery or restaurant, you're going to count on the same customers returning on a regular basis. But a heating contractor installing a new furnace or a consultant helping to implement a new order processing system probably isn't going to do that again for the same client any time soon (we hope!).

If there are certain products or services that your competitors carry but you don't, take some time to explain why so that the reader isn't left to question your judgment.

If you will be operating a retail environment, you'll want to describe the store or restaurant, as well as the items you'll offer there. You might consider adding a picture or a diagram of the layout in your appendix, as well, unless you'll be discussing these things in detail in a separate "Business Facilities" section of your plan.

COMPETITIVE COMPARISONS

Your product or service description should give the reader a complete picture by comparing your offering to similar services or products offered by others. This is especially important for a new business seeking financing. The potential lender or investor will want to mentally position you among the other companies in your category, with which he or she is more familiar.

In the competitive comparison section, it's natural to focus on how your products are bigger, better, longer lasting, better tasting, or generally more exciting that those of your competitors. There's nothing wrong with being very positive about your business's offerings. However, if your competitor's products are clearly superior in some respects, you should mention that as well. Your business plan is a planning document, not a sales brochure, and readers will not be favorably impressed by unrealistic hyperbole.

As a general rule, your plan should always address potential problems, including the strengths of your competition, rather than avoiding all mention of them. The fact that you can recognize where legitimate problems might exist reflects well on your management abilities. Most lenders and outside investors will be more impressed by the fact that you can identify problems and deal with them, than they would be if no problems existed in the planning document.

SOURCING

To some extent, all businesses are dependent on their relationships with suppliers. Even if you make nearly all the products you sell, you'll need to get your raw materials from somewhere. Service providers must locate sources of supplies used in rendering those services. And if you resell products, the source of those products can be extremely important.

Your business plan should address the type of vendors you will use, and if possible, identify them by name. You'll want to show that the issues of price, quality, and availability have been covered. Knowing which vendors you want to use, what products or services they can provide, and what business terms they require is an important part of getting your business on its feet.

In some cases, the readers of your plan will be more familiar with the vendors you use than they are with you, and you have the opportunity to gain favorably by association. You might include copies of important contracts in the appendix of your business plan, to reinforce this favorable impression.

FUTURE PRODUCTS AND SERVICES

Successful small businesses generally find that other businesses will eventually discover their formula and attempt to imitate them. Particularly if you've done a good job of identifying an important unmet need of your target market, you'll find that copycats seem to spring out of the woodwork all too quickly, and some of them may even threaten your hard-won market share.

So, small business owners need to embrace and seek out change, rather than avoid it or wait until change is forced upon them by competitors. One way to do this is to constantly be on the lookout for ways to expand your business by offering new products or services to your customers, or by combining products or services in new ways.

Your business plan should address the future in some fashion, by outlining the opportunities you see for growth beyond your current capabilities. To some extent, you've done that by creating an expansive mission statement. But you should also include at least a few paragraphs, in the product or service section of the plan, that describe your expectations for the next round of new products or services, or an update/upgrade of your current ones.

Work Smart

Timing is also an issue to address. Be realistic about the time it will take to develop the new product or service.

It's generally better to set a far-off deadline and come in early, than to continually have to revise and extend your introduction date (witness the credibility gap that some giant software companies have experienced when promised software takes months or years longer than expected to materialize).

Chapter 6

Marketing and Sales Plans

Your marketing and sales plans explain how you plan to reach your targeted customers and how you will effectively market your product or service to those customers. In essence, the marketing plan provides an answer to the market analysis that you've done. It sets forth the specific steps you will take to promote and sell your product or service and provides a timetable for those actions to occur.

Traditionally, the marketing plan portion of the business plan addresses four main topics: product, price, place, and promotion.

PRODUCT

What are the goods or services that your business will offer? How are your offerings better than those against which they will compete? Why will people buy from you? These questions will be answered in the "product" section of your marketing and sales plan.

First, you'll want to provide a very brief overview of your products or services, primarily to set the stage for readers who may not yet have read the detailed product or service description that you've provided in a separate section of the business plan (see Chapter 5).

Then, highlight the aspects of your offerings that will surpass those of your competitors. For example, if you offer a superior warranty or a broader range of services, this is the place to say that.

PRICE

How much will you charge? How will you strike a balance between sales volume and price to maximize net income? Will you be testing a variety of price points? Will you offer discounts and, if so, under what circumstances? This section of your business plan will discuss your pricing policy in some detail.

All pricing strategies depend on balancing three influences:

- Cost — to produce the item and to cover your overhead

- Competition — what other businesses are charging for comparable offerings

- Demand — what customers are willing to pay, and how many of them are willing to pay it

The basic concern for almost all small businesses is to price products at a level that will cover all expenses and that customers will accept, which generally means pricing that's fairly close to that of your competitors.

Analyzing Market Size and Composition

In setting prices for your product or service, one of the first calculations you must do is to estimate approximately how large your potential sales volume could be, based on a reasonable assessment of your potential market share in the product category, at different price levels. Knowing the size of the existing market is critical to determining if there are enough customers to establish and grow a business.

In an established market, in order to sell your product you must cut into your competitors' market shares. Who will you compete against? What are their strengths and weaknesses? Are any direct competitors vulnerable to your products? Are any competitive products priced too high or not providing product "value" for the price? The competitive analysis, described in Chapter 4, should help you to answer these questions.

Researching Product Price Elasticity

If demand for your product or service changes significantly with slight changes in price, the product category is considered to be *elastic* with respect to price.

If no significant volume changes occur, even with significant price changes, the category is *inelastic.*

Grocery store items are often very price sensitive, with a 10 percent price increase or decrease resulting in significant share and volume changes per brand. Consumers are less price-conscious when shopping for gourmet foods, and a price increase or decrease of 50 percent may be required to create any perceptible changes in consumers' behavior.

The greater the price elasticity for a product you offer, the closer you should price your products to similar competitive products and vice versa. While your product may be unique, consumers will not pay much of a premium for it if there are similar competitive choices at lower prices.

To find out more about price elasticity, you might study secondary data sources for your industry or talk to trade association experts.

Evaluating Your Product's Uniqueness

The closer your product resembles competitive products, the smaller the price differences that buyers will tolerate. And the closer the product differences between brands, the greater the likelihood that brand-switching will occur when products go on sale.

Product uniqueness does not guarantee a significant price premium over a competitive product, if the product differences aren't recognizable and meaningful to consumers. And depending on the category of product or service, even recognizable and meaningful product differences may not be enough to get buyers to switch to the new product at equivalent pricing, let alone at a premium price over the competition.

Field testing on a small market basis is highly recommended for testing new product differences or unique new products.

Analyzing Your Costs and Overhead

The most common errors in pricing are:

- pricing products or services based only on the cost to produce them

- pricing products based only on competitors' prices

Instead, you need to take both of these strategies into account and find the proper balance between them. At the very least, your pricing policy must allow you to meet your breakeven point. For more on how to calculate breakeven, see Chapter 8.

Wholesaling and Retailing Markups

Retailers and wholesalers need to consider the issue of markups in their pricing structure, and manufacturers or other product producers need to be aware of the average markup in their industry.

A Few Definitions

- *"Markup" is the percentage of the selling price (or sometimes the cost) of a product which is added to the cost in order to arrive at a selling price.*

- *"Markdown" is a percentage reduction from the selling price.*

Be aware that there are two different ways to calculate markup — on cost or on selling price. So when someone asks you about your markup on an item, you must specify whether it is "20 percent of *cost*" or "20 percent of *selling price*." In retailing, the industry standard is to compute markup as a percentage of selling price.

Example

Joel received a shipment of clocks that he will sell in his gift store. He paid $12.00 for each clock and plans to make $4.00 on each one. The selling price is then $16.00.

The markup percentage on cost is the dollar markup (4.00) divided by cost (12.00) = **33%.**

However, the markup percentage on selling price is the dollar markup (4.00) divided by selling price (16.00) = **25%.**

As a product wends its way through a distribution channel, each step along the journey adds a "markup" before selling the product to the next step. Here's an example of how markups work based on selling price:

Level	Category	$	%
Producer	Cost	20.00	80.0
	Markup	5.00	20.0
	Selling Price	25.00	100.0

Level	Category	$	%
Wholesale Outlet	Cost	25.00	71.5
	Markup	10.00	28.5
	Selling Price	35.00	100.0
Retailer	Cost	35.00	70.0
	Markup	15.00	30.0
	Selling Price	50.00	100.0

Markups vary widely among industries. For example, average retail markups (on selling price) are 14 percent on tobacco products, 50 percent on greeting cards, 8 percent on baby food, and often more than 50 percent on high-end meats.

Considering Other Pricing Strategies

In addition to the primary goal of making money, a company can have many different pricing objectives and strategies. Larger companies may utilize product pricing in a predatory or defensive fashion, to attack or defend against a competitor.

Example

Maxwell House Coffee introduced a second, low-priced brand into their own dominant eastern United States markets during the 1970s to slow and confuse the introduction of Folger's Coffee into their markets. This new product was packaged and designed to resemble Folger's familiar red can, with pricing set below Folger's Coffee. The new temporary product clogged grocer shelves and made it more difficult and expensive for Folger's to introduce their coffee into new eastern markets.

If you have a premium quality product, with premium packaging, graphics, and unique features and benefits, perhaps a premium price is necessary to reinforce the premium brand image. Higher margins than normal may be one benefit. High prices confirm perceptions of high value in consumer minds.

A good pricing strategy will also indicate guidelines for action in the case of price increases or decreases. For example, "We will price at or near the share leader's pricing on a per unit basis. We will increase prices to follow a share leader price increase, but only if we can preserve margin objectives."

Work Smart

Be sure to consider variations that may come up to affect your pricing. You may wish to use discounting for prompt cash payment or for quantity purchases. Seasonal items may warrant special pricing from time to time. How about senior citizen and student discounts? And promotional incentives may motivate your dealers. These are but a few of many variables you'll want to consider when you formulate your pricing strategy.

The pricing levels you finally select for your products should have flexibility for both increases and discounts to customers. Price increases may be inevitable because of component, ingredient, and processing cost increases. The market may or may not absorb price increases without decreasing volume effects.

Work Smart

If in doubt, price on the high side, where possible. It is always easier to discount prices than to raise them.

PLACE

Which sales channels will you use? Will you sell by telephone or will your product be carried in retail outlets? Which channel will let you economically reach your target audience? The "place" discussion in your marketing plan should explain the distribution choices you've made, and how you will go about implementing those choices.

Small businesses may have products that would appeal to many different markets, or channels of distribution in a single market. However, when you have limited resources, it's often best to select a single distribution channel or a limited number of distribution channels that offer:

- greatest ease of entry against the competition

- least financial risk and long-term commitment

- sufficient volume potential to reach short-term company goals

- pricing levels to provide acceptable profit margins

PROMOTION

Whatever you're selling, you'll need to communicate about it with your target buyers. Most businesses find that they need all three components of marketing communications (promotion, advertising, public relations), in some combination. But how do you narrow down the available choices and build a communications program that makes sense? Here's how:

1. **Know who the target buyer is.** Identify the target buyer in demographic, lifestyle, and other descriptive terms.

2. **Determine what is meaningfully unique about your product.** "Meaningful" differences are those business or brand attributes *that buyers or end users consider in making purchase decisions* among different available choices.

3. **Construct a business positioning strategy statement.** It is important to be consistent in all promotion, advertising, and PR programs, particularly with the scarce resources of most small businesses. A good business positioning strategy statement will address who the target buyer or end user is, what the competitive environment is, and what the meaningful differences in the products or services are when compared to the competition. The statement might also communicate some idea of a business "personality" that will be created and fostered in all marketing programs.

4. **Determine the best message to communicate your product positioning to target buyers.** Use your positioning statement to construct a memorable "slogan" or ad message that correlates with the needs and wants of your target buyer.

5. **Determine promotion options and costs in terms of available budget.** There is never enough money to do everything desirable to build the business. Often a promotional budget reality check means a choice between a little promotion, advertising, or PR, but not all three at the same time. Here are some options to consider.

   — Advertising — consider print, radio, cable television, billboard, and Internet ads; packaging; display and point-of-purchase signs; direct mail; catalogs; brochures and flyers; doorhangers; posters; and the yellow pages and other directories.

— Sales promotions — consider grand openings, games and contests, premiums and gifts, coupons, rebates or "frequent buyer" programs, product demonstrations, low-interest financing, and trade shows.

— Publicity and public relations — consider press releases and press kits; public service activities; and speeches or seminars. These types of activities are often "free" except for the time you'll spend on them.

The marketing and sales plan usually includes a calendar that ties marketing and sales activities to specific operational events. For example, an advertising campaign may begin some months before a new product is ready to be sold. As the date of the new product introduction approaches, the ad campaign would be stepped up. Once the new product hits the market, additional advertising is used to support specific sales objectives.

If your target market is divided among several different types of customers (for instance, you sell both wholesale and retail), you may find it necessary to address promotions for each group separately.

YOUR SALES PLANS

Your sales plans may be included in the "promotions" part of your marketing plans; however, if personal selling is a large part of your strategy and especially if your business will have a sales force, you may wish to devote a separate section to your sales plans.

One challenge that you face in developing your business plan is selecting the sales channel that is most effective. For instance, if you're in a business where you provide services personally, your participation in the sales process can be extensive. In contrast, if your business deals in the sale and production of large quantities of product with little associated service, then you face a different challenge. Customers may not know or care who you are.

Planning for selling is, therefore, based on the particular mix of goods and services that you plan to offer and on the way you intend to reach potential customers. Some tools to consider are sales presentations, product samples and giveaways, and incentive programs for sales reps.

If you are going to have a sales force of some kind, be sure you know what you will expect them to do. When making hiring decisions, do your best to find people who can do what you want. If *you* will be the entire sales force, at least initially, try to quantify the activities and time involved.

Chapter 7

Operations and Management Plans

The operations and management portions of your business plan will explain how you will actually produce the goods and services your business will deliver to its customers. These sections also address the back office or "overhead" activities that all businesses must undertake.

Operations and management include activities such as:

- hiring and managing employees or contract workers

- choosing and maintaining your business facility

- supervising and improving your production processes

- filling orders

- collecting money from customers

- providing customer service and support after the sale

- dealing with unexpected occurrences or changing conditions

These types of issues can be grouped into two major categories for purposes of dealing with them in your plan. The categories are: the operations plan, and the management and human resources plan.

PLANNING YOUR OPERATIONS

Creating the operations plan forces you to think through each step that must be completed before your customers receive whatever it is that they purchase from you, and also how you will interface with customers after the sale. For the reader of your business plan, the operations planning section should provide a good overview of the types of activities your business must routinely perform in its core business activities.

The types of operational issues that you'll face will vary tremendously based on the type of business you own. For example, a consultant who deals primarily in assisting customers with network communications isn't going to have an extensive manufacturing or inventory control plan.

For some service businesses, the operations issues may be adequately addressed in the section of your business plan in which you describe your services. It may be most efficient to describe how you're planning to provide services in the same place where you describe exactly what they are. In that case, the services description section (see page 43), in combination with the human resources section (see page 59), may avert the need for a separate operations section.

Production Plans

A fast food vendor, in contrast, will have to carefully plan for purchasing the food and related supplies, inventory storage and turnover, the cooking process, employee sanitation, disposal, etc. Similarly, a manufacturer will generally have to plan for facilities, equipment, and inventories of raw materials and finished goods, not to mention the production processes themselves. Owners of these types of businesses should include a fairly detailed operations section in their business plan. They may even want to divide the operations section into several subsections, such as production, facilities, inventory control, and customer service/order fulfillment.

In writing the production section of the business plan, you may find it useful to look at your business as if it were a linear process that starts with raw materials and ends with a delivery to a satisfied customer. You'll probably be surprised at how many steps there are and how critical the timing and duration of each step is.

While it is easy to relate to production issues in a manufacturing process where goods are fabricated, the concept may also be applicable to other types of businesses.

Example

As a consultant you are engaged to help a company convert from a paper-based billing system to a computer-based system. The end "product" that you will deliver is assistance in selecting the appropriate software and hardware, training on that new equipment, and supervision of the process by which the data is converted to electronic format.

You can do a great job without "producing" anything tangible beyond, perhaps, documentation of the process. This doesn't mean that you can ignore "production." Consider all the work that you would have to do. First, a working knowledge of the client's existing system has to be acquired. Then, software and hardware combinations are evaluated in light of the client's needs and budget. A conversion process has to be developed so that those portions of the existing data that carry over to the new system are available in the new format. Documentation must be prepared to train the client's employees in using the new system. Whether you thought of them that way or not, each of these activities would be part of your production process.

Business Facility Assessment

There are a number of issues you should address in your business plan regarding the choice of a facility.

The first question to address is why you need a business facility, and what kind. At one extreme, a consultant may perform most services in space provided by clients. That consultant may not need a facility at all and may maintain a small home office to store reference materials and business records. At the other extreme, a manufacturing business may require access to rail transport, room for manufacturing operations and storage, parking facilities for a lot of employees, etc.

The success of a retail outlet or a restaurant may depend to a large extent on its location. Is it situated in the right part of town, on a street with sufficient foot traffic, parking, or public transportation? Are the neighbors conducive to drawing customers who might also patronize your business? Don't give these issues short shrift, either in actually choosing your location, or in explaining your choice in your business plan.

Your business plan should also describe the basic aspects of your facility (age, square footage, location on first or second floor, etc.), as well as the important aspects of any equipment, furniture, or fixtures that you may need for operation. You may want to augment your explanations with maps, site plans, floor plans, or even architectural drawings.

If you've already obtained a lease, you may want to attach a copy to the plan in an appendix. If you're seeking financing in order to purchase a facility, you'll want to include a lot of detail about the property you're considering and how it suits your needs.

Inventory Control

Businesses that are required to carry an inventory often find that a significant amount of their working capital is tied up in inventory. This applies to those engaged in retailing, wholesaling, and manufacturing, but may also apply to some service businesses. For example, restaurants must maintain inventory of the food they will be serving and perhaps also supplies such as napkins, straws, sugar packets, etc.

If your business maintains an inventory, we suggest that your business plan should discuss how you plan to manage it. For example, how many weeks' or months' worth of raw materials will you attempt to keep on hand? How many months' supply of finished or retail products? Who will be in charge of keeping track? Will you have a computerized system? Will your suppliers help you to stay on top of your inventory?

Being able to answer these questions in your plan will show that you've considered the implications of maintaining adequate stock, without tying up too much money in inventory that may become obsolete or unsalable. If you're just starting out, your suppliers should be able to give you ballpark estimates of what you'll need; trade associations may also provide some helpful information.

Order Fulfillment and Customer Service

Providing superlative customer service is often the most important way in which small businesses can distinguish themselves from the competition. If you've established a customer service policy, be sure to include it in your plan. Your policy may be as simple as saying that "all customers will be treated in a friendly, professional manner" — and if you have employees, you may need to reinforce it often.

If your business is one in which customers place advance orders and then receive their products later, consider including a section in your business plan that discusses your procedures for taking and fulfilling orders. What shipping methods will you use? Will you charge a flat rate for shipping, or will you base your shipping charges on what the carrier charges, plus (or minus) a fixed percentage?

Will you set a target fulfillment period within which the customer should receive the order? Will you set a time limit on returns, or will you state that only exchanges are available (i.e., no cash returns)?

MANAGEMENT AND HUMAN RESOURCE PLANS

A business plan should help you to organize the roles and responsibilities of all the people involved in your business. Therefore, virtually every plan will have a section describing its management. Some businesses will also need a description of their other staffing or the independent contractors they plan to use.

Management Plans

Whether your business has one owner/employee — you — or dozens, you'll need to describe the management strengths and expertise of your business in your business plan.

If your plan is designed to be shown to an outside investor or lender, the quality of management can be a deciding factor in whether you get the desired capital or not. Generally "quality" is interpreted as meaning "experience," so be sure to explain any previous related job experience, any pertinent experience working for community or other voluntary organizations, and even your family background if that will indicate that you know what you are doing in running the business. Also highlight any special skills or education you have. You may wish to include a formal resume in your appendix.

If your business has more than one owner or manager, you should explain how the important roles and duties will be divided between you. For example, will one of you focus on sales, while the other takes care of the production plant? Or will each of you be in charge of a separate business facility, such as a store or restaurant?

It's generally better to establish business roles with some definition, rather than just assuming that "everyone will pitch in with whatever needs doing." Although in fact you may all need to cover each other's roles from time to time, most owners find that the business runs more smoothly if everyone knows what their primary responsibilities are.

Also consider the "key person" concept. Is there anyone whose presence in the business is vital? For instance, yourself? If so, it makes sense to consider what your business would do in the event that a key player is lost. This may be especially important to lenders who would be concerned if the business's revenue stream were interrupted.

Management Gaps

For some businesses, particularly those just starting out, there may be important positions in the business that remain to be filled, or there may be some gaps in the owner's experience or skills that need to be addressed.

If that's true in your case, your plan should explain the situation. If, for example, you're launching a new magazine but are still searching for the right managing editor, you should explain the importance of the position and the fact that finding the right person is crucial to your success. You may want to outline the qualities and experience you're looking for. Be sure to list a ballpark salary that you expect to pay — you'll need it to complete your financial projections.

If you recognize gaps in your own experience, you should explain what they are and how you expect to compensate. In many cases, you can hire a business or an individual to take care of the tasks that are not your strengths. For instance, you can hire an accountant if you don't know much about recordkeeping, and you can hire a salesperson if personal selling is not your strong suit. The fact that you admit your potential weaknesses will generally not diminish your business's potential in the eyes of an outside reader, as long as you have a realistic plan to fill the gaps.

Staffing Plans

It can be difficult to predict how many people your business is going to need, particularly if you're in a new business. You should find that the process of creating a business plan will be very helpful in this respect. As you consider each of the key areas, you'll develop a picture of all the activities that go into running your business. Then you can estimate how many and what kind of employees you'll need, how much you'll need to pay them, and what your total payroll and contractor costs will be.

At one extreme, your business plan can make it clear that you won't ever have any employees. What little you can't do, you'll contract out. Many businesses built around performing services tend to be near this end of the spectrum. At the other extreme, your plan may reveal a need for an exponentially expanding sales force until you have reps in every major city in the United States.

Even if it's just for your own benefit, a description or even a checklist of all the different tasks performed by individuals (or classes of individuals, if you have many employees) may be useful. You may want to include an organization chart to show who reports to whom, if that is a part of your business's structure.

Chapter 8

Financial Plans

Unless you are thinking of starting a religious or charitable organization, the main reason you're starting a business is because you think you can make money at it. The drive to be your own boss might have caused you to quit being an employee and *start* your business, but the quest for income is what keeps it going. When you develop a business plan, financial projections and cash flow analysis are among the most critical elements.

You have a close personal interest in the financial performance of your business. So does everyone else who might be looking at your business plan. Not surprisingly, the portions of your plan dealing with expected financial performance will usually come under the closest scrutiny. A potential lender will want to know what you'll be doing with the money it lends you and how you plan to generate the necessary income to pay the money back.

Fortunately, or perhaps unfortunately, the financial projections are the most formalistic and stylized documents that you will have to prepare. There are certain accounting conventions that you are expected to follow. Simple accounting or business planning software can be extremely helpful in formatting the statements and doing the math. For example, four of the plans in this book were originally formatted using Ultimate Business Planner™ from Atlas Business Solutions (www.abs-usa.com). You can generally purchase such software for under $100, and it's well worth the price.

In some cases, you may need to prepare the financial portions of your plan in conformance with "generally accepted accounting principles" (GAAP). This usually occurs when the business owner is creating a plan in an effort to obtain a loan or line of credit, and the bank or potential investor requests that you follow these formally established accounting rules. It also means that you'll need to get an accountant involved in preparing that portion of the plan. If the financial material was created in conformance with GAAP, that should be noted within the plan. The same is true if the financial statements have been audited.

Important Financial Information to Include

- **Important assumptions** — *statements that must be assumed to be true as the premise for all your projections*

- **Breakeven analysis** – *a description of the sales volume needed to cover all your costs (may be omitted for businesses that have been operating for some time)*

- **Projected sales volume** – *your assessment of how much you can realistically sell at your chosen price points, in a given period of time*

- **Projected profit and loss** – *the statement that details your income, your expenses, and the difference between the two which equals your profit or loss*

- **Projected cash flow budget** – *the statement that shows the timing of cash inflows and outflows for your business*

- **Projected balance sheet** – *the statement that shows your business's projected net worth after operating for a specified period of time*

The type of financial information that you're going to need to prepare your analysis will depend on whether your business is an established enterprise or is just starting out.

As a general rule, however, you should plan to include three years of projected financial statements, unless your lender requests five years. The first year's statements should be broken down by month; later years' information can be presented on a quarterly or annual basis.

STARTUP BUSINESS FINANCIAL INFORMATION

If you're just starting out, you face a special challenge because there is no history of operations, profitable or otherwise. You're going to have to rely almost entirely on financial projections; that is, *prospective* ("pro-forma") statements based on assumptions that you've made as to how your business will perform in the future.

You'll also have to rely heavily on your ability to sell yourself as a potentially successful business owner. In large part, your ability to capture the readers' imagination and get them excited about the possibilities is a substitute for the historical information that doesn't exist.

Startup businesses, or business expansions, frequently involve a startup budget that is different in character from the operating budget of an ongoing business. These startup costs will be detailed separately, in the startup summary of the company summary section of your plan (see page 23).

The startup funding plan will show how your personal investment will be used to fund the business (see page 27). If you plan to contribute any personal assets to the business, such as a car, truck, office machines or computers, etc., you should provide specific details on that as well. Other documents that may be required, particularly if you're trying to obtain outside financing, are a personal financial statement and your income tax returns for the last few years.

As with an established business, you're also going to need to provide a statement of important assumptions, a breakeven analysis, and projected sales forecasts, profit and loss statements, cash flow budget worksheets, and balance sheets. These documents quantify the results you expect to achieve through your operations.

HISTORICAL FINANCIAL INFORMATION

An existing business can bolster the credibility of its business plan by documenting the results of its ongoing operations. A proven track record is very persuasive evidence of your chances for continued success.

Hopefully, you've been creating and maintaining financial records since the inception of your business. If so, most of your work is done. You'll already have balance sheets, income statements, and cash flow budgets for the last three to five years (or since inception if your business is less than three years old). As always, the relative importance of each type of document will vary with the characteristics of your particular business.

These financial statements are the most objective pieces of evidence that lenders will look at to either support or contradict your forecasts for future performance. Generally speaking, the reader of your plan will expect that "history will repeat itself" and that your business's future will be an extension of the trends that are shown in your historical statements. Therefore, if you expect that the picture will improve dramatically, be sure your plan provides solid evidence as to why that will happen.

Our sample business plans (beginning on page 87) have left out the historical financial statements, in the interest of saving space. But be sure to include them in your own finished plan.

ESTABLISHING REASONABLE ASSUMPTIONS

When you draft a business plan, you need to make many different types of assumptions. Some of these are so basic that they remain, appropriately, unstated. For example, although the U.S. economy might cease to function predictably if the country were invaded by Canadian armed forces, it's safe to assume that no such invasion will occur.

Beyond that, there are several broad types of assumptions that you're going to have to make. These assumptions are what support and quantify the financial projections that you'll make in the plan.

Assumptions About the Business Environment

As you draft your business plan, you may feel somewhat overwhelmed by the sheer number of external factors that can dramatically impact your business. Most of these factors are simply beyond your control. For example, if you're planning to take out a variable-rate loan, you'll have to make an assumption about the interest rate during the planning period, which may be dependent upon the general state of the economy.

Work Smart

If you feel very uncomfortable predicting an average interest rate, you may want to draw up several sets of financial projections using best-case, worst-case, and most-likely-case interest rate assumptions. However, this is rather time-consuming and most business owners will simply choose the most-likely-case scenario, for initial planning purposes.

As another example, while Census data may tell you how many people are physically located in your geographic market, the percentage of people who will actually buy your product or service isn't so easy to nail down. But such assumptions are an absolute requirement when it comes time to project sales.

Besides the assumptions about interest rates and about market demand for your product, your business plan should list any other assumptions on which the financial statements depend. For the reader, and for yourself as well, the list serves as a warning that if an assumption later turns out to be false, your business may not perform as expected.

Here are some examples of the wide variety of types of statements you may want to include in your assumptions:

- *We assume continued stable government and political structure in the African countries we will tour.*

- *There will be no major competitive threat from a currently unknown source.*

- *No sales will be made on credit.*

- *Fifty percent of sales in our retail gift shop will occur during the last three months of the year.*

- *Personnel burden (the extra costs of payroll taxes and benefits for employees) will be 30% of total payroll.*

Despite the difficulty in ensuring that your assumptions are reasonable, there is a lot of help available. For example, a bank can provide you with historical information regarding rate changes, and possibly even a prediction about future rates. Vendors can tell you about product availability issues. Get as much information as you need to feel comfortable with your ability to make reasonable assumptions. Remember, however, that no one is likely to be right all the time. If the assumptions on which you base your planning are generally "in the ballpark," you have done a good job.

Assumptions About Your Business

As you work your way through the planning process, you will be called on to take your best guess regarding the key operational issues facing any business. You'll have to make estimates regarding productivity, capacity, cash flow, costs, and a hundred other interrelated factors. For example, if you are considering a manufacturing business, how many units of product can you expect a particular piece of equipment to produce? What assumptions can you make about the equipment's reliability and potential down-time?

From a practical standpoint, there are two potential sources for the information you need to make reasonable assumptions. If you have an existing business, you have your personal experience on which to rely. You know how much to expect from an employee or how reliable your production equipment is. Even if you're taking on a new product or trying to enter a new market, your experience in the industry in general will serve you well.

But what about the business owner who has relatively little experience in a particular field? The best bet is to tap into existing sources of information. One excellent source is industry groups or associations. These organizations exist to further the aims of business owners within a specific industry or field of endeavor. They can provide information regarding a wide variety of topics. Local chambers of commerce and other civic organizations can often provide valuable demographic information regarding the specific geographic market in which you will compete.

Potential vendors and suppliers can also be consulted to get information regarding costs, product availability, timing requirements, etc.

While there is no substitute for personal experience, you can learn a lot by drawing on the experience of those around you. Unless you're starting a wholly new type of business, there will be someone around with experience at what you're planning to do. You'd be surprised how willing even potential competitors are to share information, if asked in the right way. This is particularly true if your business will serve a limited geographic market and won't directly compete with a similar business located some distance away.

BREAKEVEN ANALYSIS

The "breakeven point" for your business is the sales volume you need to achieve in order to cover all the costs of your business. It's extremely important for you to know what your breakeven point is, and to have confidence that you can achieve that volume of sales within a reasonable period of time — otherwise, you need to do more work on the marketing portion of the plan, or to rethink your business idea altogether!

Also, it's a good idea to recalculate your breakeven point periodically, because it will change whenever your costs or your pricing structure changes. Knowing your breakeven point is a good way to keep a handle on all your costs over time.

Fixed and Variable Costs

So, how do you calculate breakeven? Start by determining all the costs of doing business. You may want to use your income statement form as an aid (see page 72).

Virtually all of your business's costs will fall, more or less neatly, into one of two categories:

- "Variable costs" increase directly in proportion to the level of sales in dollars or units sold. Depending on your type of business, some examples of variable costs would be the price you paid for the items you sold (cost of goods sold), sales commissions, shipping charges, delivery charges, costs of direct materials or supplies, wages of part-time or temporary employees, and sales or production bonuses.

- "Fixed costs" remain the same, at least in the short term, regardless of your level of sales. Depending on your type of business, some typical examples would be rent, interest on debt, insurance, plant and equipment expenses, business licenses, and salary of permanent full-time workers.

Your accountant can help you determine which of your costs are fixed and which are variable, but here the key word is "help." In order to be accurate, the ultimate classification has to be done by someone who's intimately familiar with your business operations—which probably means you.

Combination Costs

Some costs are a combination of fixed and variable: a certain minimum level will be incurred regardless of your sales levels, but the costs rise as your volume increases. As an analogy, think about your phone bill: you probably pay an access or line charge that is the same each month, and you probably also pay a charge based on the volume of calls you make. Strictly speaking, these costs should be separated into their fixed and variable components, but that may be more trouble than it's worth for a small business.

Save Time

To simplify things, just decide which type of cost (fixed or variable) is the most important for the particular item, and then classify the whole item according to the more important characteristic. For example, in a telemarketing business, if your phone call volume charges are normally greater than your line access charges, you'd classify the entire bill as variable.

Variable Costs Per Unit

If you add up all your variable costs for the accounting period, and divide by the number of units sold, you will arrive at the cost per unit. This cost should remain constant, regardless of how few or how many units you sell. If yours is a service business, you may be able to divide your variable costs by the number of jobs performed (if the jobs are essentially similar) or by the hours spent on all jobs (if the jobs vary greatly in size).

Calculating the Breakeven Point

Once you know what your variable costs are, as well as your overall fixed costs for the business, you can determine your breakeven point: the volume of sales needed to at least cover all your costs. You can also compute the new breakeven point that you'd need to meet if your cost structure changed (for example, if you undertook a major expansion project or bought some new office equipment, thus increasing your fixed costs). The computation is best explained through an example.

Example

Assume that the financial statements for Lillian's Bakery reveal that the bakery's total fixed monthly costs are $4,900, and its variable costs per unit of production (loaf of raisin coffee cake) are $.30.

Further assume that each loaf sells for $1.00. Therefore, after the $.30 per loaf variable costs are covered, each loaf sold can contribute $.70 toward covering fixed costs.

Dividing fixed costs by the contribution to those costs per unit of sales tells Lillian's Bakery at what level of sales it will break even. In this case: $4,900/$.70 = 7,000 loaves.

As sales exceed 7,000 loaves per month, Lillian's Bakery earns a profit. Sales of less than 7,000 loaves produce a loss.

Lillian's Bakery can see that a 1,000-loaf increase in sales over the break-even point to 8,000 loaves will produce a $700 profit, and a 3,000-loaf increase to 10,000 will produce a $2,100 profit. On the other hand, a decline in sales of 1,000 loaves from break-even to 6,000 loaves will produce a loss of $700, and a 3,000 decrease from the 7,000 break-even point produces a $2,100 loss.

Presenting this information in your business plan is generally done in the form of a graph, with sales units (or dollars) forming one axis of the graph and profits (and losses) forming the other axis. The reader can immediately see the effect that various sales levels will have on your bottom line.

PROJECTED SALES FORECAST

Every financial plan must include a forecast of sales for the business. Any forecast will include some uncertainty. Your sales forecast probably won't match your actual sales because of the many variables that ultimately affect the final amount. The economy, inflation, competitive influences, and a whole range of other variables will affect your actual sales. No matter how much uncertainty you associate with these variables, you must come up with an estimate of future sales.

Projecting Sales for an Existing Business

If your business has been operating for a number of years, your sales reports for the last few years are the best starting point for estimating sales for the coming year. Simply adjust last year's sales figures as necessary to reflect the conditions you expect next year.

If you anticipate making changes that will affect your sales volume in the future, the sales forecast section of the plan should explain those changes, and why they will have the effect you state. Similarly, if you expect that external changes will have an effect on your sales volume, such as a new highway, a plant closing, changing demographics in your area, or new competition entering the market, this is the place to say so.

You might also want to explain your strategy for meeting the challenges you foresee — for instance, will you hire an additional salesperson if you expect sales would otherwise drop, or will you need more production capacity if you expect sales revenue to increase dramatically?

Case Study — Sales Forecasting

John Divot owns a golf supply retail store. John will use last year's sales figures to prepare his sales forecast for the next six months. Here is the sales information from the first six months of last year:

January	$18,000
February	$18,500
March	$20,500
April	$28,900
May	$32,300
June	$36,600

John expects sales for this year to be 1 percent higher in the off season and 1.5 percent higher during the golf season, which begins in April. John forecasts his sales for the first six months of this year to be as follows:

January	$18,180
February	$18,685
March	$20,705
April	$29,333
May	$32,785
June	$37,150

Projecting Sales for a New Business

Before we take a look at some ways to estimate revenues for a startup business, a word of caution. Estimating your sales will be an inexact science. Don't count too heavily on your projections and, if you're going to err, err on the conservative side in predicting how much business you'll do in your first year.

Product vendors may be an excellent source of sales data. If your new business is one that will have high inventory levels, suppliers or warehouse facilities may be a potential source of sales data.

For example, assume you plan to open a grocery store. You would purchase the majority of your product from a primary grocery distributor. Usually a distributor of any significant size will have access to other grocery stores' sales in your trade area. This could be your starting point for your sales potential. You will have to make adjustments to the sales figure based, for example, on site selection, competition, and marketing.

Warning

Be careful when dealing with product vendors to determine sales potential. Some may just tell you what you want to hear in order to get your business. Back up their forecasts with other sources.

Most libraries have a wide range of information available for specific types of enterprises. The trade publications and trade associations are good sources of overall sales information for your specific industry. These publications will generally break out sales by geographic region and by business type.

The Bureau of the Census publications and website (www.census.gov) can provide you with a lot of information on sales volume for various business types by geographic location. This information is usually a few years out of date, so if your new business is one that will be greatly affected by the time lag, you'll want to make adjustments for it. Remember that your sales figure will still be just an educated guess. Along with the sales figure, Census data will provide other financial details, such as average cost of goods sold and payroll.

Example

Let's say you want to estimate sales for a fictitious submarine sandwich shop in Cedar Rapids, Iowa.

The Census of Retail Trade, a Census Bureau publication, showed that there were 284 eating and drinking establishments in Cedar Rapids. The average sales volume per eating establishment was $548,866. Based on other research, it was determined that this in itself was not a realistic number for the planned sub shop, and adjustments need to be made for other known facts.

Assume that the average customer will spend $4.50 per meal. Also assume that the restaurant will have between 150 to 200 customers on an average day. Multiplying the $4.50 times 175 customers (average of 150 and 200) times 365 days, the sales will compute to $287,438 per year.

PROJECTED PROFIT AND LOSS STATEMENT

Also called an income statement, a profit and loss statement lists your income, expenses, and the difference between the two, which is your net income (or loss). Your business's tax return will use a variation of the profit and loss statement to determine your potentially taxable income.

The profit and loss statement shows you a summary of the flow of transactions your business has over the entire accounting period. In other words, the statement shows you what happens during the period between balance sheets.

Three years' worth of projected income-statement data is normally presented, so that you can make comparisons and identify trends.

For a sample form that you can use to construct your own statement, see the next page. The categories provided are the ones that are most common for the average small business — be sure to add or subtract categories as appropriate to your particular company.

Your Company Projected Profit and Loss Statement - Annual by Month	JAN	FEB	MAR	APR	MAY	JUN
Revenue:						
Gross Sales						
Less: Sales Returns						
Net Sales						
Cost of Goods Sold:						
Materials						
Labor						
Other Direct Expenses						
Indirect Expenses						
Total Cost of Goods Sold						
Gross Profit (Loss)						
Expenses:						
Advertising						
Bad Debts						
Bank Charges						
Credit Card Fees						
Delivery Expenses						
Depreciation						
Dues and Subscriptions						
Equipment Rental						
Insurance						
Interest						
Maintenance						
Miscellaneous						
Office Expenses						
Operating Supplies						
Payroll Taxes						
Permits and Licenses						
Postage						
Rent						
Telephone						
Travel						
Utilities						
Wages and Benefits						
Total Expenses						
Net Operating Income						
Other Income:						
Gain (Loss) on Asset Sales						
Interest Income						
Total Other Income						
Net Income Before Tax						
Net Income After Tax						

	Your Company					
	Projected Profit and Loss Statement - Annual by Month					
JUL	AUG	SEP	OCT	NOV	DEC	TOTAL

The data on your projected profit and loss consist of the following:

- sales revenue

- sales returns and allowances

- cost of goods sold

- selling, general, and administrative expenses

- depreciation and amortization expenses

- interest expense

A detailed, month-by-month P & L should be provided for the first year. For later years, you may want to break down the information by quarter, or you may decide to provide an annual summary.

Depending on whether you are preparing a projected profit and loss statement for an existing business or a startup enterprise, you may have some difficulty coming up with reliable estimates for some of these figures. Dun & Bradstreet and other financial information purveyors may be able to provide information regarding industry average expenditures for cost of goods sold, general and administrative expenses, and other major categories as a percentage of sales. As you talk to suppliers and receive bids from them, sign leases for equipment or facilities, find out the going rate for employees in the jobs you'll be hiring for, etc., you should be able to fill in the blanks.

PROJECTED CASH FLOW BUDGETS

In its simplest form, cash flow is the movement of money in and out of your business. It could be described as the process in which your business uses cash to generate goods or services for the sale to your customers, collects the cash from the sales, and then completes this cycle all over again.

"Inflows" are the movement of money into your business, and are most likely from the sale of your goods or services to your customers. If you extend credit to your customers and allow them to charge the sale of the goods or services to their account, then an inflow occurs as you collect on the customers' accounts. The proceeds from a bank loan are also a cash inflow.

"Outflows" are the movement of money out of your business, and are generally the result of paying expenses. If your business involves reselling goods, your largest outflow is most likely to be for the purchase of retail inventory.

A manufacturing business's largest outflows will most likely be for payroll and for the purchases of raw materials and other components needed for the manufacturing of the final product. Purchasing fixed assets, paying back loans, and paying accounts payable are also cash outflows.

A good way to learn respect for the concept of cash flow is to compare it to the idea of profit. If a retail business is able to buy a retail item for $1,000 and sell it for $2,000, then it has made a $1,000 gross profit. But what if the buyer of the retail item is slow to pay his or her bill, and six months pass before the bill is paid? Using accrual accounting, the retail business still shows a profit, but what about the bills it has to pay during the six months that pass? It will not have the cash to pay them, despite the profit earned on the sale.

As you can see, profit and cash flow are two entirely different concepts, each with entirely different results. The concept of profit is somewhat narrow, and only looks at income and expenses over an entire accounting period. Cash flow, on the other hand, is more dynamic. It is concerned with the movement of money in and out of a business. More importantly, it is concerned with the time at which the movement of the money takes place. You might even say the concept of cash flow is more in line with reality!

Therefore, your cash flow projections will be the most important financial statements in your business plan. You need to include a month-by-month cash flow projection for at least the first year. For a sample form on which you can compute your own cash flow, see page 76. In using the form, note that the cash that remains at the end of the first month will become the beginning cash balance for the second month, and so on through all the months of the year.

For later years, you can project annually by quarter, or even annually by year, as you'll see in our sample business plans.

If you are preparing a cash flow budget worksheet for an existing business, you can base your estimates of cash inflows and outflows on historical information. On the other hand, if you're a startup business, you should base your estimates of cash sources and uses on the revenues and expenses listed in the projected profit and loss statements. Accordingly, we recommend that you complete a projected profit and loss statement before completing the cash flow budget worksheet.

If you are seeking a loan, an important feature of your cash flow statement is that it will show the lender exactly how you're going to afford the loan payments.

Your Company						
Cash Flow Budget Worksheet - Annual by Month						
	JAN	**FEB**	**MAR**	**APR**	**MAY**	**JUN**
Beginning Cash Balance						
Cash Inflows (Income):						
Accounts Receivable Collections						
Loan Proceeds						
Sales & Receipts						
Other						
Total Cash Inflows						
Available Cash Balance						
Cash Outflows (Expenses):						
Advertising						
Bank Service Charges						
Credit Card Fees						
Delivery						
Health Insurance						
Insurance						
Interest						
Inventory Purchases						
Miscellaneous						
Office						
Payroll						
Payroll Taxes						
Professional Fees						
Rent or Lease						
Subscriptions & Dues						
Supplies						
Taxes & Licenses						
Utilities & Telephone						
Other						
Travel						
Maintenance						
Subtotal						
Other Cash Outflows:						
Capital Purchases						
Loan Principal						
Owner's Draw						
Other:						
Subtotal						
Total Cash Outflows						
Ending Cash Balance						

			Your Company			
		Cash Flow Budget Worksheet - Annual by Month				
JUL	AUG	SEP	OCT	NOV	DEC	TOTAL

Planning Your Cash Flow

If you were able to do business in a perfect world, you'd probably like to have a cash inflow (a cash sale) occur every time you experience a cash outflow (pay an expense). But you know all too well that business takes place in the real world, and things just don't happen like that.

Instead, cash outflows and inflows rarely occur together. More often than not, it seems, cash inflows lag behind your cash outflows, leaving your business short of money. Think of this money shortage as your cash flow gap.

When creating your business plan, you have the time and opportunity to adjust your projected cash flow statements. If you notice a gap, and especially if the gap is large, try to change your operating plans until the gap disappears. For instance, if you expect a gap in October as you load up on inventory for the December selling season, consider reducing or postponing some of the expenses you'd normally pay that month. You might be able to reduce your travel expenses that month, or avoid purchasing office supplies, or change your insurance payment due dates so that none fall in October.

The point is not only to make your business plan look good (although that's important, obviously) but also to do as much as you can ahead of time to avoid any cash flow gaps and the havoc they can wreak upon your business.

PROJECTED BALANCE SHEETS

The balance sheet is a statement of your company's relative wealth or financial position *at a given point in time*. It's often referred to as a "snapshot," because it gives you a fairly clear picture of the business at that moment, but does not in itself reveal how the business arrived there or where it's going next. That's one reason why the balance sheet is not the whole story — you must also look at the information from each of the other financial statements (and at historical information as well) to get the most benefit from the data.

In your business plan, you'll want to provide at least three years of projected balance sheet information. You may want to provide detailed, month-by-month information for the first year, as our sample business plans have done.

The balance sheet consists of three categories of items: assets, liabilities, and stockholders' or owners' equity.

Assets. Assets are generally divided into two groups: current assets and noncurrent (long-term) assets. They are usually presented in order of liquidity, with current assets (cash and those that will be converted to cash within one year) appearing first. Current assets include cash, accounts and notes receivable, inventories, prepaid expenses, and any other short-term investments. Long-term assets include land, buildings, machinery and equipment, and capitalized leases, less any accumulated depreciation and amortization.

Liabilities. Liabilities are normally presented in order of their claim on the company's assets (i.e., liabilities due within one year are presented before liabilities due several years from now). Liabilities include accounts payable, notes payable, income taxes payable, the current portion of any long-term debt, and any other liabilities due within the accounting period. Long-term liabilities include a mortgage or any other debt that will become due after the relevant accounting period, deferred income taxes, or other deferred debts.

Equity. For sole proprietorships, equity is usually a one-line entry that represents the difference between the business's assets and its liabilities.

For co-owned businesses such as partnerships or limited liability companies, the statement should show the division of equity between or among the co-owners.

For corporations, stockholders' equity is presented properly when each class of stock is presented with all its relevant information (for example, number of shares authorized, shares issued, shares outstanding, and par value). If retained earnings are restricted or appropriated, this also should be shown.

See page 80 for a sample balance sheet form that you can adapt for your company. We've filled in the blanks for a fictitious company, to show you how the numbers should add up. You can also use other formats, as illustrated in the sample business plans.

SOURCES AND USES OF FUNDS STATEMENT

If your business is seeking a loan or investment by an outsider, it's important to show prospective financiers exactly how much money you need and how you expect to spend it. The sources and uses of funds statement is the best way to highlight this information. It will also indicate the extent to which you're investing your own funds in the business – something that is highly important to an investor. With your own assets on the line, you'll certainly be more motivated to make sure the business succeeds.

Joel's Chocolate Company, Inc.
Projected Balance Sheet - December 31, ____

Assets			Liabilities and Capital		
Current Assets:			**Current Liabilities:**		
Cash		$815,840	Accounts Payable	$7,500	
Accounts Receivable	$22,000		Sales Taxes Payable	800	
Less: Reserve for Bad Debts		20,020	Payroll Taxes Payable	17,500	
1,980					
Merchandise Inventory		15,000	Accrued Wages Payable	60,000	
Prepaid Expenses		5,200	Unearned Revenues	78,000	
Notes Receivable		0	Short-Term Notes Payable	0	
Total Current Assets		$856,060	Short-Term Bank Loans		
			Payable	0	
Fixed Assets:			**Total Current Liabilities**		$163,800
Vehicles	0				
Less: Accumulated Dep.	0	0	**Long-Term Liabilities:**		
Furniture and Fixtures	25,000		Long-Term Notes Payable	50,000	
Less: Accumulated Dep.	9,000	16,000	Mortgages Payable	0	
Equipment	160,000		**Total Long-Term Liabilities**		50,000
Less: Accumulated Dep.	60,000	100,000			
Buildings	0		**Total Liabilities**		213,800
Less: Accumulated Dep.	0	0			
Land	0		**Capital:**		
Total Fixed Assets		116,000	Paid-in Capital	758,260	
Other Assets:			Additional Capital	0	
Goodwill		0	**Total Capital**		758,260
Total Other Assets		0			
Total Assets		$972,060	**Total Liabilities and Capital**		$972,060

The sources and uses of funds document should start by stating the total amount of capital you need to start operations, to finance your expansion project, or to do whatever else it is that you want to accomplish with your plan.

It should detail how you expect to spend the money, in categories such as: working capital, facilities, equipment, marketing expenses, staff hiring, initial inventory, etc.

Then, it should detail how you expect to obtain the money: investment by you, sale of stock in the company, a short-term line of credit, long-term debt, a mortgage, etc. The total funds needed should equal the total funds to be sourced, of course!

Chapter 9

Using The Completed Plan

Your completed business plan is a document that you can use as a blueprint as you begin or continue to operate the company. It's also a document that you can use to communicate with both internal and external audiences.

But creating a business plan should yield many benefits over and above the actual document. Most importantly, you will have established a planning process that you can use over and over again, improving it each time by incorporating the experience you have gained. The existence of both the *document* and the *process* enable you to derive the maximum benefit from the work you put into creating the plan.

The plan can also become a tracking and evaluation tool. Because your plan will set forth a number of marketing, operational, and financial milestones, you can meaningfully interpret your actual operating results against the baseline established by the plan.

Let's take a look at how you can effectively use your business plan to run your company.

MONITORING YOUR PROGRESS

A well-written business plan defines the goals and objectives that you wish to achieve over the next few years in specific, quantifiable terms. It may project a certain level of sales by a given date, the acquisition of a certain number of clients, or any of a number of other objective measures of success. Whatever the conditions that spell success, you'll want to watch your progress toward those goals over time. If you're on track, great!

If not, you're in a position to take steps to get back on track before it's too late.

The process of monitoring your business's performance can be relatively painless. The following pages discuss the issues to consider.

How Frequently Should You Look?

As a practical matter, you'll probably have a feel for how you're doing because of your involvement with the day-to-day activities of your business. If you make the bank deposits each night, if you pay the bills each month, if you balance the books at the end of the month, then you already know a lot about how your business is doing. But it's worthwhile to supplement this familiarity with some hard and fast milestones.

Using milestones is simply a decision to take a look at a specific performance measure at a particular point in time. You should select your milestones to accommodate two competing considerations. On the one hand, milestones should be infrequent enough so that there is a meaningful amount of information available to analyze. On the other hand, milestones must occur frequently enough so that you can take appropriate action if you see that interim goals aren't being reached. With luck, you'll be able to schedule these periodic business check-ups to coincide with activities you would do anyway, such as balancing your checking account.

Many larger businesses take a look, each month, at certain performance measures that they deem especially important. We suggest that your business do the same, so that you can make any necessary corrections quickly and avoid major problems. Waiting until the end of the year, or even the calendar quarter, to check your progress may be too late.

Selecting Performance Measures

Almost every aspect of your business can probably be measured against some objective yardstick of success. The ability of a salesperson can be measured by the number of sales per month or by the cumulative amount of sales, year-to-date. If your business gets most of its profit from the more expensive products or services you provide, sales revenue (or dollar amount per sale) will be of far more interest than the raw number of sales.

If possible, try to integrate all of your performance measures into the routine of your operations. For example, if a lender requires monthly statements of income and expense, use them to monitor performance. You may want to track information the lender doesn't want, but you can piggyback that data-gathering onto your required reports.

Assessing Your Performance

Once you begin operations according to your business plan, there are two possible outcomes. One is that your projections and assumptions prove to be relatively accurate. In that case, it's likely that your business will be performing as you had hoped. More likely, however, things aren't going exactly as projected. These departures from your plan may be small and not a source of concern, or they may be substantial and require immediate action on your part.

When Things Go According to the Plan

Let's consider the first outcome: you did a good job of planning and, basically, your business is operating the way you'd like to see it. Your performance measurement system is generating data showing that the goals and objectives set forth in your business plan are being met. Congratulations! As many race car drivers say, "I'd rather be lucky than good any day." If you've written a plan and your business developed just as you projected, you're definitely one or the other. So, what do you do about it?

First, make an effort to extend your planning horizon further out in time. Begin to "firm up" the numbers for periods beyond the initial planning window. Fine-tune the plan to get an even better picture of where you're heading. For you, keeping the plan current is easy.

Second, and more importantly, begin looking for ways to improve on what you've done so far. You've begun to build a track record of success and you want to keep on building. Your basic business idea was, most likely, sound (never completely discount the luck factor), and you now have an opportunity to expand, refine, and innovate. If you haven't considered the long-term future of your business, start thinking. If you've set aggressive goals (and most business owners do), consider what you'll have if your business stays on track for three years, or five.

When Things Go Wrong

Despite your best efforts, sometimes a business just doesn't take off the way you expected. The unfortunate fact is that a large percentage of new small businesses fail. But then, most small business owners don't bother to create a written business plan unless they are absolutely required to (as is usually the case if you need outside investors or bank financing). Without a written plan, it's just that much harder to cope when your business isn't meeting your goals.

You, however, will have a written plan, so let's see how it can help you out when things go wrong.

Deviation Analysis

We've included a chart, below, that you can use to compare your expected results against your actual results for any given month, and for the year to date. The difference between the actual and expected results is the deviation – and it can be positive (in your favor) or negative. In the columns labeled "Budget," you can insert the data from the pro-forma income statements in your business plan. Comparing the "actual" data with the "budget" will tell you the deviation, either positive or negative. Once you know the extent of your deviation from what you had hoped to achieve, you can decide what to do about it.

Financial Results	This Month	This Month	This Month	Year to Date	Year to Date	Year to Date	Prior Year to Date
(In 1000's)	Actual	Budget	Deviation	Actual	Budget	Deviation	Actual
Sales Revenue							
Direct Costs							
Marketing Costs							
Marketing Contribution							
New Units Sold: Line A							
New Units Sold: Line B							

When things don't go well for a business, it isn't always easy to figure out why. It could be that your business plan contains some faulty assumptions or conclusions. Or it could be that your business is having operational difficulties of some sort. In either event, you have to isolate the cause of the problem before you can correct it.

Some problems will be internal to your business, while others will result from external factors beyond your direct control.

External factors can be very widespread, such as a downturn in the entire local economy, or they can be specific to your business, such as a vendor's failure to deliver on time. Internal factors relate to the specific processes and activities that you use in running your business. An employee may not be performing as you'd like, or operating cost estimates contained in the business plan might have been too low.

In all probability, there won't be just a single root cause for your business's problems. As you look for the source of your problems, don't be surprised if you have to address several issues. The key concern is to identify all of the reasons why your business isn't going the way you'd like. Then you can consider what to do about them.

KEEPING YOUR PLAN CURRENT

You should treat your business plan as a dynamic document that should be kept current as your business evolves. You've invested a good deal of your time and effort to create the plan in the first place. If you don't keep the plan current, you can look forward to a similar effort the next time you need a written plan. Remember, it's almost always easier to edit an existing document than to create a new one from scratch.

Planning Interval

Many people think of "planning" as an annual process. Thousands of companies publish an annual plan each year, outlining their expectations about operating results for the coming 12 months.

Realistically, though, you're probably planning all the time. Most business owners are always thinking about ways to make their business better. In discussing a "planning interval," what we're really suggesting is periodically setting aside a certain amount of time to create or update your written business plan.

So how do you select a reasonable planning interval? Start with the assumption that you'd like to have at least one planning period each year. Many factors that affect your business will be tied to some annual cycle. For example, income taxes are due yearly, and federal safety rules require posting annual summaries of information. Also, many employees will expect annual raises or bonuses. This and other factors make annual planning after tax time a reasonable starting point, though your circumstances may require a different planning interval.

Example

 Consider a business located on a small chain of lakes. It operates a marina and boat repair facility from spring to fall. As the boating season ends, the business switches to servicing snowmobiles and supporting ice fishers. Even though the results of marina operations are available as of the end of the season, that information is of limited value in planning for the coming winter.

The information that is meaningful to the business owner trying to plan for winter relates to the prior winter's operations. Planning for summer operations and for winter operations wouldn't have to occur at the same time, and there would likely be benefits from scheduling two planning sessions.

Part II

Five Sample Business Plans

Now you have a good understanding of the elements that a good business plan should include and the purposes that each section serves. So, it's time to take a look at some sample business plans that illustrate how the elements of a plan are written in light of the unique circumstances of individual businesses.

In Part II, we provide you with five sample business plans written for different types of businesses, in various stages of the business lifecycle. We include a plan for a growing manufacturer, a two-person start-up, a specialty food and drink retailer, a venture-capital-financed transportation service and a custom clothing company. Four of the plans are for startups, and one is for a business that is already operating but wants to expand its scope (and profitability).

Appleton Moldings, Inc. Appleton Moldings, Inc. is a six-year old business engaged in injection molding of parts for a variety of manufacturers. In order to expand the business, the plan seeks to obtain $125,000 in bank financing to purchase additional molding equipment. One important point is that Appleton has already obtained $75,000 in vendor financing for the purchase.

The plan emphasizes the experience and abilities of the individuals who serve as the company's management team.

The Appleton Moldings, Inc plan is instructional in several areas:

- This is a good example of a plan for an existing manufacturing business that has unused space in its production facility.

- A careful analysis of the primary competitors demonstrates that Appleton, which is smaller than its major competitors, is nimble and better capable of reacting to changes in customer demands than others in the same business.

- The business has a well thought out promotional plan to aggressively target new customer.

- The plan addresses other business changes required to succeed, including hiring additional production and sales staff.

- This plan is designed to increase the production capacity in a very short time after financing is acquired.

Crime & Accident Scene Cleanup, Inc. This is a company seeking funding to begin business in a carefully selected niche market. Few cleaning services offer bio-hazardous waste removal, so competition is limited. One very interesting feature of the plan is that the owners plan to operate the business for a relatively short period of time (six years) and then sell it to employees or competitors.

The plan for Crime & Accident Scene Cleanup, Inc. provides several important insights:

- This business targets a single metropolitan area for its initial operations, with plans to expand into other large cities as the business grows.

- The plan also targets three focused groups of potential customers, including insurance companies, a number of very specific industries (police, medical service providers, coroners, funeral homes) and, finally, property owners.

- This plan discusses the experience of its two principals, and demonstrates that they have already done their homework and also arranged for professional advisors to assist them.

- The business will initially operate out of one owner's garage in order to minimize the indirect costs associated with operations.

- This is primarily a service organization, with much of the requested funding to be used to acquire two specially equipped vehicles designed specifically to perform bio-hazardous waste cleanup.

HydroHut LLC. This start-up business intends to operate a single retail facility in Austin, Texas. Its products will consist of still water drinks and baked goods for health-conscious consumers. The plan is designed to support a request for a line of credit, rather than a lump-sum. This will allow the owners to draw upon funds without having to pay interest on the entire amount requested unless they actually use the full amount requested.

Like the other plans presented here, the plan for HydroHut has much to offer:

- Great emphasis is placed on the experience and knowledge of the owners. They have both worked in similar industries, and they spent substantial time researching existing still water businesses in other locations.

- The cash flow projections suggest that no additional financing will be required once the business is up and running.

- This business will not produce any of the products to be sold. Instead, everything will be acquired from third-party vendors, many of whom have already been identified.

- Because the owners project that they will probably only need one-third of the amount requested, they are both willing to invest their own money as well as pledge personal assets as collateral for the loan.

- The choice of location was driven by Austin's high per capita consumption of healthy food, the proximity of a university, and the fact that there are currently no competitors in the market.

Royal Limousine. This is another start-up that intends to provide luxury limousine services in the Omaha, Nebraska market. The owners designed the business around meeting personal goals, permitting one of them to attend college while still being a 50 percent participant in the business.

It's a well-structured plan with some important lessons:

- The owners carefully researched the competitors and deliberately built the plan on providing a higher quality of service and a larger capacity limousine.

- The business has already entered into an agreement with a local casino, giving them access to an existing audience for scheduled limousine trips.

- This plan targets several types of potential customers in addition to its scheduled casino trips, including weddings and hourly rentals.

- This business needed $150,000 in startup capital from an outside source. The plan was finished on a Friday afternoon, presented to the angel investor that evening, and the full $150,000 was approved and available the next day!

The T-Shirt Shop. The T-Shirt Shop plan seeks funding to open a proposed silk screening and embroidery business, to be operated as a sole proprietorship. Research indicated that there was only one competitor in the target market of Billings, Montana.

- The business will rely on its ability to obtain discounts on bulk purchases, and undercut the competition by passing along the savings to its corporate customers.

- Both the owner and primary employee have substantial experience in and knowledge of the retail clothing industry, so the business will have the advantage of providing products that are more leading edge than its competitor

- Although it will be located in a highly trafficked retail mall, 75% of sales will be targeted at corporate customers. The 25% of retail customers won't enjoy the discounts passed on to corporate customers.

- The plan is unusual in that it seeks three distinctly different types of financing: a loan, a line of credit, and a second loan to be used for personal purposes.

- The plan contemplates an aggressive promotional plan designed to quickly acquire local businesses as customers.

- The plan does a particularly good job of addressing the "Four Ps of Marketing:" Product, Price, Place and Promotion.

The Business Plan for

Appleton Moldings, Inc.

A Wisconsin C Corporation

Contact Information:

Steve Johnson

1234 River Lane

Appleton, WI 12345

(123) 456-7890

(123) 456-7891 Fax

sjohnson@appletonmoldings.net

This is a business plan and does not imply an offering of securities.

Copy Number __ of Five.

Non-Disclosure and Confidentiality Agreement

The undersigned ("Recipient") hereby agrees that all financial and other information ("Information") that it has and will receive concerning Appleton Moldings, Inc. is confidential and will not be disclosed to any individual or entity without prior written consent.

The Information shall remain the property of Appleton Moldings, Inc. and shall be returned to Appleton Moldings, Inc. promptly at its request together with all copies made thereof.

Recipient acknowledges that no remedy of law may be adequate to compensate Appleton Moldings, Inc. for a violation of this Agreement and Recipient hereby agrees that in addition to any legal or other rights that may be available in the event of a breach hereunder, Appleton Moldings, Inc. may seek equitable relief to enforce this Agreement in any Court of competent jurisdiction.

_____   _____

Date   Signature of Recipient

THE PLAN FOR APPLETON MOLDINGS, INC.

1.0 EXECUTIVE SUMMARY

Steve Johnson had an idea in 2000 to start an injection molding business that would provide plastic products to manufacturing companies throughout the Midwest. Appleton Moldings, Inc. was formed in 2002 out of Steve's vision, and now has been successfully operating in the Appleton area for the past 5 years.

Steve has built Appleton Moldings, Inc. into a profitable business by maintaining a small, skilled workforce and low operating costs. Although the business has remained profitable, sales have become stagnant. The company is operating at 100 percent capacity and needs to expand operations in order to meet the demand from current customers and to acquire new ones. Appleton Moldings, Inc. can meet this demand by adding new equipment and increasing its marketing efforts.

1.1 Business Opportunity

In the past, Appleton Moldings, Inc. has only targeted small and mid-level sized manufacturing companies located within the state of Wisconsin. The company has the opportunity to broaden its scope by moving outside of the state and into the greater Midwest market. The Midwest market is estimated to be a $125 million industry each year.

1.2 Injection Molding Products

Appleton Moldings, Inc. currently manufactures and markets plastic injection molded products for lawnmowers, irrigation systems, golf carts, and vacuum cleaners. Once the pieces have been molded, the plastic pieces are then shipped to the manufacturer to be incorporated into the finished product.

1.3 Current Business Position

Appleton Moldings, Inc. is a C Corporation registered in the state of Wisconsin. Steve Johnson formed the corporation in 2002. Steve is the CEO and is a twenty-year veteran of the injection molding industry. Steve started the business with a cash investment of $75,000 and a building.

Steve Johnson owns 60% of Appleton Moldings, Inc., while Charles Wright, one of the board members and a local banker, owns 25%. Peter Whitney, a board member and local farmer, owns a 10% stake in the company. The company's employees own the remaining 5% of Appleton Moldings, Inc.

The funds Steve used to capitalize the firm were primarily used to purchase two used injection molding machines, plastic materials and some office equipment. Steve started the business when he inherited a 52,000 square foot building where Appleton Moldings, Inc. conducts business operations.

1.4 Financial Potential

Based upon the financial projections for the next three years, Appleton Moldings, Inc. expects to significantly increase revenues and profitability if the company is able to secure the funds needed to purchase additional molding equipment. Annual sales have remained constant over the past few years averaging at or near $1,500,000.

Appleton Moldings, Inc. ownership strongly believes that by doubling the amount of operating equipment, adding additional personnel, and increasing marketing efforts the business will increase revenues to $2,975,000 in year one, and $3,420,000 in years two and three. Operating income before taxes and interest during the three years projected are estimated at $243,695 in year one, and $436,245 in years two and three.

The following chart is a breakdown of projected revenues and expenses for Appleton Moldings, Inc. over the next three years:

-6-

Profit & Loss Statement

For years ending December - 2008, 2009, 2010			
	Year 1	Year 2	Year 3
Income	2,975,000	3,420,000	3,420,000
Less COGS:			
Material	652,500	750,000	750,000
Labor	783,000	900,000	900,000
Other	248,500	282,000	282,000
Total COGS	1,684,000	1,932,000	1,932,000
Gross profit	1,291,000	1,488,000	1,488,000
Operating expenses:			
Insurance	32,000	32,000	32,000
Utilities	180,000	180,000	180,000
Telephone	24,000	24,000	24,000
Marketing	120,000	120,000	120,000
Travel	72,000	72,000	72,000
Management Salaries	255,000	255,000	255,000
Sales Salaries	112,500	112,500	112,500
Office Supplies	6,000	6,000	6,000
Repairs & Maintenance	18,000	18,000	18,000
Professional Services	9,000	9,000	9,000
Bad debts	29,750	34,200	34,200
Depreciation	189,055	189,055	189,055
Total operating expenses	1,047,305	1,051,755	1,051,755
Operating income	243,695	436,245	436,245
Interest expense	32,495	24,646	16,327
Net income before taxes	211,200	411,599	419,918
Estimated taxes	52,800	102,900	104,980
Net income	158,400	308,699	314,939

The following is a graph showing Appleton Moldings, Inc.'s balance sheet projections for the next three years:

-7-

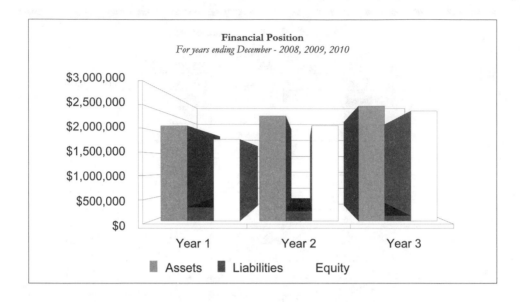

Financial Position
For years ending December - 2008, 2009, 2010

Legend: Assets | Liabilities | Equity

1.5 The Request

Appleton Moldings, Inc. is seeking $125,000 from National Bank in order to assist with the purchase of new injection molding equipment. Appleton Moldings, Inc. has already arranged vendor financing from an equipment supplier in the amount of $75,000.

2. COMPANY BACKGROUND

Before the company started in 2002, Steve Johnson worked for one of the largest injection molding companies in the Midwest, PBI Molding. Steve began his career as a machinist for PBI and quickly moved into a sales position. Steve was a salesperson for ten years until 1999 when he began working on Appleton Moldings, Inc.

2.1 Current Position and Business Objectives

Currently, only half of Appleton's production facility is being used; and in order to make Appleton more profitable, the company must fill the remaining warehouse space with new injection molding equipment. The sales staff and operating personnel will also have to be increased in order bring new business to the company.

-8-

3. PRODUCTS

Injection molding is a manufacturing process where a solid plastic is heated and forced into a mold within an injection molding machine. After being heated, the plastic is placed under extreme pressure to fill the shape of the mold. The plastic slowly cools within the cavity of the mold and is dropped into a cooling bin to change from a liquid to a solid. After the product is finished cooling, it is cleaned and prepared for shipping.

3.1 Product Overview

Appleton Moldings, Inc. currently produces plastic pieces for lawnmowers, irrigation systems, golf carts, and vacuums. Appleton's largest customers include Toro and Green Rain. Toro, a lawnmower manufacturer, contributes 35% of Appleton's sales each year, while Green Rain, an irrigation system manufacturer, contributes 45% of Appleton's sales. The remainder of the sales come from Club, a golf cart manufacturer, DryVac, an industrial vacuum maker, and a few other small companies throughout Wisconsin. All of these manufacturers are expanding and would like Appleton Moldings, Inc. to produce additional products for their companies.

3.2 Competitive Analysis

There are several injection molding companies located across the United States. The Midwest market, where Appleton plans on expanding, is dominated by few major companies. Some of these companies focus strictly on injection molding, while others have in-house machine shops to produce molds for the different plastic products. Appleton Moldings, Inc. currently outsources this work and will continue to do so after expansion. Appleton Moldings, Inc. then passes its costs plus a mark-up onto the customer.

Appleton Moldings, Inc. is much smaller than most of the firms competing in the Midwest, but this serves as a competitive advantage. The company can be more flexible and able to adapt quickly to changes in the market, where larger companies cannot change their production methods easily. Appleton Moldings, Inc. also possesses adequate warehouse space without having to pay the high costs for renovation. Appleton's workforce is very skilled and the cost of labor is much cheaper than other Midwest locations. This inexpensive labor has allowed Appleton Moldings, Inc. to pass its labor savings onto the customer.

3.3 Suppliers and Inventory

For the last decade, Appleton Molding's raw materials supplier has been Ashton Plastics. This company is one of the largest raw plastic suppliers in the Midwest and supplies several other injection molding companies. Ashton Plastics will continue to support Appleton's growth and expansion in the years to come.

4. SERVICES

One of Appleton Moldings, Inc.'s top priorities is to keep every customer satisfied. Appleton Moldings, Inc. will not only grow its operation by adding new customers, the company will need to maintain the satisfaction of existing customers. Appleton Moldings, Inc. has put into place the following standards in order to ensure customer satisfaction:

1. All estimates will be processed within 48 hours.

2. Appleton Moldings, Inc. will use the highest quality of materials available.

3. Calls will be placed following every job in order to ensure customer satisfaction.

5. THE INJECTION MOLDING INDUSTRY

The plastic injection molding industry is a very large industry that changes daily. The industry has an annual growth rate of 4.8%. Companies within the injection molding industry are continuously improving manufacturing techniques and developing new products in order to remain competitive.

5.1 Industry Definition

The overall size of the U.S. plastics industry is $345 billion annually. Because the industry includes a very diverse group of products with significantly different characteristics, it is more meaningful to classify the products into eight different product groups:

Transportation: This industry is expected to grow only one percent according to industry reports and trade publications over the next year.

Electrical and Electronics: This industry is expected to grow approximately 12.1%.

Medical: This industry is expected to slow down to 7.0% to 7.5% within the year, down from 9.7% growth in the previous year.

Toys: This industry is expected to slow down and decline as much as 2.4%.

-10-

Packaging: This industry is expected to slow as much as 2.6% with a recession or 3.6% with a minor industry slowdown.

Building and construction: This industry is expected to remain stable at a 3.0% growth rate.

Furniture and furnishings: This industry is expected to grow to 3.3% to 3.6%.

Appliances/durable goods: This industry is expected to decline to a 2.9% growth rate with a recession or a 4.1% growth rate with a minor industry slowdown.

5.2 Primary Competitors

Some of the large competitors in the Midwest region include Midwest Tooling, Midwest Plastics, PBI Plastics, and Ryan Injection Molding. Out of the four companies listed, Midwest Plastics and PBI Plastics are the market leaders followed by Midwest Tooling and Ryan Injection Molding. Midwest Plastics has 27% of the market share, while PBI Plastics controls 23%. The Midwest market for injection molding is approximately $125 million annually, and these two companies capture $62 million.

5.3 Market Changes

The most significant developments in the injection molding business include the relocation of U.S. facilities to foreign countries. Foreign countries provide a competitive advantage for large injection molding companies because of labor, rent, and overall production savings. Injection molding companies have become pressured to become full-service manufacturers.

5.4 Customer Profile

The typical steps a buyer goes through when purchasing injection-molded products for inclusion into manufactured goods include:

1. The buyer contacts the injection molding company to provide the size and dimensions for the object.

2. A prototype or drawing is created to match the size and shape of the product.

3. The type of plastic is selected depending upon the intended use of the product.

4. The amount of units per month and time of delivery is selected.

5. A price quote is submitted to the customer.

6. The customer places the order.

6. MARKETING PLAN

Appleton's goal is to bring the plant to 100% capacity after new machinery is acquired and additional personnel has been hired. In order to accomplish this, the business must keep a strong focus on marketing efforts in the years to come.

6.1 Competitive Advantage

Appleton uses an aggressive, yet personal, approach when targeting new customers. This personal touch has gone a long way toward helping Appleton Moldings, Inc. grow to where it is today.

6.2 Pricing

When manufacturers contact Appleton Moldings, Inc. for a custom price quote, they usually provide the company with drawings for the product. The cost of production is estimated by taking the dimensions, cost of the mold, how many units will need to be produced, and the type of plastic material to be used. On average, Appleton's prices are 5-10% less than the competition. The reason why the prices are lower is because the cost of labor is less and the savings are passed onto the customer.

6.3 Distribution Channels

The company currently has only one salesperson, who is responsible for all Appleton Molding's customers. The company will hire two additional salespersons in order to add new customers and increase business from existing customers.

6.4 Promotional Plan

The sales staff will try to arrange meetings with important buyers from large manufacturing companies throughout the Midwest. Other marketing activities will also be geared towards getting potential customers to meet with Appleton's sales team. Appleton Moldings, Inc. has a monthly marketing budget of $10,000, and marketing efforts will consist of the following:

Advertise in the Thomas Register catalog ($1,000): Appleton Moldings, Inc. will pay an annual fee to be listed under plastic injection molding companies in the Thomas Register catalog.

-12-

Advertise in industry trade publications and the Internet ($7,000):

1. Plastics Technology ($1,500)

2. IMM Magazine ($1,500)

3. Plastic News ($1,000)

4. Modern Plastics ($1,000)

5. Plastics Magazine ($1,000)

6. Advanced Manufacturing Magazine ($1,000)

Direct business mailings ($2,000): Direct mail pieces will be sent to manufacturing companies throughout the Midwest. The cost includes the mailing list price, postage, and the cost to produce the postcard.

Trade shows ($4,000): The sales team will attend the following trade shows and expos during the first month of expansion:

1. The International Lawn, Garden, and Power Equipment Expo ($1,200)

2. The International Manufacturing Technology Show ($1,500)

3. Pacific Design and Manufacturing Show ($1,300)

Meetings with potential customers ($2,000): Appleton's sales team will set up appointments and travel to meet potential customers.

7. OPERATING PLAN

7.1 Facility

Appleton Moldings, Inc. currently owns and operates in a building located in Appleton, Wisconsin. This facility is 23 years old and has 52,000 square feet. About 25,000 square feet is used for production and 2,000 square feet is used for administrative headquarters.

7.2 Operating Equipment

Below is a list of the machines owned by the company and currently used to produce plastic products. Appleton Moldings, Inc. will purchase new models of the same equipment it already uses.

1. Van Dorn 75 Ton Press ($30,000)

2. Battenfeld 170 Ton Press ($45,000)

3. Engel 275 Ton Press ($75,000)

4. Reed 350 Ton Press ($90,000)

5. Lombard 450 Ton Press ($105,000)

6. Hartig Extrusion Line ($25,000)

7.3 Personnel Plan

There are five full-time employees at Appleton Moldings, Inc. and this number will double when the business purchases additional equipment. Appleton Moldings, Inc. will strive to hire individuals who work well in a team environment.

8.0 MANAGEMENT, ORGANIZATION & OWNERSHIP

8.1 Appleton's Management

Steve Johnson: Steve graduated from the University of Minnesota in 1978 with a B.S. in Engineering. Steve brings over twenty years of experience to Appleton Moldings, Inc.. He has successfully grown Appleton Moldings, Inc. from a two person operation to a five employee firm with annual sales over $1.5 million.

Andrew Nalgene: Andrew graduated from the University of Wisconsin in 1994 with a B.S. in Accounting. Andrew is responsible for all bookkeeping activities.

Jim Shook: Jim is the Plant Manger. He is responsible for the operations within the production facilities. Jim graduated from the University of Minnesota in 1985 with a B.S. in Engineering. He has worked for Appleton Moldings, Inc. for over seven years, and his duties include project estimation and overseeing the production facility, where he is responsible for three injection molding machine operators.

8.2 Ownership

Steve Johnson owns 60% of Appleton Moldings, Inc., while Charles Wright, one of the board members and a local banker, owns 25%. Peter Whitney, a board member and local farmer, owns a 10% stake in the company. The company's employees own the remaining 5% of Appleton Moldings, Inc.

-14-

8.3 Organization

Appleton Moldings, Inc. is a C Corporation registered in the state of Wisconsin.

9. GOALS AND STRATEGIES

9.1 Business Goals

Appleton Molding's most important goal is to achieve full capacity with the new equipment within seven months of purchase. In order to ensure the success of Appleton Moldings, Inc., the company is going to put a full effort behind its marketing strategies to achieve this goal.

9.2 Future Plans

After reaching its business goal, Appleton Moldings, Inc. will re-evaluate its business position with board members and consider further expansion. The company will look at entering other U.S. regions, as well as explore overseas opportunities.

10.0 FINANCIAL ASSUMPTIONS

The financial projections for Appleton Moldings, Inc. are based upon previous financial statements for the business:

Below are the projected annual sales for Appleton Moldings, Inc.:

Income Projection

For years ending December - 2008, 2009, 2010			
Income Category	Year 1	Year 2	Year 3
Unit Production	2,610,000	3,000,000	3,000,000
Mold Setup Fees	200,000	240,000	240,000
Shipping	165,000	180,000	180,000
Total Income	2,975,000	3,420,000	3,420,000

Below are the projected annual expenses before Bad Debts and Depreciation for Appleton Moldings, Inc.:

Expense Projection

For years ending December - 2008, 2009, 2010			
Expense Category	Year 1	Year 2	Year 3
Insurance	32,000	32,000	32,000
Utilities	180,000	180,000	180,000
Telephone	24,000	24,000	24,000
Marketing	120,000	120,000	120,000
Travel	72,000	72,000	72,000
Management Salaries	255,000	255,000	255,000
Sales Salaries	112,500	112,500	112,500
Office Supplies	6,000	6,000	6,000
Repairs & Maintenance	18,000	18,000	18,000
Professional Services	9,000	9,000	9,000
Total Expenses	828,500	828,500	828,500

In addition to the above projected sales and expenses, Appleton Moldings, Inc.'s financials include the following assumptions:

Loans for the purchase of Equipment:

National Bank - $125,000 @ 8.75% over 36 months

Van Dorn Financing - $75,000 @ 10.0% over 72 months

-16-

10.1 Assumptions

The following information explains the financial projections for Appleton Moldings, Inc.:

Beginning Balance Sheet

For year beginning January, 2008		
Assets:		
Current assets:		
Cash	5,000	
Total current assets	5,000	
Fixed assets (net)	2,000,000	
Total assets		2,005,000
Liabilities:		
Current liabilities:		
Current maturities of long-term liabilities	78,148	
Total current liabilities	78,148	
Long-term liabilities (net)	296,852	
Total liabilities		375,000
Equity:		
Total equity		1,630,000
Total liabilities and equity		2,005,000
Debt-to-equity ratio		0.23

PPE:

Existing building = $1,200,000

Existing molding equipment = $375,000

Existing office furniture & accessories = $30,000

Existing computers & other hardware = $25,000

2 Van Dorn presses = $75,000

1 Van Dorn extrusion line = $25,000

3 Engel presses = $270,000

Total PPE = $2,000,000

Liabilities:

Existing equipment loan = $175,000 @ 9.75%, 57 monthly payments remaining

New equipment loan (Van Dorn) = $75,000 @ 10%, 72 monthly payments

Additional bank financing = $125,000 @ 8.75%, 36 monthly payments

Total Liabilities = $375,000

Equity:

Additional $175,000 invested by Appleton Moldings, Inc.

Balance Sheets (Year 1, 2, and 3)

Line of credit activity = $23,023 paid back in month 8 of Year 1

-18-

Profit & Loss

For years ending December - 2008, 2009, 2010			
	Year 1	Year 2	Year 3
Income	2,975,000	3,420,000	3,420,000
Less COGS:			
Material	652,500	750,000	750,000
Labor	783,000	900,000	900,000
Other	248,500	282,000	282,000
Total COGS	1,684,000	1,932,000	1,932,000
Gross profit	1,291,000	1,488,000	1,488,000
Operating expenses:			
Insurance	32,000	32,000	32,000
Utilities	180,000	180,000	180,000
Telephone	24,000	24,000	24,000
Marketing	120,000	120,000	120,000
Travel	72,000	72,000	72,000
Management Salaries	255,000	255,000	255,000
Sales Salaries	112,500	112,500	112,500
Office Supplies	6,000	6,000	6,000
Repairs & Maintenance	18,000	18,000	18,000
Professional Services	9,000	9,000	9,000
Bad debts	29,750	34,200	34,200
Depreciation	189,055	189,055	189,055
Total operating expenses	1,047,305	1,051,755	1,051,755
Operating income	243,695	436,245	436,245
Interest expense	32,495	24,646	16,327
Net income before taxes	211,200	411,599	419,918
Estimated taxes	52,800	102,900	104,980
Net income	158,400	308,699	314,939

Sales: Projected monthly sales are based on existing monthly sales. After the expansion, Appleton Moldings, Inc. expects monthly sales to increase to $285,000 in month 7.

Cost of Sales:

Material: 25% of unit sales

Labor/benefits/taxes: 30% of unit sales plus 25% for benefits and taxes

Other:

Mold Setup Fees:

Selling price is $5,000, cost is $2,500

Shipping Expenses: 10% of the actual cost to ship products (90% of shipping cost is recovered from customers)

Operating Expenses:

Marketing: See Promotional Plan in the Marketing Plan section.

Travel: Tradeshows and client meetings.

Bad debt: All Appleton Molding sales are on credit. Historically, the company has encountered a 1 percent uncollectible rate.

Estimated taxes: 25% of net income before taxes.

Cash Plan

For years ending December - 2008, 2009, 2010			
	Year 1	Year 2	Year 3
Cash receipts	2,945,250	3,385,800	3,385,800
Operating cash expenses:			
Cost of sales	1,684,000	1,932,000	1,932,000
Other expenses	828,500	828,500	828,500
Estimated taxes	52,800	102,900	104,980
Total operating cash expenses	2,565,300	2,863,400	2,865,480
Cash from operations	379,950	522,400	520,320
Debt activities:			
Principal payments	(78,148)	(85,729)	(94,048)
Interest payments	(32,495)	(24,646)	(16,327)
Total debt activities	(110,643)	(110,375)	(110,375)
Net cash after debt service	269,307	412,025	409,946
Change in cash	269,307	412,025	409,946
Beginning cash	5,000	274,307	686,332
Cash before borrowing	274,307	686,332	1,096,278
Line of credit activity	0	0	0
Ending cash	274,307	686,332	1,096,278

All figures are derived from the assumptions above.

-20-

11.0 APPENDIX

This section contains the following reports and supporting documentation:

- Income Projection
- Expense Projection
- Profit & Loss
- Balance Sheet
- Cash Plan
- Ratio Analysis

Income Projection - Year 1

Income Category	Jan	Feb	Mar	Apr	May	Jun	Jul	Aug	Sep	Oct	Nov	Dec	Year 1
Unit Production	150000	160000	175000	190000	210000	225000	250000	250000	250000	250000	250000	250000	2610000
Mold Setup Fees	10000	10000	10000	15000	15000	20000	20000	20000	20000	20000	20000	20000	200000
Shipping	10000	11000	12000	13000	14000	15000	15000	15000	15000	15000	15000	15000	165000
Total Income	170000	181000	197000	218000	239000	260000	285000	285000	285000	285000	285000	285000	2975000

Income Projection - Year 2

Income Category	Jan	Feb	Mar	Apr	May	Jun	Jul	Aug	Sep	Oct	Nov	Dec	Year 2
Unit Production	250000	250000	250000	250000	250000	250000	250000	250000	250000	250000	250000	250000	3000000
Mold Setup Fees	20000	20000	20000	20000	20000	20000	20000	20000	20000	20000	20000	20000	240000
Shipping	15000	15000	15000	15000	15000	15000	15000	15000	15000	15000	15000	15000	180000
Total Income	285000	285000	285000	285000	285000	285000	285000	285000	285000	285000	285000	285000	3420000

Income Projection - Year 3

Income Category	Jan	Feb	Mar	Apr	May	Jun	Jul	Aug	Sep	Oct	Nov	Dec	Year 3
Unit Production	250000	250000	250000	250000	250000	250000	250000	250000	250000	250000	250000	250000	3000000
Mold Setup Fees	20000	20000	20000	20000	20000	20000	20000	20000	20000	20000	20000	20000	240000
Shipping	15000	15000	15000	15000	15000	15000	15000	15000	15000	15000	15000	15000	180000
Total Income	285000	285000	285000	285000	285000	285000	285000	285000	285000	285000	285000	285000	3420000

Expense Projection - Year 1

Expense Category	Jan	Feb	Mar	Apr	May	Jun	Jul	Aug	Sep	Oct	Nov	Dec	Year 1
Insurance	8000	0	0	8000	0	0	8000	0	0	8000	0	0	32000
Utilities	15000	15000	15000	15000	15000	15000	15000	15000	15000	15000	15000	15000	180000
Telephone	2000	2000	2000	2000	2000	2000	2000	2000	2000	2000	2000	2000	24000
Marketing	10000	10000	10000	10000	10000	10000	10000	10000	10000	10000	10000	10000	120000
Travel	6000	6000	6000	6000	6000	6000	6000	6000	6000	6000	6000	6000	72000
Management Salaries	21250	21250	21250	21250	21250	21250	21250	21250	21250	21250	21250	21250	255000
Sales Salaries	9375	9375	9375	9375	9375	9375	9375	9375	9375	9375	9375	9375	112500
Office Supplies	500	500	500	500	500	500	500	500	500	500	500	500	6000
Repairs & Maintenance	1500	1500	1500	1500	1500	1500	1500	1500	1500	1500	1500	1500	18000
Professional Svcs.	750	750	750	750	750	750	750	750	750	750	750	750	9000
Total Expenses	74375	66375	66375	74375	66375	66375	74375	66375	66375	74375	66375	66375	828500

Expense Projection - Year 2

Expense Category	Jan	Feb	Mar	Apr	May	Jun	Jul	Aug	Sep	Oct	Nov	Dec	Year 2
Insurance	8000	0	0	8000	0	0	8000	0	0	8000	0	0	32000
Utilities	15000	15000	15000	15000	15000	15000	15000	15000	15000	15000	15000	15000	180000
Telephone	2000	2000	2000	2000	2000	2000	2000	2000	2000	2000	2000	2000	24000
Marketing	10000	10000	10000	10000	10000	10000	10000	10000	10000	10000	10000	10000	120000
Travel	6000	6000	6000	6000	6000	6000	6000	6000	6000	6000	6000	6000	72000
Management Salaries	21250	21250	21250	21250	21250	21250	21250	21250	21250	21250	21250	21250	255000
Sales Salaries	9375	9375	9375	9375	9375	9375	9375	9375	9375	9375	9375	9375	112500
Office Supplies	500	500	500	500	500	500	500	500	500	500	500	500	6000
Repairs & Maintenance	1500	1500	1500	1500	1500	1500	1500	1500	1500	1500	1500	1500	18000
Professional Svcs.	750	750	750	750	750	750	750	750	750	750	750	750	9000
Total Expenses	74375	66375	66375	74375	66375	66375	74375	66375	66375	74375	66375	66375	828500

Expense Projection - Year 3

Expense Category	Jan	Feb	Mar	Apr	May	Jun	Jul	Aug	Sep	Oct	Nov	Dec	Year 3
Insurance	8000	0	0	8000	0	0	8000	0	0	8000	0	0	32000
Utilities	15000	15000	15000	15000	15000	15000	15000	15000	15000	15000	15000	15000	180000
Telephone	2000	2000	2000	2000	2000	2000	2000	2000	2000	2000	2000	2000	24000
Marketing	10000	10000	10000	10000	10000	10000	10000	10000	10000	10000	10000	10000	120000
Travel	6000	6000	6000	6000	6000	6000	6000	6000	6000	6000	6000	6000	72000
Management Salaries	21250	21250	21250	21250	21250	21250	21250	21250	21250	21250	21250	21250	255000
Sales Salaries	9375	9375	9375	9375	9375	9375	9375	9375	9375	9375	9375	9375	112500
Office Supplies	500	500	500	500	500	500	500	500	500	500	500	500	6000
Repairs & Maintenance	1500	1500	1500	1500	1500	1500	1500	1500	1500	1500	1500	1500	18000
Professional Svcs.	750	750	750	750	750	750	750	750	750	750	750	750	9000
Total Expenses	74375	66375	66375	74375	66375	66375	74375	66375	66375	74375	66375	66375	828500

Profit & Loss - Year 1

	Jan	Feb	Mar	Apr	May	Jun	Jul	Aug	Sep	Oct	Nov	Dec	Year 1
Income	170000	181000	197000	218000	239000	260000	285000	285000	285000	285000	285000	285000	2975000
Less COGS:													
Material	37500	40000	43750	47500	52500	56250	62500	62500	62500	62500	62500	62500	652500
Labor	45000	48000	52500	57000	63000	67500	75000	75000	75000	75000	75000	75000	783000
Other	14000	14900	15800	19200	20100	23500	23500	23500	23500	23500	23500	23500	248500
Total COGS	96500	102900	112050	123700	135600	147250	161000	161000	161000	161000	161000	161000	1684000
Gross profit	73500	78100	84950	94300	103400	112750	124000	124000	124000	124000	124000	124000	1291000
Operating expenses:													
Insurance	8000	0	0	8000	0	0	8000	0	0	8000	0	0	32000
Utilities	15000	15000	15000	15000	15000	15000	15000	15000	15000	15000	15000	15000	180000
Telephone	2000	2000	2000	2000	2000	2000	2000	2000	2000	2000	2000	2000	24000
Marketing	10000	10000	10000	10000	10000	10000	10000	10000	10000	10000	10000	10000	120000
Travel	6000	6000	6000	6000	6000	6000	6000	6000	6000	6000	6000	6000	72000
Management Salaries	21250	21250	21250	21250	21250	21250	21250	21250	21250	21250	21250	21250	255000
Sales Salaries	9375	9375	9375	9375	9375	9375	9375	9375	9375	9375	9375	9375	112500
Office Supplies	500	500	500	500	500	500	500	500	500	500	500	500	6000
Repairs & Maintenance	1500	1500	1500	1500	1500	1500	1500	1500	1500	1500	1500	1500	18000
Professional Svcs.	750	750	750	750	750	750	750	750	750	750	750	750	9000
Bad debts	1700	1810	1970	2180	2390	2600	2850	2850	2850	2850	2850	2850	29750
Depreciation	15755	15755	15755	15755	15755	15755	15755	15755	15755	15755	15755	15755	189060
Total operating expenses	91830	83940	84100	92310	84520	84730	92980	84980	84980	92980	84980	84980	1047310
Operating income	-18330	-5840	850	1990	18880	28020	31020	39020	39020	31020	39020	39020	243690
Interest expense	2958	3028	2973	2851	2763	2713	2663	2612	2561	2510	2458	2406	32496
Net income before taxes	-21288	-8868	-2123	-861	16117	25307	28357	36408	36459	28510	36562	36614	211194
Estimated taxes	0	0	0	0	0	2072	7089	9102	9115	7128	9141	9154	52801
Net income	-21288	-8868	-2123	-861	16117	23235	21268	27306	27344	21382	27421	27460	158393

Profit & Loss - Year 2

	Jan	Feb	Mar	Apr	May	Jun	Jul	Aug	Sep	Oct	Nov	Dec	Year 2
Income	285000	285000	285000	285000	285000	285000	285000	285000	285000	285000	285000	285000	3420000
Less COGS:													
Material	62500	62500	62500	62500	62500	62500	62500	62500	62500	62500	62500	62500	750000
Labor	75000	75000	75000	75000	75000	75000	75000	75000	75000	75000	75000	75000	900000
Other	23500	23500	23500	23500	23500	23500	23500	23500	23500	23500	23500	23500	282000
Total COGS	161000	161000	161000	161000	161000	161000	161000	161000	161000	161000	161000	161000	1932000
Gross profit	124000	124000	124000	124000	124000	124000	124000	124000	124000	124000	124000	124000	1488000
Operating expenses:													
Insurance	8000	0	0	8000	0	0	8000	0	0	8000	0	0	32000
Utilities	15000	15000	15000	15000	15000	15000	15000	15000	15000	15000	15000	15000	180000
Telephone	2000	2000	2000	2000	2000	2000	2000	2000	2000	2000	2000	2000	24000
Marketing	10000	10000	10000	10000	10000	10000	10000	10000	10000	10000	10000	10000	120000
Travel	6000	6000	6000	6000	6000	6000	6000	6000	6000	6000	6000	6000	72000
Management Salaries	21250	21250	21250	21250	21250	21250	21250	21250	21250	21250	21250	21250	255000
Sales Salaries	9375	9375	9375	9375	9375	9375	9375	9375	9375	9375	9375	9375	112500
Office Supplies	500	500	500	500	500	500	500	500	500	500	500	500	6000
Repairs & Maintenance	1500	1500	1500	1500	1500	1500	1500	1500	1500	1500	1500	1500	18000
Professional Svcs.	750	750	750	750	750	750	750	750	750	750	750	750	9000
Bad debts	2850	2850	2850	2850	2850	2850	2850	2850	2850	2850	2850	2850	34200
Depreciation	15755	15755	15755	15755	15755	15755	15755	15755	15755	15755	15755	15755	189060
Total operating expenses	92980	84980	84980	92980	84980	84980	92980	84980	84980	92980	84980	84980	1051760
Operating income	31020	39020	39020	31020	39020	39020	31020	39020	39020	31020	39020	39020	436240
Interest expense	2353	2300	2247	2193	2139	2084	2029	1973	1917	1861	1804	1747	24647
Net income before taxes	28667	36720	36773	28827	36881	36936	28991	37047	37103	29159	37216	37273	411593
Estimated taxes	7167	9180	9193	7207	9220	9234	7248	9262	9276	7290	9304	9318	102899
Net income	21500	27540	27580	21620	27661	27702	21743	27785	27827	21869	27912	27955	308694

Profit & Loss - Year 3

	Jan	Feb	Mar	Apr	May	Jun	Jul	Aug	Sep	Oct	Nov	Dec	Year 3
Income	285000	285000	285000	285000	285000	285000	285000	285000	285000	285000	285000	285000	3420000
Less COGS:													
Material	62500	62500	62500	62500	62500	62500	62500	62500	62500	62500	62500	62500	750000
Labor	75000	75000	75000	75000	75000	75000	75000	75000	75000	75000	75000	75000	900000
Other	23500	23500	23500	23500	23500	23500	23500	23500	23500	23500	23500	23500	282000
Total COGS	161000	161000	161000	161000	161000	161000	161000	161000	161000	161000	161000	161000	1932000
Gross profit	124000	124000	124000	124000	124000	124000	124000	124000	124000	124000	124000	124000	1488000
Operating expenses:													
Insurance	8000	0	0	8000	0	0	8000	0	0	8000	0	0	32000
Utilities	15000	15000	15000	15000	15000	15000	15000	15000	15000	15000	15000	15000	180000
Telephone	2000	2000	2000	2000	2000	2000	2000	2000	2000	2000	2000	2000	24000
Marketing	10000	10000	10000	10000	10000	10000	10000	10000	10000	10000	10000	10000	120000
Travel	6000	6000	6000	6000	6000	6000	6000	6000	6000	6000	6000	6000	72000
Management Salaries	21250	21250	21250	21250	21250	21250	21250	21250	21250	21250	21250	21250	255000
Sales Salaries	9375	9375	9375	9375	9375	9375	9375	9375	9375	9375	9375	9375	112500
Office Supplies	500	500	500	500	500	500	500	500	500	500	500	500	6000
Repairs & Maintenance	1500	1500	1500	1500	1500	1500	1500	1500	1500	1500	1500	1500	18000
Professional Svcs.	750	750	750	750	750	750	750	750	750	750	750	750	9000
Bad debts	2850	2850	2850	2850	2850	2850	2850	2850	2850	2850	2850	2850	34200
Depreciation	15755	15755	15755	15755	15755	15755	15755	15755	15755	15755	15755	15755	189060
Total operating expenses	92980	84980	84980	92980	84980	84980	92980	84980	84980	92980	84980	84980	1051760
Operating income	31020	39020	39020	31020	39020	39020	31020	39020	39020	31020	39020	39020	436240
Interest expense	1689	1631	1572	1513	1454	1394	1333	1272	1211	1149	1086	1024	16328
Net income before taxes	29331	37389	37448	29507	37566	37626	29687	37748	37809	29871	37934	37996	419912
Estimated taxes	7333	9347	9362	7377	9392	9407	7422	9437	9452	7468	9483	9499	104979
Net income	21998	28042	28086	22130	28174	28219	22265	28311	28357	22403	28451	28497	314933

Balance Sheet - Year 1

	Jan	Feb	Mar	Apr	May	Jun	Jul	Aug	Sep	Oct	Nov	Dec	Year 1
Assets:													
Current assets:													
Cash	5000	5000	5000	9630	35067	67573	98060	134535	170998	201447	237834	274307	274307
Total current assets	5000	5000	5000	9630	35067	67573	98060	134535	170998	201447	237834	274307	274307
Fixed assets (net)	1984245	1968491	1952736	1936982	1921227	1905472	1889718	1873963	1858209	1842454	1826700	1810945	1810945
Total assets	1989245	1973491	1957736	1946612	1956294	1973045	1987778	2008498	2029207	2043901	2064534	2085252	2085252
Liabilities and equity:													
Current liabilities:													
Line of credit	11773	11174	3878	0	0	0	0	0	0	0	0	0	0
Notes payable	0	0	0	0	0	0	0	0	0	0	0	0	0
Current maturities	78753	79363	79978	80597	81221	81850	82484	83123	83767	84416	85070	85729	85729
Total current liabilities	90526	90537	83856	80597	81221	81850	82484	83123	83767	84416	85070	85729	85729
Long-term liabilities (net)	290007	283110	276158	269153	262094	254980	247811	240586	233306	225968	218575	211123	211123
Total liabilities	380533	373647	360014	349750	343315	336830	330295	323709	317073	310384	303645	296852	296852
Equity	1608712	1599844	1597722	1596862	1612979	1636215	1657483	1684789	1712134	1733517	1760889	1788400	1788400
Total liabilities and equity	1989245	1973491	1957736	1946612	1956294	1973045	1987778	2008498	2029207	2043901	2064534	2085252	2085252

Balance Sheet - Year 2

	Jan	Feb	Mar	Apr	May	Jun	Jul	Aug	Sep	Oct	Nov	Dec	Year 2
Assets:													
Current assets:													
Cash	304717	341114	377498	407868	444225	480568	510897	547212	583513	613801	650074	686332	686332
Total current assets	304717	341114	377498	407868	444225	480568	510897	547212	583513	613801	650074	686332	686332
Fixed assets (net)	1795190	1779436	1763681	1747927	1732172	1716417	1700663	1684908	1669154	1653399	1637645	1621890	1621890
Total assets	2099907	2120550	2141179	2155795	2176397	2196985	2211560	2232120	2252667	2267200	2287719	2308222	2308222
Liabilities and equity:													
Current liabilities:													
Line of credit	0	0	0	0	0	0	0	0	0	0	0	0	0
Notes payable	0	0	0	0	0	0	0	0	0	0	0	45347	45347
Current maturities	86393	87062	87737	88416	89101	89792	90488	91189	91895	92607	93325	48701	48701
Total current liabilities	86393	87062	87737	88416	89101	89792	90488	91189	91895	92607	93325	94048	94048
Long-term liabilities (net)	203614	196047	188422	180737	172993	165188	157323	149398	141410	133361	125250	117075	117075
Total liabilities	290007	283109	276159	269153	262094	254980	247811	240587	233305	225968	218575	211123	211123
Equity	1809900	1837441	1865020	1886642	1914303	1942005	1963749	1991533	2019362	2041232	2069144	2097099	2097099
Total liabilities and equity	2099907	2120550	2141179	2155795	2176397	2196985	2211560	2232120	2252667	2267200	2287719	2308222	2308222

Balance Sheet - Year 3

	Jan	Feb	Mar	Apr	May	Jun	Jul	Aug	Sep	Oct	Nov	Dec	Year 3
Assets:													
Current assets:													
Cash	716577	752806	789021	819222	855407	891577	921733	957873	993997	1024106	1060200	1096278	1096278
Total current assets	716577	752806	789021	819222	855407	891577	921733	957873	993997	1024106	1060200	1096278	1096278
Fixed assets (net)	1606135	1590381	1574626	1558872	1543117	1527362	1511608	1495853	1480099	1464344	1448590	1432835	1432835
Total assets	2322712	2343187	2363647	2378094	2398524	2418939	2433341	2453726	2474096	2488450	2508790	2529113	2529113
Liabilities and equity:													
Current liabilities:													
Line of credit	0	0	0	0	0	0	0	0	0	0	0	0	0
Notes payable	41718	38061	34378	30669	26932	23168	19376	15557	11710	7835	3932	0	0
Current maturities	49099	49500	49905	50313	50724	51139	51557	51978	52403	52832	53264	53699	53699
Total current liabilities	90817	87561	84283	80982	77656	74307	70933	67535	64113	60667	57196	53699	53699
Long-term liabilities (net)	112798	108486	104138	99755	95337	90882	86390	81862	77297	72695	68054	63376	63376
Total liabilities	203615	196047	188421	180737	172993	165189	157323	149397	141410	133362	125250	117075	117075
Equity	2119097	2147140	2175226	2197357	2225531	2253750	2276018	2304329	2332686	2355088	2383540	2412038	2412038
Total liabilities and equity	2322712	2343187	2363647	2378094	2398524	2418939	2433341	2453726	2474096	2488450	2508790	2529113	2529113

Cash Plan - Year 1

	Jan	Feb	Mar	Apr	May	Jun	Jul	Aug	Sep	Oct	Nov	Dec	Year 1
Cash receipts	168300	179190	195030	215820	236610	257400	282150	282150	282150	282150	282150	282150	2945250
Operating cash expenses:													
Cost of sales	96500	102900	112050	123700	135600	147250	161000	161000	161000	161000	161000	161000	1684000
Other expenses	74375	66375	66375	74375	66375	66375	74375	66375	66375	74375	66375	66375	828500
Estimated taxes	0	0	0	0	0	2072	7089	9102	9115	7128	9141	9154	52801
Total operating cash exp.	170875	169275	178425	198075	201975	215697	242464	236477	236490	242503	236516	236529	2565301
Cash from operations	-2575	9915	16605	17745	34635	41703	39686	45673	45660	39647	45634	45621	379949
Debt activities:													
Principal payments	-6240	-6288	-6337	-6386	-6435	-6485	-6535	-6586	-6637	-6688	-6740	-6792	-78149
Interest payments	-2958	-3028	-2973	-2851	-2763	-2713	-2663	-2612	-2561	-2510	-2458	-2406	-32496
Total debt activities	-9198	-9316	-9310	-9237	-9198	-9198	-9198	-9198	-9198	-9198	-9198	-9198	-110645
Net cash after debt service	-11773	599	7295	8508	25437	32505	30488	36475	36462	30449	36436	36423	269304
Change in cash	-11773	599	7295	8508	25437	32505	30488	36475	36462	30449	36436	36423	269304
Beginning cash	5000	5000	5000	5000	9630	35067	67573	98060	134535	170998	201447	237884	5000
Cash before borrowing	-6773	5599	12295	13508	35067	67572	98061	134535	170997	201447	237883	274307	274304
Line of credit activity	11773	-599	-7295	-3878	0	0	0	0	0	0	0	0	1
Ending cash	5000	5000	5000	9630	35067	67572	98061	134535	170997	201447	237883	274307	274307

Cash Plan - Year 2

	Jan	Feb	Mar	Apr	May	Jun	Jul	Aug	Sep	Oct	Nov	Dec	Year 2
Cash receipts	282150	282150	282150	282150	282150	282150	282150	282150	232150	282150	282150	282150	3385800
Operating cash expenses:													
Cost of sales	161000	161000	161000	161000	161000	161000	161000	161000	151000	161000	161000	161000	1932000
Other expenses	74375	66375	66375	74375	66375	66375	74375	66375	66375	74375	66375	66375	828500
Estimated taxes	7167	9180	9193	7207	9220	9234	7248	9262	9276	7290	9304	9318	102899
Total operating cash exp.	242542	236555	236568	242582	236595	236609	242623	236637	236651	242665	236679	236693	2863399
Cash from operations	39608	45595	45582	39568	45555	45541	39527	45513	45499	39485	45471	45457	522401
Debt activities:													
Principal payments	-6845	-6898	-6951	-7005	-7059	-7114	-7169	-7225	-7281	-7337	-7394	-7451	-85729
Interest payments	-2353	-2300	-2247	-2193	-2139	-2084	-2029	-1973	-1917	-1861	-1804	-1747	-24647
Total debt activities	-9198	-9198	-9198	-9198	-9198	-9198	-9198	-9198	-9198	-9198	-9198	-9198	-110376
Net cash after debt service	30410	36397	36384	30370	36357	36343	30329	36315	36301	30287	36273	36259	412025
Change in cash	30410	36397	36384	30370	36357	36343	30329	36315	36301	30287	36273	36259	412025
Beginning cash	274307	304717	341114	377498	407868	444225	480568	510897	547212	583513	613801	650074	274307
Cash before borrowing	304717	341114	377498	407868	444225	480568	510897	547212	583513	613800	650074	686333	686332
Line of credit activity	0	0	0	0	0	0	0	0	0	0	0	0	0
Ending cash	304717	341114	377498	407868	444225	480568	510897	547212	583513	613800	650074	686333	686333

Cash Plan - Year 3

	Jan	Feb	Mar	Apr	May	Jun	Jul	Aug	Sep	Oct	Nov	Dec	Year 3
Cash receipts	282150	282150	282150	282150	282150	282150	282150	282150	282150	282150	282150	282150	3385800
Operating cash expenses:													
Cost of sales	161000	161000	161000	161000	161000	161000	161000	161000	161000	161000	161000	161000	1932000
Other expenses	74375	66375	66375	74375	66375	66375	74375	66375	66375	74375	66375	66375	828500
Estimated taxes	7333	9347	9362	7377	9392	9407	7422	9437	9452	7468	9483	9499	104979
Total operating cash exp.	242708	236722	236737	242752	236767	236782	242797	236812	236827	242843	236858	236874	2865479
Cash from operations	39442	45428	45413	39398	45383	45368	39353	45338	45323	39307	45292	45276	520321
Debt activities:													
Principal payments	-7509	-7567	-7626	-7685	-7744	-7804	-7865	-7926	-7987	-8049	-8111	-8174	-94047
Interest payments	-1689	-1631	-1572	-1513	-1454	-1394	-1333	-1272	-1211	-1149	-1086	-1024	-16328
Total debt activities	-9198	-9198	-9198	-9198	-9198	-9198	-9198	-9198	-9198	-9198	-9197	-9198	-110375
Net cash after debt service	30244	36230	36215	30200	36185	36170	30155	36140	36125	30109	36095	36078	409946
Change in cash	30244	36230	36215	30200	36185	36170	30155	36140	36125	30109	36094	36078	409945
Beginning cash	686332	716577	752806	789021	819222	855407	891577	921733	957873	993997	1024106	1060200	686332
Cash before borrowing	716576	752807	789021	819221	855407	891577	921732	957873	993998	1024106	1060200	1096278	1096277
Line of credit activity	0	0	0	0	0	0	0	0	0	0	0	0	0
Ending cash	716576	752807	789021	819221	855407	891577	921732	957873	993998	1024106	1060200	1096278	1096278

Ratio Analysis - Year 1

	Jan	Feb	Mar	Apr	May	Jun	Jul	Aug	Sep	Oct	Nov	Dec	Year 1
Profitability ratios:													
Gross profit margin	43.24%	43.15%	43.12%	43.26%	43.26%	43.37%	43.51%	43.51%	43.51%	43.51%	43.51%	43.51%	43.39%
Operating profit margin	-10.78%	-3.23%	0.43%	0.91%	7.90%	10.78%	10.88%	13.69%	13.69%	10.88%	13.69%	13.69%	8.19%
Net profit margin	-12.52%	-4.90%	-1.08%	-0.39%	6.74%	8.94%	7.46%	9.58%	9.59%	7.50%	9.62%	9.64%	5.32%
Return on equity	-1.31%	-0.55%	-0.13%	-0.05%	1.00%	1.43%	1.29%	1.63%	1.61%	1.24%	1.57%	1.55%	9.55%
Return on assets	-0.92%	-0.29%	0.04%	0.10%	0.97%	1.32%	1.21%	1.50%	1.48%	1.17%	1.45%	1.44%	9.55%
Liquidity ratios:													
Current ratio	0.06	0.06	0.06	0.12	0.43	0.83	1.19	1.62	2.04	2.39	2.80	3.20	3.20
Quick ratio (Acid-test)	0.06	0.06	0.06	0.12	0.43	0.83	1.19	1.62	2.04	2.39	2.80	3.20	3.20
Working capital ratio	-0.50	-0.47	-0.40	-0.33	-0.19	-0.05	0.05	0.18	0.31	0.41	0.54	0.66	0.06
Activity ratios:													
Accounts receivable days	0.00	0.00	0.00	0.00	0.00	0.00	0.00	0.00	0.00	0.00	0.00	0.00	0.00
Inventory days	0.00	0.00	0.00	0.00	0.00	0.00	0.00	0.00	0.00	0.00	0.00	0.00	0.00
Inventory turnover	n/a	n/a	n/a	n/a	n/a	n/a	n/a	n/a	n/a	n/a	n/a	n/a	n/a
Sales-to-assets	0.09	0.09	0.10	0.11	0.12	0.13	0.14	0.14	0.14	0.14	0.14	0.14	1.49
Leverage ratios:													
Debt-to-equity	0.24	0.23	0.23	0.22	0.21	0.21	0.20	0.19	0.19	0.18	0.17	0.17	0.17
Debt ratio	0.19	0.19	0.18	0.18	0.18	0.17	0.17	0.16	0.16	0.15	0.15	0.14	0.14
Times-interest (TI) earned:													
Operating income	-18330	-5840	850	1990	18880	28020	31020	39020	39020	31020	39020	39020	243695
Interest expense ($\div$)	2958	3028	2973	2851	2763	2713	2663	2612	2561	2510	2458	2406	32495
TI earned ratio	-6.20	-1.93	0.29	0.70	6.83	10.33	11.65	14.94	15.24	12.36	15.87	16.22	7.4994615

Ratio Analysis - Year 2

	Jan	Feb	Mar	Apr	May	Jun	Jul	Aug	Sep	Oct	Nov	Dec	Year 2
Profitability ratios:													
Gross profit margin	43.51%	43.51%	43.51%	43.51%	43.51%	43.51%	43.51%	43.51%	43.51%	43.51%	43.51%	43.51%	43.51%
Operating profit margin	10.88%	13.69%	13.69%	10.88%	13.69%	13.69%	10.88%	13.69%	13.69%	10.88%	13.69%	13.69%	12.76%
Net profit margin	7.54%	9.66%	9.68%	7.59%	9.71%	9.72%	7.63%	9.75%	9.76%	7.67%	9.79%	9.81%	9.03%
Return on equity	1.20%	1.51%	1.49%	1.15%	1.46%	1.44%	1.11%	1.40%	1.39%	1.08%	1.36%	1.34%	15.91%
Return on assets	1.14%	1.41%	1.40%	1.11%	1.38%	1.36%	1.08%	1.34%	1.33%	1.05%	1.30%	1.29%	15.19%
Liquidity ratios:													
Current ratio	3.53	3.92	4.30	4.61	4.99	5.35	5.65	6.00	6.35	6.63	6.97	7.30	7.30
Quick ratio (Acid-test)	3.53	3.92	4.30	4.61	4.99	5.35	5.65	6.00	6.35	6.63	6.97	7.30	7.30
Working capital ratio	0.77	0.89	1.02	1.12	1.25	1.37	1.48	1.60	1.73	1.83	1.95	2.08	0.17
Activity ratios:													
Accounts receivable days	0.00	0.00	0.00	0.00	0.00	0.00	0.00	0.00	0.00	0.00	0.00	0.00	0.00
Inventory days	0.00	0.00	0.00	0.00	0.00	0.00	0.00	0.00	0.00	0.00	0.00	0.00	0.00
Inventory turnover	n/a	n/a	n/a	n/a	n/a	n/a	n/a	n/a	n/a	n/a	n/a	n/a	n/a
Sales-to-assets	0.14	0.14	0.13	0.13	0.13	0.13	0.13	0.13	0.13	0.13	0.13	0.12	1.56
Leverage ratios:													
Debt-to-equity	0.16	0.15	0.15	0.14	0.14	0.13	0.13	0.12	0.12	0.11	0.11	0.10	0.10
Debt ratio	0.14	0.13	0.13	0.12	0.12	0.12	0.11	0.11	0.10	0.10	0.10	0.09	0.09
Times-interest (TI) earned:													
Operating income	31020	39020	39020	31020	39020	39020	31020	39020	39020	31020	39020	39020	436245
Interest expense ($\div$)	2353	2300	2247	2193	2139	2084	2029	1973	1917	1861	1804	1747	24646
TI earned ratio	13.18	16.97	17.37	14.15	18.24	18.72	15.29	19.78	20.35	16.67	21.63	22.34	17.700438

Ratio Analysis - Year 3

	Jan	Feb	Mar	Apr	May	Jun	Jul	Aug	Sep	Oct	Nov	Dec	Year 3
Profitability ratios:													
Gross profit margin	43.51%	43.51%	43.51%	43.51%	43.51%	43.51%	43.51%	43.51%	43.51%	43.51%	43.51%	43.51%	43.51%
Operating profit margin	10.88%	13.69%	13.69%	10.88%	13.69%	13.69%	10.88%	13.69%	13.69%	10.88%	13.69%	13.69%	12.76%
Net profit margin	7.72%	9.84%	9.85%	7.77%	9.89%	9.90%	7.81%	9.93%	9.95%	7.86%	9.98%	10.00%	9.21%
Return on equity	1.04%	1.31%	1.30%	1.01%	1.27%	1.26%	0.98%	1.24%	1.22%	0.96%	1.20%	1.19%	13.98%
Return on assets	1.02%	1.27%	1.26%	1.00%	1.24%	1.23%	0.97%	1.21%	1.20%	0.95%	1.18%	1.17%	13.71%
Liquidity ratios:													
Current ratio	7.89	8.60	9.36	10.12	11.02	12.00	12.99	14.18	15.50	16.88	18.54	20.42	20.42
Quick ratio (Acid-test)	7.89	8.60	9.36	10.12	11.02	12.00	12.99	14.18	15.50	16.88	18.54	20.42	20.42
Working capital ratio	2.20	2.33	2.47	2.59	2.73	2.87	2.99	3.12	3.26	3.38	3.52	3.66	0.30
Activity ratios:													
Accounts receivable days	0.00	0.00	0.00	0.00	0.00	0.00	0.00	0.00	0.00	0.00	0.00	0.00	0.00
Inventory days	0.00	0.00	0.00	0.00	0.00	0.00	0.00	0.00	0.00	0.00	0.00	0.00	0.00
Inventory turnover	n/a	n/a	n/a	n/a	n/a	n/a	n/a	n/a	n/a	n/a	n/a	n/a	n/a
Sales-to-assets	0.12	0.12	0.12	0.12	0.12	0.12	0.12	0.12	0.12	0.11	0.11	0.11	1.42
Leverage ratios:													
Debt-to-equity	0.10	0.09	0.09	0.08	0.08	0.07	0.07	0.06	0.06	0.06	0.05	0.05	0.05
Debt ratio	0.09	0.08	0.08	0.08	0.07	0.07	0.06	0.06	0.06	0.05	0.05	0.05	0.05
Times-interest (TI) earned:													
Operating income	31020	39020	39020	31020	39020	39020	31020	39020	39020	31020	39020	39020	436245
Interest expense (÷)	1689	1631	1572	1513	1454	1394	1333	1272	1211	1149	1086	1024	16327
TI earned ratio	18.37	23.92	24.82	20.50	26.84	27.99	23.27	30.68	32.22	27.00	35.93	38.11	26.719238

The Business Plan for

Crime & Accident Scene Cleanup, Inc.

A Delaware Subchapter S Corporation

Contact Information:

Mr. Pete Miller

1248 Hyde Street

Washington, D.C. 12345

Ms. Lisa Anderson

56 Pine Street

Washington, D.C. 12345

Copy Number ___ of Five.

Non-Disclosure and Confidentiality Agreement

The undersigned ("Recipient") hereby agrees that all financial and other information ("Information") that it has and will receive concerning Crime & Accident Scene Cleanup, Inc. is confidential and will not be disclosed to any other individual or entity without prior written consent.

The Information shall remain the property of Crime & Accident Scene Cleanup, Inc. and shall be returned to Crime & Accident Scene Cleanup, Inc. promptly at its request together with all copies made thereof.

Recipient acknowledges that no remedy of law may be adequate to compensate Crime & Accident Scene Cleanup, Inc. for a violation of this Agreement and Recipient hereby agrees that in addition to any legal or other rights that may be available in the event of a breach hereunder, Crime & Accident Scene Cleanup, Inc. may seek equitable relief to enforce this Agreement in any Court of competent jurisdiction.

_____   _____
Date   Signature of Recipient

-2-

THE PLAN FOR CRIME & ACCIDENT SCENE CLEANUP

1.0 EXECUTIVE SUMMARY

Bio-hazardous cleanup entails cleaning and/or the removal of anything contaminated with bio-hazardous waste. These wastes may include blood, tissue, and other human or animal fluids and wastes. Bio-hazardous wastes can carry diseases such as blood-borne pathogens, making them a serious health risk when left exposed.

There are several businesses scattered throughout the U.S. that do bio-hazardous cleanup on a part-time basis, but most perform very little to no marketing. Many people are not aware such services exist and think it is a disgusting practice. Market research indicated this business can fit a unique niche to succeed. Many cleanup companies that perform similar services are not even listed in the phone book. Furthermore, many people are unaware insurance companies will pay for bio-hazardous cleanup. Crime & Accident Scene Cleanup, Inc. (CASC) believes, if it can effectively market its cleanup services, it will experience soaring revenues.

1.1 Business Opportunity

CASC has a huge business opportunity to succeed in this market. First of all, the market has very few competitors and most of these competitors do not advertise effectively. Secondly, if the owners are able to build close relationships with local authorities, emergency personnel, the coroner's office, funeral home directors, and insurance companies, CASC will quickly become a market leader in Washington D.C.

1.2 Service Description

CASC will sanitize an area that has been infected with bio-hazardous waste by disinfecting and deodorizing the contaminated area. CASC's services won't necessarily be more appealing than the competition; however, CASC will take a professional approach to the cleanup and market its services to three distinct groups to give it a competitive advantage.

The three primary groups CASC will target are insurance companies, emergency personnel, and property owners. It will be important to develop relationships with all three groups because they are either the first ones to the scene of an accident or have the final decision in the cleanup process.

1.3 Current Business Position

CASC is a concept scheduled to start in January of 2008. It will be an S Corporation with ownership involving Peter Miller, whose initial investment is $12,000 (60% ownership), and Lisa Anderson, whose initial investment is $8,000 (40% ownership). The business will be operated in Washington D.C. Expansion will begin into other U.S. cities after necessary market research has been conducted and the markets are proven to be ready for such a service.

1.4 Financial Potential

CASC projects sales of $180,000 in year one, $216,000 in year two, and $252,000 in year three. This results in a net income of $23,140 in year one, $33,638 at the end of year two, and a projected net income of $65,330 after year three.

1.5 The Request

The primary shareholders of CASC are seeking financing for $50,000 from a bank to begin operations.

2.0 COMPANY BACKGROUND

2.1 Current Position and Business Objectives

At the present time, CASC has completed the necessary marketing research to move the business into start-up phase. The owners have been able to fund the marketing research, but will need additional funds to purchase equipment and to cover costs the business will occur in the first year.

2.2 Ownership

Peter Miller and Lisa Anderson are the primary shareholders of the business. Mr. Miller's contributions to the company give him 60% of the shares outstanding, and Ms. Anderson's contributions give her 40% of the outstanding shares.

3.0 PRODUCTS

Product sales are not anticipated initially.

-6-

4.0 SERVICES

4.1 Service Descriptions

CASC's primary service will be the cleanup and disposal of bio-hazardous waste from accident scenes. CASC's owners have talked to industry professionals for advice to gain understanding of how a business of this type operates. One individual in particular, Mr. Jon Schuut, has provided sufficient start-up advice. Mr. Schuut has been in the industry for over twenty years and runs a business in Los Angeles. He said he typically cleans up after murders, suicides, discovered bodies, and dead animals. He says part of the bio-recovery process is preparing the contaminated environment for renovation. This includes stripping the surroundings down to the frame. The cleanup services will allow property owners to avoid the extreme hassle and safety risks of cleaning up after an incident of this nature.

4.2 Competitive Comparison

The competition in the D.C. area is limited to only a couple of competitors. A list of area service providers was obtained from the County Coroner's Office, which includes one carpet cleaning company, called Clematic, and Delta Forensic Sanitation. Clematic was listed in the phone book, but didn't list bio-hazardous waste cleanup. Delta Forensic Sanitation wasn't even listed in the phone book.

There are three competitive advantages that CASC will offer:

1. Cleaning will be available at any hour of the day.

2. The staff will be professionally trained to deal with the scene.

3. CASC will help complete the necessary paperwork for insurance companies, so the owner will not have to deal with the scene.

4.3 Service Process

When an accident occurs or is discovered, it is reported to authorities. The scene is then documented and the coroner is called in. After the coroner pays a visit, CASC will be called to clean and disinfect the scene.

5.0 THE INDUSTRY, COMPETITION AND MARKET

Bio-recovery services have an extremely unique niche in the cleaning industry. Not too many cleaning services specialize in bio-hazardous cleaning.

5.1 Industry Definition

The bio-hazardous waste cleanup industry is really undefined and, typically, unheard of. Many people don't think of what happens to an accident scene after the accident has occurred. After the scene has been cleaned, the scene, in most cases, looks as if nothing occurred.

5.2 Primary Competitors

The two primary competitors, who occupy CASC's market space, are Clematic and Delta Forensic Sanitation. Both of these competitors were contacted during market research. A message was left with Clematic, but the call wasn't returned. Delta Forensic Sanitation's telephone number was no longer in service.

5.3 Market Size

The overall number of fatalities has been slowly growing over the years, while the suicide and homicide rates have been declining. This may sound bad for business, but the population in Washington D.C. is growing. There has been a continuing 2.5% increase of deaths per year in the city, according to the US Census Bureau.

5.4 Market Growth

The Washington D.C. area has a population of approximately 2.2 million. The latest projections show the city growing at a rate of 9% annually over the last five years (www.census.gov).

In 2006, there were 97 homicides in the D.C. area. Approximately 90% of these were committed in a manner that would create work for CASC. Murder rates tend to rise in the summer months when the weather is warmer.

Due to the lack of statistics on how suicides were committed in the D.C. area, estimates have been developed using state and national data. In 2000, the suicide rate in Washington D.C. was 10.1 per 100,000 residents, resulting in approximately 157 suicides. Our interviews with members of the bio-recovery field indicated that suicides tend to increase significantly in the months of November and December.

A portion of business will also come from the cleanup of undiscovered decomposed bodies. Many of the bodies discovered will be elderly citizens living alone. Current population estimates show there are 565,000 adults above the age of 65 living in the metro D.C. area. According to the American Association of Retired Persons, there is an increasing number of elderly living alone. With the population becoming older and more elderly living alone, the likelihood of undiscovered, decomposing bodies will undoubtedly increase.

5.5 Customer Profile

The CASC target market includes three distinct groups. The first group is insurance companies. Insurance companies were selected as a target market because they traditionally pay for the bio-recovery services. Property insurance will cover the costs of cleaning and the renovation of the area that has been affected.

The second targeted group will be referrals from the following:

1. Police departments

2. Emergency medical service employees

3. Coroner's office

4. Funeral homes

The owners of CASC will meet these individuals in person to tell them about their services. Traditional cleaning businesses will also be included in this group.

The third group is property owners. Property owners make the final decision of who will perform the cleanup. A listing in the yellow pages and a small advertisement in the general cleaning section are the most effective way of reaching this group.

6.0 MARKETING PLAN

CASC firmly believes after the first year of business, it can become the market leader in this type of service. Based upon statistics, CASC expects to perform 60 jobs in year one, 72 jobs in year two, and 84 jobs in year three.

6.1 Competitive Advantage

Most of the competition in this industry doesn't intend on performing these services, therefore, they do not market their business for such services. CASC will have a competitive advantage by marketing the availability of their business for these services.

6.2 Pricing

The nature of business allows a premium price strategy. CASC will charge $3,000 minimum for each cleanup job. This may sound high, but the price is comparable to other cleaning services in metropolitan cities.

For extraordinary accidental or natural incidents, or multiple crime scenes, the project cost may be bid on a time and materials basis.

6.3 Promotional Plan

An advertisement will be placed in the yellow pages to promote the business, and CASC will focus on public relations to increase awareness of the business. The uniqueness of the company should gain media attention. The business will pay a $100 referral fee to other cleaning businesses.

6.4 Premium Service

Premium service will come with the high price. Trained professionals will be sent to job sites and all the necessary paperwork will be completed by CASC employees. The customer will have little interaction with the cleaners and insurance company.

7.0 OPERATING PLAN

7.1 Location

The business will be operated initially out of Peter Miller's home with calls being directed to a separate telephone line. His garage will be used as storage for the business.

7.2 Operating Equipment

CASC will purchase two black 1/2 ton GMC extended cab trucks. These trucks will be fitted with emergency lights and toppers. Magnetic decals will be put on the doors and on the tailgate. There will be the company's logo, which is a red splatter with the bio-hazard symbol and the company's name over the top in yellow. An enclosed matching trailer will be purchased to haul the equipment. The decals can be removable in case the customer is concerned about confidentiality and don't want to attract attention to their property. Other major equipment and supplies will include a steamer, wet-dry vacuum, chemicals, protective clothing, disposable gloves, general tools, fans, mops, brooms, and bio-hazardous bags and containers.

-10-

7.3 Suppliers and Disposal

General supplies will be purchased from local retail stores. The chemicals will need to be purchased through ChemPro. Bio-hazardous Waste Disposal will dispose all of the waste for a fee of $100 for each job. These costs will be calculated as cost of sales.

7.4 Personnel Plan

One employee will be hired in the second year of business in order to assist with cleaning. This employee will be paid $20/hour and will work between 30 to 36 hours per month.

8.0 MANAGEMENT, ORGANIZATION AND OWNERSHIP

Mr. Miller and Ms. Anderson will share all of the management responsibilities along with the cleaning duties during the first year of business. Compensation for the two will be executed in the form of salary. They will each be paid a monthly salary of $2,500 for the first six months. After this six-month period, each will be paid a monthly salary of $3,500.

8.1 Field Experience

Both founders have experience in clean-up work. Mr. Miller's parents own a steam cleaning business, which he has worked at for several years. Ms. Anderson has worked for a home cleaning service. The two met each other in a college course at George Washington University, where they created the concept for CASC.

8.2 Organizational Structure

Both Mr. Miller and Ms. Anderson will be co-owners of the business with share dependent upon their initial investment in the business. For the first three years, the two will run the business operations and conduct the cleaning services. A third employee will be hired in year two to prepare for future expansion to other cities.

8.3 Professional Support Services / Boards

Mr. Jon Schuut will be an operations advisor. He founded Crime Sweep, which is now Cleanup Services of America, located in Los Angeles, CA.

Mr. Gordon Hyde will be the legal advisor for the business. Mr. Hyde has been an attorney and legal advisor for over 100 small businesses.

-11-

Mr. Scott Dunn will be an accounting and financial advisor for the business. He has experience working with many small organizations as a Certified Public Accountant (CPA) in the D.C. area for over 16 years. Mr. Dunn will be compensated $1,000 each month to maintain the books.

CASC will also work very closely with Mr. Jeff Harrison in the Washington D.C. Pollution Control Department. Mr. Harrison has agreed to advise the company on legal disposal issues.

9.0 GOALS AND STRATEGIES

9.1 Business Goals

The company has established revenue targets of $180,000 in year one, $216,000 in year two, and $252,000 in year three. Net income is projected to be $23,140 for year one, $33,638 for year two, and $65,330 in year three. Both owners are confident of attaining these profit levels.

9.2 Keys to Success

The two most important items, which must be accomplished in order to achieve success in this industry, are:

1. Creating awareness of the business

2. Establishing relationships with insurance companies, public authorities, emergency personnel, and the coroner's office.

9.3 Future Plans

The cities of Chicago, IL, Detroit, MI, Milwaukee, WI, and Kansas City, MO are currently being studied for expansion. All have large populations, resulting in potentially large markets for this business. Statistics have shown that as the population increases so do crime, violence, accidents, suicides, and deaths per capita annually.

A harvest strategy has been put into place, where the owners anticipate exiting after six years. The owners would first try to sell the business as one unit to employees, or to a business owner who already owned a bio-hazardous cleanup operation. The sale of the business will hinge around its profitability. Obviously, this is not the type of work that many people enjoy doing.

10.0 FINANCIAL ASSUMPTIONS

The financial projections for CASC are based on conservative sales and industry average expenses throughout the first three years of business. The following projections allow for long-term loan repayments and adequate cash flow:

Below are the estimated sales for CASC:

Income Projection

For years ending December - 2008, 2009, 2010			
Income Category	Year 1	Year 2	Year 3
Cleanup Sales	180,000	216,000	252,000
Total Income	180,000	216,000	252,000

Below are the estimated expenses for CASC:

Expense Projection

For years ending December - 2008, 2009, 2010			
Expense Category	Year 1	Year 2	Year 3
Advertising	6,000	6,000	6,000
License	2,640	2,640	2,640
Insurance	9,600	9,600	9,600
Telephone	2,400	2,400	2,400
Office Supplies	600	600	600
Accountant Fees	12,000	12,000	12,000
Repairs & Maintenance	600	600	600
Fuel Expense	2,400	2,400	2,400
Equipment Rental	3,000	3,000	3,000
Salary Expense	84,960	99,120	99,120
Part-time Wages	0	8,496	9,912
Total Expenses	124,200	146,856	148,272

-13-

Below is a chart representing the expenses by category:

Expenses by Category

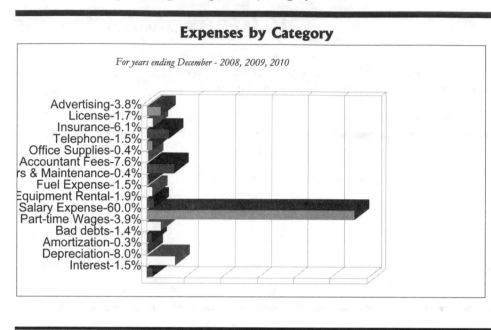

For years ending December - 2008, 2009, 2010

Advertising-3.8%
License-1.7%
Insurance-6.1%
Telephone-1.5%
Office Supplies-0.4%
Accountant Fees-7.6%
rs & Maintenance-0.4%
Fuel Expense-1.5%
Equipment Rental-1.9%
Salary Expense-60.0%
Part-time Wages-3.9%
Bad debts-1.4%
Amortization-0.3%
Depreciation-8.0%
Interest-1.5%

10.1 Assumptions

The following information explains the financial projections for CASC:

-14-

Beginning Balance Sheet

For year beginning January, 2008		
Assets:		
Current assets:		
Cash	7,000	
Total current assets	7,000	
Fixed assets (net)	62,900	
Other assets (net)	2,000	
Total assets		71,900
Liabilities:		
Current liabilities:		
Current maturities of long-term liabilities	7,138	
Total current liabilities	7,138	
Long-term liabilities (net)	42,862	
Total liabilities		50,000
Equity:		
Total equity		21,900
Total liabilities and equity		71,900
Debt-to-equity ratio		2.28

PPE:

2 - GMC Trucks = $50,000

1 - Enclosed trailer = $4,500

Cleaning Equipment = $5,000

Tools = $1,500

Supplies = $500

-15-

Other Assets:

Incorporation costs = $1,500

Liabilities:

Start-up Loan: Credit Union - $50,000 @ 6.0% for 72 months

Balance Sheet Summary

For years ending December - 2008, 2009, 2010			
	Year 1	Year 2	Year 3
Assets:			
Current assets:			
Cash	21,139	57,216	124,519
Accounts receivable (net)	14,850	17,820	20,790
Total current assets	35,989	75,036	145,309
Fixed assets (net)	50,320	37,740	25,160
Other assets (net)	1,600	1,200	800
Total assets	87,909	113,976	171,269
Liabilities and equity:			
Current liabilities:			
Line of credit	0	0	0
Current maturities	7,578	8,045	8,542
Total current liabilities	7,578	8,045	8,542
Long-term liabilities (net)	35,284	27,239	18,697
Total liabilities	42,862	35,284	27,239
Equity	45,046	78,692	144,030
Total liabilities and equity	87,909	113,976	171,269

-16-

Profit & Loss Summary

For years ending December - 2008, 2009, 2010			
	Year 1	Year 2	Year 3
Income	180,000	216,000	252,000
Less COGS:			
Other	14,994	17,993	20,992
Total COGS	14,994	17,993	20,992
Gross profit	165,006	198,007	231,008
Operating expenses:			
Advertising	6,000	6,000	6,000
License	2,640	2,640	2,640
Insurance	9,600	9,600	9,600
Telephone	2,400	2,400	2,400
Office Supplies	600	600	600
Accountant Fees	12,000	12,000	12,000
Repairs & Maintenance	600	600	600
Fuel Expense	2,400	2,400	2,400
Equipment Rental	3,000	3,000	3,000
Salary Expense	84,960	99,120	99,120
Part-time Wages	0	8,496	9,912
Bad debts	1,800	2,160	2,520
Amortization	400	400	400
Depreciation	12,580	12,580	12,580
Total operating expenses	138,980	161,996	163,772
Operating income	26,026	36,011	67,236
Interest expense	2,880	2,366	1,898
Net income	23,146	33,646	65,338

Sales:

Year 1: 60 jobs at $3,000 each

Year 2: 72 jobs at $3,000 each

Year 3: 84 jobs at $3,000 each

Cost of Sales = $250 per job

Chemicals: ($100)

Protective Gear: ($50)

Disposal: ($100)

-17-

Operating Expenses:

Advertising: $6,000 each year. This amount covers the cost to place an ad in the yellow pages and to pay referral fees to other cleaning companies.

License: $2,640 is required annually by the city of Washington D.C. to dispose of the bio-hazardous waste.

Accountant Fees: Mr. Scott Dunn will be hired to maintain the books for $12,000 annually.

Salary Expenses: Mr. Miller and Ms. Anderson will be compensated $2,500 each for the first six months. Their salaries will increase to $3,500 after month six and remain the same for the remainder of the forecast.

Part-time wages: One part-time employee will be hired in year two. This employee will be paid $20 per hour and work an average of 30 to 36 hours per month.

Cash Plan

For years ending December - 2008, 2009, 2010			
	Year 1	Year 2	Year 3
Cash receipts	163,350	210,870	246,510
Operating cash expenses:			
Cost of sales	14,994	17,993	20,992
Other expenses	124,200	146,856	148,272
Total operating cash exp.	139,194	164,849	169,264
Cash from operations	24,156	46,021	77,246
Debt activities:			
Principal payments	(7,138)	(7,578)	(8,046)
Interest payments	(2,880)	(2,366)	(1,898)
Total debt activities	(10,017)	(9,944)	(9,944)
Net cash after debt service	14,139	36,078	67,303
Change in cash	14,139	36,078	67,303
Beginning cash	7,000	21,139	57,216
Cash before borrowing	21,139	57,216	124,519
Line of credit activity	0	0	0
Ending cash	21,139	57,216	124,519

All figures on the Cash Plan are derived from the assumptions above.

-18-

11. APPENDIX

This section contains the following reports and supporting documentation:

- Income Projection
- Expense Projection
- Profit & Loss
- Balance Sheet
- Cash Plan
- Ratio Analysis

Income Projection - Year 1

Income Category	Jan	Feb	Mar	Apr	May	Jun	Jul	Aug	Sep	Oct	Nov	Dec	Year 1
Cleanup Sales	15000	15000	15000	15000	15000	15000	15000	15000	15000	15000	15000	15000	180000
Total Income	15000	15000	15000	15000	15000	15000	15000	15000	15000	15000	15000	15000	180000

Income Projection - Year 2

Income Category	Jan	Feb	Mar	Apr	May	Jun	Jul	Aug	Sep	Oct	Nov	Dec	Year 2
Cleanup Sales	18000	18000	18000	18000	18000	18000	18000	18000	18000	18000	18000	18000	216000
Total Income	18000	18000	18000	18000	18000	18000	18000	18000	18000	18000	18000	18000	216000

Income Projection - Year 3

Income Category	Jan	Feb	Mar	Apr	May	Jun	Jul	Aug	Sep	Oct	Nov	Dec	Year 3
Cleanup Sales	21000	21000	21000	21000	21000	21000	21000	21000	21000	21000	21000	21000	252000
Total Income	21000	21000	21000	21000	21000	21000	21000	21000	21000	21000	21000	21000	252000

Expense Projection - Year 1

Expense Category	Jan	Feb	Mar	Apr	May	Jun	Jul	Aug	Sep	Oct	Nov	Dec	Year 1
Advertising	500	500	500	500	500	500	500	500	500	500	500	500	6000
License	220	220	220	220	220	220	220	220	220	220	220	220	2640
Insurance	800	800	800	800	800	800	800	800	800	800	800	800	9600
Telephone	200	200	200	200	200	200	200	200	200	200	200	200	2400
Office Supplies	50	50	50	50	50	50	50	50	50	50	50	50	600
Accountant Fees	1000	1000	1000	1000	1000	1000	1000	1000	1000	1000	1000	1000	12000
Repairs & Maintenance	50	50	50	50	50	50	50	50	50	50	50	50	600
Fuel Expense	200	200	200	200	200	200	200	200	200	200	200	200	2400
Equipment Rental	250	250	250	250	250	250	250	250	250	250	250	250	3000
Salary Expense	5900	5900	5900	5900	5900	5900	8260	8260	8260	8260	8260	8260	84960
Part-time Wages	0	0	0	0	0	0	0	0	0	0	0	0	0
Total Expenses	9170	9170	9170	9170	9170	9170	11530	11530	11530	11530	11530	11530	124200

Expense Projection - Year 2

Expense Category	Jan	Feb	Mar	Apr	May	Jun	Jul	Aug	Sep	Oct	Nov	Dec	Year 2
Advertising	500	500	500	500	500	500	500	500	500	500	500	500	6000
License	220	220	220	220	220	220	220	220	220	220	220	220	2640
Insurance	800	800	800	800	800	800	800	800	800	800	800	800	9600
Telephone	200	200	200	200	200	200	200	200	200	200	200	200	2400
Office Supplies	50	50	50	50	50	50	50	50	50	50	50	50	600
Accountant Fees	1000	1000	1000	1000	1000	1000	1000	1000	1000	1000	1000	1000	12000
Repairs & Maintenance	50	50	50	50	50	50	50	50	50	50	50	50	600
Fuel Expense	200	200	200	200	200	200	200	200	200	200	200	200	2400
Equipment Rental	250	250	250	250	250	250	250	250	250	250	250	250	3000
Salary Expense	8260	8260	8260	8260	8260	8260	8260	8260	8260	8260	8260	8260	99120
Part-time Wages	708	708	708	708	708	708	708	708	708	708	708	708	8496
Total Expenses	12238	12238	12238	12238	12238	12238	12238	12238	12238	12238	12238	12238	146856

Expense Projection - Year 3

Expense Category	Jan	Feb	Mar	Apr	May	Jun	Jul	Aug	Sep	Oct	Nov	Dec	Year 3
Advertising	500	500	500	500	500	500	500	500	500	500	500	500	6000
License	220	220	220	220	220	220	220	220	220	220	220	220	2640
Insurance	800	800	800	800	800	800	800	800	800	800	800	800	9600
Telephone	200	200	200	200	200	200	200	200	200	200	200	200	2400
Office Supplies	50	50	50	50	50	50	50	50	50	50	50	50	600
Accountant Fees	1000	1000	1000	1000	1000	1000	1000	1000	1000	1000	1000	1000	12000
Repairs & Maintenance	50	50	50	50	50	50	50	50	50	50	50	50	600
Fuel Expense	200	200	200	200	200	200	200	200	200	200	200	200	2400
Equipment Rental	250	250	250	250	250	250	250	250	250	250	250	250	3000
Salary Expense	8260	8260	8260	8260	8260	8260	8260	8260	8260	8260	8260	8260	99120
Part-time Wages	826	826	826	826	826	826	826	826	826	826	826	826	9912
Total Expenses	12356	12356	12356	12356	12356	12356	12356	12356	12356	12356	12356	12356	148272

Profit & Loss - Year 1

	Jan	Feb	Mar	Apr	May	Jun	Jul	Aug	Sep	Oct	Nov	Dec	Year 1
Income	15000	15000	15000	15000	15000	15000	15000	15000	15000	15000	15000	15000	180000
Less COGS:													
Other	1250	1250	1250	1250	1250	1250	1250	1250	1250	1250	1250	1250	15000
Total COGS	1250	1250	1250	1250	1250	1250	1250	1250	1250	1250	1250	1250	15000
Gross profit	13750	13750	13750	13750	13750	13750	13750	13750	13750	13750	13750	13750	165000
Operating expenses:													
Advertising	500	500	500	500	500	500	500	500	500	500	500	500	6000
License	220	220	220	220	220	220	220	220	220	220	220	220	2640
Insurance	800	800	800	800	800	800	800	800	800	800	800	800	9600
Telephone	200	200	200	200	200	200	200	200	200	200	200	200	2400
Office Supplies	50	50	50	50	50	50	50	50	50	50	50	50	600
Accountant Fees	1000	1000	1000	1000	1000	1000	1000	1000	1000	1000	1000	1000	12000
Repairs & Maintenance	50	50	50	50	50	50	50	50	50	50	50	50	600
Fuel Expense	200	200	200	200	200	200	200	200	200	200	200	200	2400
Equipment Rental	250	250	250	250	250	250	250	250	250	250	250	250	3000
Salary Expense	5900	5900	5900	5900	5900	5900	8260	8260	8260	8260	8260	8260	84960
Part-time Wages	0	0	0	0	0	0	0	0	0	0	0	0	0
Bad debts	150	150	150	150	150	150	150	150	150	150	150	150	1800
Amortization	33	33	33	33	33	33	33	33	33	33	33	33	396
Depreciation	1048	1048	1048	1048	1048	1048	1048	1048	1048	1048	1048	1048	12576
Total operating expenses	10401	10401	10401	10401	10401	10401	12761	12761	12761	12761	12761	12761	138972
Operating income	3349	3349	3349	3349	3349	3349	989	989	989	989	989	989	26028
Interest expense	250	295	269	242	238	235	232	229	226	223	220	217	2876
Net income	3099	3054	3080	3107	3111	3114	757	760	763	766	769	772	23152

Profit & Loss - Year 2

	Jan	Feb	Mar	Apr	May	Jun	Jul	Aug	Sep	Oct	Nov	Dec	Year 2
Income	18000	18000	18000	18000	18000	18000	18000	18000	18000	18000	18000	18000	216000
Less COGS:													
Other	1499	1499	1499	1499	1499	1499	1499	1499	1499	1499	1499	1499	17988
Total COGS	1499	1499	1499	1499	1499	1499	1499	1499	1499	1499	1499	1499	17988
Gross profit	16501	16501	16501	16501	16501	16501	16501	16501	16501	16501	16501	16501	198012
Operating expenses:													
Advertising	500	500	500	500	500	500	500	500	500	500	500	500	6000
License	220	220	220	220	220	220	220	220	220	220	220	220	2640
Insurance	800	800	800	800	800	800	800	800	800	800	800	800	9600
Telephone	200	200	200	200	200	200	200	200	200	200	200	200	2400
Office Supplies	50	50	50	50	50	50	50	50	50	50	50	50	600
Accountant Fees	1000	1000	1000	1000	1000	1000	1000	1000	1000	1000	1000	1000	12000
Repairs & Maintenance	50	50	50	50	50	50	50	50	50	50	50	50	600
Fuel Expense	200	200	200	200	200	200	200	200	200	200	200	200	2400
Equipment Rental	250	250	250	250	250	250	250	250	250	250	250	250	3000
Salary Expense	8260	8260	8260	8250	8260	8260	8260	8260	8260	8260	8260	8260	99120
Part-time Wages	708	708	708	738	708	708	708	708	708	708	708	708	8496
Bad debts	180	180	180	180	180	180	180	180	180	180	180	180	2160
Amortization	33	33	33	33	33	33	33	33	33	33	33	33	396
Depreciation	1048	1048	1048	1048	1048	1048	1048	1048	1048	1048	1048	1048	12576
Total operating expenses	13499	13499	13499	13499	13499	13499	13499	13499	13499	13499	13499	13499	161988
Operating income	3002	3002	3002	3002	3002	3002	3002	3002	3002	3002	3002	3002	36024
Interest expense	214	211	208	205	202	199	196	192	189	186	183	180	2365
Net income	2788	2791	2794	2797	2800	2803	2806	2810	2813	2816	2819	2822	33659

Profit & Loss - Year 3

	Jan	Feb	Mar	Apr	May	Jun	Jul	Aug	Sep	Oct	Nov	Dec	Year 3
Income	21000	21000	21000	21000	21000	21000	21000	21000	21000	21000	21000	21000	252000
Less COGS:													
Other	1749	1749	1749	1749	1749	1749	1749	1749	1749	1749	1749	1749	20988
Total COGS	1749	1749	1749	1749	1749	1749	1749	1749	1749	1749	1749	1749	20988
Gross profit	19251	19251	19251	19251	19251	19251	19251	19251	19251	19251	19251	19251	231012
Operating expenses:													
Advertising	500	500	500	500	500	500	500	500	500	500	500	500	6000
License	220	220	220	220	220	220	220	220	220	220	220	220	2640
Insurance	800	800	800	800	800	800	800	800	800	800	800	800	9600
Telephone	200	200	200	200	200	200	200	200	200	200	200	200	2400
Office Supplies	50	50	50	50	50	50	50	50	50	50	50	50	600
Accountant Fees	1000	1000	1000	1000	1000	1000	1000	1000	1000	1000	1000	1000	12000
Repairs & Maintenance	50	50	50	50	50	50	50	50	50	50	50	50	600
Fuel Expense	200	200	200	200	200	200	200	200	200	200	200	200	2400
Equipment Rental	250	250	250	250	250	250	250	250	250	250	250	250	3000
Salary Expense	8260	8260	8260	8260	8260	8260	8260	8260	8260	8260	8260	8260	99120
Part-time Wages	826	826	826	826	826	826	826	826	826	826	826	826	9912
Bad debts	210	210	210	210	210	210	210	210	210	210	210	210	2520
Amortization	33	33	33	33	33	33	33	33	33	33	33	33	396
Depreciation	1048	1048	1048	1048	1048	1048	1048	1048	1048	1048	1048	1048	12576
Total operating expenses	13647	13647	13647	13647	13647	13647	13647	13647	13647	13647	13647	13647	163764
Operating income	5604	5604	5604	5604	5604	5604	5604	5604	5604	5604	5604	5604	67248
Interest expense	176	173	170	167	163	160	157	153	150	146	143	140	1898
Net income	5428	5431	5434	5437	5441	5444	5447	5451	5454	5458	5461	5464	65350

Balance Sheet - Year 1

	Jan	Feb	Mar	Apr	May	Jun	Jul	Aug	Sep	Oct	Nov	Dec	Year 1
Assets:													
Current assets:													
Cash	3000	3000	3000	6484	10086	13687	14929	16171	17413	18655	19897	21139	21139
Accounts receivable (net)	14850	14850	14850	14850	14850	14850	14850	14850	14850	14850	14850	14850	14850
Total current assets	17850	17850	17850	21334	24936	28537	29779	31021	32263	33505	34747	35989	35989
Fixed assets (net)	61852	60803	59755	58707	57658	56610	55562	54513	53465	52417	51368	50320	50320
Other assets (net)	1967	1933	1900	1867	1833	1800	1767	1733	1700	1667	1633	1600	1600
Total assets	81669	80586	79505	81908	84427	86947	87108	87267	87428	87589	87748	87909	87909
Liabilities and equity:													
Current liabilities:													
Line of credit	7248	3695	117	0	0	0	0	0	0	0	0	0	0
Current maturities	7174	7209	7245	7282	7318	7355	7391	7428	7466	7503	7540	7578	7578
Total current liabilities	14422	10904	7362	7282	7318	7355	7391	7428	7466	7503	7540	7578	7578
Long-term liabilities (net)	42248	41630	41010	40386	39760	39130	38497	37861	37221	36579	35933	35284	35284
Total liabilities	56670	52534	48372	47668	47078	46485	45888	45289	44687	44082	43473	42862	42862
Equity	24999	28052	31133	34240	37349	40462	41220	41978	42741	43507	44275	45047	45047
Total liabilities and equity	81669	80586	79505	81908	84427	86947	87108	87267	87428	87589	87748	87909	87909

Balance Sheet - Year 2

	Jan	Feb	Mar	Apr	May	Jun	Jul	Aug	Sep	Oct	Nov	Dec	Year 2
Assets:													
Current assets:													
Cash	21423	24677	27930	31184	34438	37692	40946	44200	47454	50708	53962	57216	57216
Accounts receivable (net)	17820	17820	17820	17820	17820	17820	17820	17820	17820	17820	17820	17820	17820
Total current assets	39243	42497	45750	49004	52258	55512	58766	62020	65274	68528	71782	75036	75036
Fixed assets (net)	49272	48223	47175	46127	45078	44030	42982	41933	40885	39837	38788	37740	37740
Other assets (net)	1567	1533	1500	1467	1433	1400	1367	1333	1300	1267	1233	1200	1200
Total assets	90082	92253	94425	96598	98769	100942	103115	105286	107459	109632	111803	113976	113976
Liabilities and equity:													
Current liabilities:													
Line of credit	0	0	0	0	0	0	0	0	0	0	0	0	0
Current maturities	7616	7654	7692	7731	7769	7808	7847	7887	7926	7966	8005	8045	8045
Total current liabilities	7616	7654	7692	7731	7769	7808	7847	7887	7926	7966	8005	8045	8045
Long-term liabilities (net)	34632	33976	33318	32656	31990	31321	30649	29974	29295	28613	27928	27239	27239
Total liabilities	42248	41630	41010	40387	39759	39129	38496	37861	37221	36579	35933	35284	35284
Equity	47834	50623	53415	56211	59010	61813	64619	67425	70238	73053	75870	78692	78692
Total liabilities and equity	90082	92253	94425	96598	98769	100942	103115	105286	107459	109632	111803	113976	113976

Balance Sheet - Year 3

	Jan	Feb	Mar	Apr	May	Jun	Jul	Aug	Sep	Oct	Nov	Dec	Year 3
Assets:													
Current assets:													
Cash	60102	65958	71814	77670	83526	89382	95239	101095	106951	112807	118663	124519	124519
Accounts receivable (net)	20790	20790	20790	20790	20790	20790	20790	20790	20790	20790	20790	20790	20790
Total current assets	80892	86748	92604	98460	104316	110172	116029	121885	127741	133597	139453	145309	145309
Fixed assets (net)	36692	35643	34595	33547	32498	31450	30402	29353	28305	27257	26208	25160	25160
Other assets (net)	1167	1133	1100	1067	1033	1000	967	933	900	867	833	800	800
Total assets	118751	123524	128299	133074	137847	142622	147398	152171	156946	161721	166494	171269	171269
Liabilities and equity:													
Current liabilities:													
Line of credit	0	0	0	0	0	0	0	0	0	0	0	0	0
Current maturities	8086	8126	8167	8208	8249	8290	8331	8373	8415	8457	8499	8542	8542
Total current liabilities	8086	8126	8167	8208	8249	8290	8331	8373	8415	8457	8499	8542	8542
Long-term liabilities (net)	26546	25850	25151	24448	23742	23032	22318	21601	20880	20156	19428	18697	18697
Total liabilities	34632	33976	33318	32656	31991	31322	30649	29974	29295	28613	27927	27239	27239
Equity	84119	89548	94981	100418	105856	111300	116749	122197	127651	133108	138567	144030	144030
Total liabilities and equity	118751	123524	128299	133074	137847	142622	147398	152171	156946	161721	166494	171269	171269

Cash Plan - Year 1

	Jan	Feb	Mar	Apr	May	Jun	Jul	Aug	Sep	Oct	Nov	Dec	Year 1
Cash receipts	0	14850	14850	14850	14850	14850	14850	14850	14850	14850	14850	14850	163350
Operating cash expenses:													
Cost of sales	1250	1250	1250	1250	1250	1250	1250	1250	1250	1250	1250	1250	15000
Other expenses	9170	9170	9170	9170	9170	9170	11530	11530	11530	11530	11530	11530	124200
Total operating cash exp.	10420	10420	10420	10420	10420	10420	12780	12780	12780	12780	12780	12780	139200
Cash from operations	-10420	4430	4430	4430	4430	4430	2070	2070	2070	2070	2070	2070	24150
Debt activities:													
Principal payments	-579	-582	-584	-587	-590	-593	-596	-599	-602	-605	-608	-611	-7136
Interest payments	-250	-295	-269	-242	-238	-235	-232	-229	-226	-223	-220	-217	-2876
Total debt activities	-829	-877	-853	-829	-828	-828	-828	-828	-828	-828	-828	-828	-10012
Net cash after debt service	-11249	3553	3577	3601	3602	3602	1242	1242	1242	1242	1242	1242	14138
Change in cash	-11248	3554	3577	3601	3602	3602	1242	1242	1242	1242	1242	1242	14140
Beginning cash	7000	3000	3000	3000	6484	10086	13687	14929	16171	17413	18655	19897	7000
Cash before borrowing	-4248	6554	6577	6601	10086	13688	14929	16171	17413	18655	19897	21139	21140
Line of credit activity	7248	-3554	-3577	-117	0	0	0	0	0	0	0	0	0
Ending cash	3000	3000	3000	6484	10086	13688	14929	16171	17413	18655	19897	21139	21139

Cash Plan - Year 2

	Jan	Feb	Mar	Apr	May	Jun	Jul	Aug	Sep	Oct	Nov	Dec	Year 2
Cash receipts	14850	17820	17820	17820	17820	17820	17820	17820	17820	17820	17820	17820	210870
Operating cash expenses:													
Cost of sales	1499	1499	1499	1499	1499	1499	1499	1499	1499	1499	1499	1499	17988
Other expenses	12238	12238	12238	12238	12238	12238	12238	12238	12238	12238	12238	12238	146856
Total operating cash exp.	13737	13737	13737	13737	13737	13737	13737	13737	13737	13737	13737	13737	164844
Cash from operations	1113	4083	4083	4083	4083	4083	4083	4083	4083	4083	4083	4083	46026
Debt activities:													
Principal payments	-614	-617	-620	-624	-627	-630	-633	-636	-639	-643	-646	-649	-7578
Interest payments	-214	-211	-208	-205	-202	-199	-196	-192	-189	-186	-183	-180	-2365
Total debt activities	-828	-828	-828	-829	-829	-829	-829	-828	-828	-829	-829	-829	-9943
Net cash after debt service	285	3255	3255	3254	3254	3254	3254	3255	3255	3254	3254	3254	36083
Change in cash	284	3254	3254	3254	3254	3254	3254	3254	3254	3254	3254	3254	36078
Beginning cash	21139	21423	24677	27930	31184	34438	37692	40946	44200	47454	50708	53962	21139
Cash before borrowing	21423	24677	27931	31184	34438	37692	40946	44200	47454	50708	53962	57216	57217
Line of credit activity	0	0	0	0	0	0	0	0	0	0	0	0	0
Ending cash	21423	24677	27931	31184	34438	37692	40946	44200	47454	50708	53962	57216	57216

Cash Plan - Year 3

	Jan	Feb	Mar	Apr	May	Jun	Jul	Aug	Sep	Oct	Nov	Dec	Year 3
Cash receipts	17820	20790	20790	20790	20790	20790	20790	20790	20790	20790	20790	20790	246510
Operating cash expenses:													
Cost of sales	1749	1749	1749	1749	1749	1749	1749	1749	1749	1749	1749	1749	20988
Other expenses	12356	12356	12356	12356	12356	12356	12356	12356	12356	12356	12356	12356	148272
Total operating cash exp.	14105	14105	14105	14105	14105	14105	14105	14105	14105	14105	14105	14105	169260
Cash from operations	3715	6685	6685	6685	6685	6685	6685	6685	6685	6685	6685	6685	77250
Debt activities:													
Principal payments	-652	-655	-659	-662	-665	-669	-672	-675	-679	-682	-686	-689	-8045
Interest payments	-176	-173	-170	-167	-163	-160	-157	-153	-150	-146	-143	-140	-1898
Total debt activities	-828	-828	-829	-829	-828	-829	-829	-828	-829	-828	-829	-829	-9943
Net cash after debt service	2887	5857	5856	5856	5857	5856	5856	5857	5856	5857	5856	5856	67307
Change in cash	2886	5856	5856	5856	5856	5856	5856	5856	5856	5856	5856	5856	67302
Beginning cash	57216	60102	65958	71814	77670	83526	89382	95239	101095	106951	112807	118663	57216
Cash before borrowing	60102	65958	71814	77670	83526	89382	95238	101095	106951	112807	118663	124519	124518
Line of credit activity	0	0	0	0	0	0	0	0	0	0	0	0	0
Ending cash	60102	65958	71814	77670	83526	89382	95238	101095	106951	112807	118663	124519	124519

Ratio Analysis - Year 1

	Jan	Feb	Mar	Apr	May	Jun	Jul	Aug	Sep	Oct	Nov	Dec	Year 1
Profitability ratios:													
Gross profit margin	91.67%	91.67%	91.67%	91.67%	91.67%	91.67%	91.67%	91.67%	91.67%	91.67%	91.67%	91.67%	91.67%
Operating profit margin	22.33%	22.33%	22.33%	22.33%	22.33%	22.33%	6.59%	6.59%	6.59%	6.59%	6.59%	6.59%	14.46%
Net profit margin	20.66%	20.36%	20.53%	20.71%	20.74%	20.76%	5.04%	5.06%	5.08%	5.10%	5.12%	5.14%	12.86%
Return on equity	13.21%	11.51%	10.41%	9.51%	8.69%	8.00%	1.85%	1.83%	1.80%	1.77%	1.75%	1.73%	62.64%
Return on assets	4.36%	4.13%	4.18%	4.15%	4.03%	3.91%	1.14%	1.13%	1.13%	1.13%	1.13%	1.13%	30.86%
Liquidity ratios:													
Current ratio	1.24	1.64	2.42	2.93	3.41	3.88	4.03	4.18	4.32	4.47	4.61	4.75	4.75
Quick ratio (Acid-test)	1.24	1.64	2.42	2.93	3.41	3.88	4.03	4.18	4.32	4.47	4.61	4.75	4.75
Working capital ratio	0.23	0.46	0.70	0.94	1.17	1.41	1.49	1.57	1.65	1.73	1.81	1.89	0.16
Activity ratios:													
Accounts receivable days	29.70	29.70	29.70	29.70	29.70	29.70	29.70	29.70	29.70	29.70	29.70	29.70	29.70
Inventory days	n/a	n/a	n/a	n/a	n/a	n/a	n/a	n/a	n/a	n/a	n/a	n/a	n/a
Inventory turnover	n/a	n/a	n/a	n/a	n/a	n/a	n/a	n/a	n/a	n/a	n/a	n/a	n/a
Sales-to-assets	0.20	0.18	0.19	0.19	0.18	0.18	0.17	0.17	0.17	0.17	0.17	0.17	2.13
Leverage ratios:													
Debt-to-equity	2.27	1.87	1.55	1.39	1.26	1.15	1.11	1.08	1.05	1.01	0.98	0.95	0.95
Debt ratio	0.69	0.65	0.61	0.58	0.56	0.53	0.53	0.52	0.51	0.50	0.50	0.49	0.49
Times-interest (TI) earned:													
Operating income	3349	3349	3349	3349	3349	3349	989	989	989	989	989	989	26026
Interest expense (÷)	250	295	269	242	238	235	232	229	226	223	220	217	2880
TI earned ratio	13.40	11.35	12.45	13.84	14.07	14.25	4.26	4.32	4.38	4.43	4.50	4.56	9.0368056

Ratio Analysis - Year 2

	Jan	Feb	Mar	Apr	May	Jun	Jul	Aug	Sep	Oct	Nov	Dec	Year 2
Profitability ratios:													
Gross profit margin	91.67%	91.67%	91.67%	91.67%	91.67%	91.67%	91.67%	91.67%	91.67%	91.67%	91.67%	91.67%	91.67%
Operating profit margin	16.67%	16.67%	16.67%	16.67%	16.67%	16.67%	16.67%	16.67%	16.67%	16.67%	16.67%	16.67%	16.67%
Net profit margin	15.48%	15.50%	15.52%	15.53%	15.55%	15.57%	15.58%	15.60%	15.62%	15.64%	15.66%	15.67%	15.58%
Return on equity	6.00%	5.67%	5.37%	5.10%	4.86%	4.64%	4.44%	4.25%	4.08%	3.93%	3.78%	3.65%	54.41%
Return on assets	3.37%	3.29%	3.22%	3.14%	3.07%	3.01%	2.94%	2.88%	2.82%	2.76%	2.71%	2.66%	35.68%
Liquidity ratios:													
Current ratio	5.15	5.55	5.95	6.34	6.73	7.11	7.49	7.86	8.24	8.60	8.97	9.33	9.33
Quick ratio (Acid-test)	5.15	5.55	5.95	6.34	6.73	7.11	7.49	7.86	8.24	8.60	8.97	9.33	9.33
Working capital ratio	1.76	1.94	2.11	2.29	2.47	2.65	2.83	3.01	3.19	3.36	3.54	3.72	0.31
Activity ratios:													
Accounts receivable days	29.70	29.70	29.70	29.70	29.70	29.70	29.70	29.70	29.70	29.70	29.70	29.70	29.70
Inventory days	n/a	n/a	n/a	n/a	n/a	n/a	n/a	n/a	n/a	n/a	n/a	n/a	n/a
Inventory turnover	n/a	n/a	n/a	n/a	n/a	n/a	n/a	n/a	n/a	n/a	n/a	n/a	n/a
Sales-to-assets	0.20	0.20	0.19	0.19	0.18	0.18	0.18	0.17	0.17	0.17	0.16	0.16	2.14
Leverage ratios:													
Debt-to-equity	0.88	0.82	0.77	0.72	0.67	0.63	0.60	0.56	0.53	0.50	0.47	0.45	0.45
Debt ratio	0.47	0.45	0.43	0.42	0.40	0.39	0.37	0.36	0.35	0.33	0.32	0.31	0.31
Times-interest (TI) earned:													
Operating income	3001	3001	3001	3001	3001	3001	3001	3001	3001	3001	3001	3001	36011
Interest expense (÷)	214	211	208	205	202	199	196	192	189	186	183	180	2366
TI earned ratio	14.02	14.22	14.43	14.64	14.86	15.08	15.31	15.63	15.88	16.13	16.40	16.67	15.220203

Ratio Analysis - Year 3

	Jan	Feb	Mar	Apr	May	Jun	Jul	Aug	Sep	Oct	Nov	Dec	Year 3
Profitability ratios:													
Gross profit margin	91.67%	91.67%	91.67%	91.67%	91.67%	91.67%	91.67%	91.67%	91.67%	91.67%	91.67%	91.67%	91.67%
Operating profit margin	26.68%	26.68%	26.68%	26.68%	26.68%	26.68%	26.68%	26.68%	26.68%	26.68%	26.68%	26.68%	26.68%
Net profit margin	25.84%	25.86%	25.87%	25.89%	25.90%	25.92%	25.94%	25.95%	25.97%	25.98%	26.00%	26.02%	25.93%
Return on equity	6.67%	6.25%	5.89%	5.56%	5.27%	5.01%	4.78%	4.56%	4.37%	4.19%	4.02%	3.87%	58.69%
Return on assets	4.82%	4.63%	4.45%	4.29%	4.14%	4.00%	3.86%	3.74%	3.63%	3.52%	3.41%	3.32%	47.14%
Liquidity ratios:													
Current ratio	10.00	10.68	11.34	12.00	12.65	13.29	13.93	14.56	15.18	15.80	16.41	17.01	17.01
Quick ratio (Acid-test)	10.00	10.68	11.34	12.00	12.65	13.29	13.93	14.56	15.18	15.80	16.41	17.01	17.01
Working capital ratio	3.47	3.74	4.02	4.30	4.57	4.85	5.13	5.41	5.68	5.96	6.24	6.51	0.54
Activity ratios:													
Accounts receivable days	29.70	29.70	29.70	29.70	29.70	29.70	29.70	29.70	29.70	29.70	29.70	29.70	29.70
Inventory days	n/a	n/a	n/a	n/a	n/a	n/a	n/a	n/a	n/a	n/a	n/a	n/a	n/a
Inventory turnover	n/a	n/a	n/a	n/a	n/a	n/a	n/a	n/a	n/a	n/a	n/a	n/a	n/a
Sales-to-assets	0.18	0.17	0.17	0.16	0.16	0.15	0.14	0.14	0.14	0.13	0.13	0.12	1.77
Leverage ratios:													
Debt-to-equity	0.41	0.38	0.35	0.33	0.30	0.28	0.26	0.25	0.23	0.22	0.20	0.19	0.19
Debt ratio	0.29	0.28	0.26	0.25	0.23	0.22	0.21	0.20	0.19	0.18	0.17	0.16	0.16
Times-interest (TI) earned:													
Operating income	5603	5603	5603	5603	5603	5603	5603	5603	5603	5603	5603	5603	67236
Interest expense (÷)	176	173	170	167	163	160	157	153	150	146	143	140	1898
TI earned ratio	31.84	32.39	32.96	33.55	34.37	35.02	35.69	36.62	37.35	38.38	39.18	40.02	35.424658

The Business Plan for
HydroHut LLC
A Texas Limited Liability Corporation

Contact Information:

HydroHut LLC

12709 Enfield Terrace

Austin, TX 78704

(512) 555-1212

HydroHutLLC@internet.com

Allis Walter

Matthew Strang

This is a business plan and does not imply an offering of securities.

Copy Number___ of Five.

Non-Disclosure and Confidentiality Agreement

The undersigned ("Recipient") hereby agrees that all financial and other information ("Information") that it has and will receive concerning HydroHut LLC is confidential and will not be disclosed to any other individual or entity without prior written consent.

The Information shall remain the property of HydroHut LLC and shall be returned to HydroHut LLC promptly at its request together with all copies made thereof.

Recipient acknowledges that no remedy of law may be adequate to compensate HydroHut LLC for a violation of this Agreement and Recipient hereby agrees that in addition to any legal or other rights that may be available in the event of a breach hereunder, HydroHut LLC may seek equitable relief to enforce this Agreement in any Court of competent jurisdiction.

_____   _____
Date   Signature of Recipient

-2-

THE PLAN FOR HYDROHUT LLC

-4-

1.0 EXECUTIVE SUMMARY

HydroHut LLC is a unique concept ready to enter the Austin, Texas retail restaurant and bar market. Its products will consist of still water drinks and baked goods for health-conscious consumers. The owners, who bring more than 12 years of retail restaurant and bar operations experience to the venture, are seeking a line-of-credit of $15,000 to facilitate the opening and operation of HydroHut LLC.

Income Projection

For years ending December - 2008, 2009, 2010			
Income Category	Year 1	Year 2	Year 3
Retail Walk-In	100,100	107,000	189,100
Corporate	0	8,000	13,000
Special Events	9,500	17,000	20,300
Total Income	109,600	132,000	222,400

1.1 Business Opportunity

Still (non-carbonated) water beverages are the trendiest new drinks since gourmet coffee. The market for still water drinks has been building strongly for three years and now appears ready to enter a new, accelerated period of growth.

1.2 Product/Service Description

Still water drinks are much different from the mass-produced carbonated beverages sold by the soft drink giants. They are usually produced in small quantities by entrepreneurial organizations and product quality is extremely high. Still water drinks include functional additives, including nutriceuticals, which further differentiate them from mass-market soft drinks and appeal to health-conscious consumers.

The product line, all purchased from outside vendors, will consist of approximately 20 different still water beverages and functional beverages, in addition to a selection of freshly baked breads, muffins, cookies, and other locally produced items.

[Insert picture of bottled water]

1.3 Current Business Position

HydroHut LLC will be owned by Allis Walter and Matthew Strang. The business will be structured as an LLC, with Walter and Strang being the only two Members. Mr. Walter and Mr. Strang are experienced in retail restaurant and bar operations.

1.4 Financial Potential

Revenues of $109,600 are expected in HydroHut LLC's first year of operations, with a 20 percent revenue increase in year two. Early in year three, a second location is planned, which will increase HydroHut LLC's potential for success. Revenues are expected to increase considerably after the second location is opened, to a projected $222,400. Bank financing is not expected to be required after HydroHut LLC's first year of operation, based on the projected cash flows.

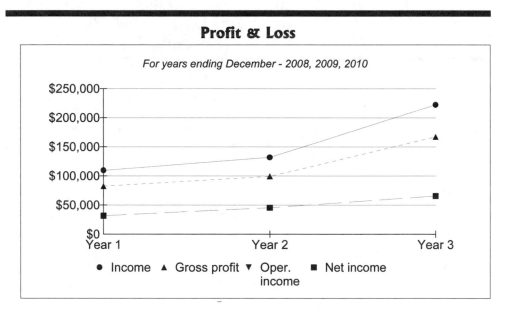

Profit & Loss

1.5 The Request

HydroHut LLC is seeking to establish a $15,000 line-of-credit loan to cover start-up costs, purchase needed equipment, and provide working capital until the business can support itself financially. HydroHut LLC is requesting this amount be formalized as a line of credit, which the company can draw from as needed.

-6-

Even though the amount requested is $15,000, HydroHut LLC projects it will only require funds equal to $4,250. However, such a line of credit will help HydroHut LLC cover operating expenses should the forecast fall short. The owners are prepared to pledge personal assets in the amount of the loan to collateralize the transaction. In addition, they are willing to invest $10,000 of their own cash to help get HydroHut LLC up and running.

2.0 COMPANY BACKGROUND

The two members that will own HydroHut LLC are Mr. Allis Walter and Mr. Matthew Strang, who together bring more than 12 years of restaurant hospitality experience to the business. The partners recognized the progressive, health-conscious lifestyles of much of Austin's population, and view the functional still water market as one with strong potential. Research of functional still water beverage locations elsewhere in the United States supported the partner's beliefs about its potential for success. There are no other such facilities in Austin at the current time.

2.1 Business Description

HydroHut LLC will sell still water beverages through a retail outlet in Austin, Texas. The outlet will consist of a bar and seating area, as well as a service counter. It will serve beverages prepared on the premises for consumption either in the beverage bar or off-site. In addition, it will offer prepackaged products, including baked goods.

HydroHut LLC will target its products to Austin's educated, progressive population. Austin has one of the country's highest per-capita rates of consumption of natural foods and beverages.

A retail business, including a small bar and seating area and drive-through window area, will be located in an existing facility near the intersection of Loop 1 and Enfield Road in central Austin.

2.2 Company History

Allis Walter and Matthew Strang became associated in the summer of 1996, through mutual memberships in a regional hospitality trade association. A combination of a mutual passion for health-conscious products with shared entrepreneurial attitudes eventually led them to discuss becoming business partners. After doing considerable market research in the health products industry, the partners discovered the absence of functional still water products in Austin. Further research into existing functional water facilities in the United States showed the partners the potential for success in this type of business.

2.3 Current Position and Business Objectives

HydroHut LLC is currently in the start-up phase of its business life. The first HydroHut LLC location will be located near the intersection of Loop 1 and Enfield Road, one of the city's busiest intersections and hottest retail environments. The store will be the first of its kind in Austin, a major metro area of more than one million people.

HydroHut LLC's mission statement is as follows:

"HydroHut LLC will sell still water drinks and functional beverages to health-conscious consumers in Austin, Texas. Retail customers will consist of students, faculty, and staff from the nearby University of Texas campus, the nation's largest, and residents of the well-educated, affluent surrounding neighborhoods."

Long-term goals for HydroHut LLC include an expansion to three locations by the end of its fifth year of operations, as well as the possibility of the creation of company-owned or franchised outlets thereafter.

2.4 Ownership

HydroHut LLC will be owned by Allis Walter and Matthew Strang. The business will be structured as an LLC. Mr. Walter and Mr. Strang are experienced in retail restaurant bar operations.

3.0 PRODUCTS

Still water is the fastest growing segment of the alternative beverage industry. Sales for 2006, the most recent year for which data is available, were up 25 percent, almost double the industry average of 13 percent. Other alternative beverage segments include juices, teas, sport drinks, sparkling waters, and natural sodas.

3.1 Product Overview

The primary products to be sold through HydroHut LLC will be functional still water drinks in three categories:

1. Nutriceuticals

Nutriceutical waters include still waters to which have been added minerals such as potassium, calcium, vitamins including A, C, and D, and other substances, such as caffeine.

-8-

2. <u>Bacteria-Free Still Water</u>

Bacteria-free still waters are processed using techniques that eliminate microorganisms, including associated flavors and particles, from the water.

3. <u>Exotic Waters</u>

Exotic waters are bottled and imported from locations such as Alaska, Canada, France, Hawaii, Sweden, and Russia.

Functional still water fountain drinks will be offered at the following prices:

Small: $1.00

Medium: $1.50

Large: $2.50

In addition, larger sizes of water will be sold for customer carryout or delivery. They will range from 1-liter bottles to 20-liter plastic jugs at prices ranging from $2.50 to $25.00.

HydroHut LLC will sell these products, as well as prepackaged products (including baked goods), for consumption both in the beverage bar and off-site. The location will also have a drive-through window area for customer convenience.

3.2 Competitive Analysis

Currently, no other business in Austin focuses exclusively on the functional still water market. This will provide considerable flexibility in pricing and allow for the creation of a great deal of customer awareness and brand loyalty, erecting significant barriers to entry for potential competitors.

While no retail businesses devoted exclusively to functional water beverages exist in Austin, functional water beverages are sold at Whole Foods, Whole Earth Provision, Randall's Markets, and other grocery retailers.

3.3 Suppliers and Inventory

HydroHut LLC's products will be supplied by various vendors, including the following: Aqua Health, Water for Life, H2Ah!, Nutri-Water, Hydration Technologies, Guava Cool, Soft Beverages, and Millennium Moisture. These vendors supply a variety of beverages with features such as nutriceutical content, bacteria-free processing, and a number of natural, organic flavorings, including berries, fruits, and spices.

These suppliers are, for the most part, located in the continental United States. While they are not currently available for wholesale distribution in Austin, which partially explains the lack of local retail distribution, all operate existing distribution systems with representatives in other Texas cities, including Houston, San Antonio, and Dallas. No problems in obtaining adequate supplies of important products are anticipated. A projected inventory level of 30 days' worth of product will be on hand at all times.

3.4 Research and Development

HydroHut LLC's success will come from educating customers about the appeal and benefits of functional still water beverages, and from providing a quality service and products not available in grocery stores. Price competition will be a minimal influence given current market conditions.

Expansion will begin in year three and includes the planned opening of a second location, an expansion of corporate sales, and added emphasis on special outside event promotions.

4.0 SERVICES

No special services are contemplated initially.

5.0 THE INDUSTRY, COMPETITION AND MARKET

HydroHut LLC will take advantage of the rapidly growing still water beverage market niche. The market for these products has been building strongly for over three years, appealing mainly to health-conscious consumers of all age groups. While Austin, Texas contains one of the highest demographic target markets for these products, the community currently has no still water beverage retailer. The following sections discuss the opportunities for HydroHut LLC in the Austin area.

5.1 Industry Definition

Still water is the fastest growing segment of the alternative beverage industry. Sales for 2006, the most recent year for which data is available, were up 25 percent, almost double the industry average of 13 percent. Other alternative beverage segments include juices, teas, sport drinks, sparkling waters, and natural sodas.

Still water sales totaled 731 million cases, making the category by far the dominant player in alternative beverages, whose total sales neared 1.9 billion cases. Still water's share of the alternative beverage market exceeded 39 percent, up 3.7 percent from the previous year, when 585 million cases of still waters were sold. Other strong categories included sport drinks and teas.

-10-

5.2 Primary Competitors

No other business in Austin focuses exclusively on the functional still water market. This will provide considerable flexibility in pricing and allow for the creation of a great deal of customer awareness and brand loyalty, erecting significant barriers to entry for potential competitors.

While no retail businesses devoted exclusively to functional water beverages exist in Austin, functional water beverages are sold at Whole Foods, Whole Earth Provision, Randall's Markets, and other grocery retailers.

5.3 Market Size

Austin is the capital of Texas, located near the center of the state approximately 70 miles north of San Antonio and 200 miles south of Dallas. The city has a population of roughly 500,000 and is the hub of a metropolitan area of more than 1 million people. It is home to the nation's largest university, as well as many offices related to the state government and also a booming business community, including the headquarters of Dell Computer Corp. and Whole Foods Market, the nation's largest retailer of natural foods.

5.4 Market Growth

HydroHut LLC is an ideal business for Austin, given the market including size and demographics. Based on average individual transactions of approximately $2.25, including functional still water drinks and ancillary products, the business has the potential to gross over $220,000 in sales by its third year of operation. Three additional locations are planned by the end of HydroHut LLC's fifth year of operations.

5.5 Customer Profile

Austin has one of the highest percentages of adults possessing a college degree of any American city, and is generally regarded as a center of progressive lifestyles in the Southwest. The city has one of the country's highest per-capita rates of consumption of natural foods and beverages. The facility will be located near desirable residential areas, the state capital complex, and the University of Texas main campus.

6.0 MARKETING PLAN

HydroHut LLC's overall marketing strategy will be to educate consumers about the benefits of still water and functional water beverages, and to promote the availability of these products through HydroHut LLC. Customers will be reached through fliers, newspaper advertisements, publicity efforts, and special event promotions.

HydroHut LLC will target health-conscious, progressive, and generally well-educated and affluent customers who are interested in trying new products and experiences and are dissatisfied with the limited selection and lack of personal service found in grocery store-type water retailers.

6.1 Competitive Advantage

No other business in Austin focuses exclusively on the functional still water market. This will provide considerable flexibility in pricing and allow for the creation of a great deal of customer awareness and brand loyalty, erecting significant barriers to entry for potential competitors. HydroHut LLC will be located in a high-traffic area of Austin, in the middle of its target market.

6.2 Pricing

Research in San Francisco, California, indicated that six functional still water beverage retail locations existed. The oldest has been in operation for slightly more than two years. These businesses were thriving, selling functional still water drinks units at prices ranging from $1.25 for small counter-prepared beverages to be consumed on the premises, to $24.00 for larger bottles to be installed off-premises in water coolers.

HydroHut LLC's still water fountain drinks will be offered at the following prices:

Small: $1.00

Medium: $1.50

Large: $2.50

In addition, larger sizes of water will be sold for customer carryout or delivery. They will range from 1-liter bottles to 20-liter plastic jugs at prices ranging from $2.50 to $25.00.

-12-

6.3 Distribution Channels

Primary distribution of functional still water drinks will be through the retail facility, centrally located within HydroHut LLC's target market area. Secondary distribution will consist of deliveries of bottled water beverages to restaurants, retailers, and corporate locations. The partners' previous presence in the Austin hospitality industry will contribute to HydroHut LLC's success in this market. Additional distribution will be accomplished through temporary booths set up at athletic and cultural events, such as bicycle races and concerts.

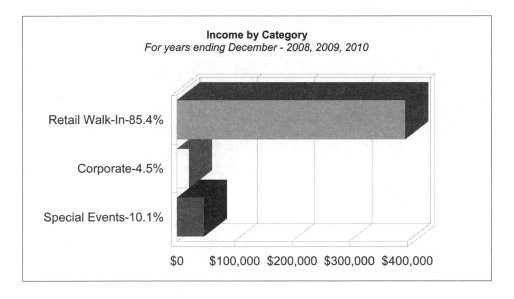

Income by Category
For years ending December - 2008, 2009, 2010

6.4 Promotional Plan

HydroHut LLC will promote functional still water drinks to customers via:

Newspaper Advertisements:

Regular newspaper advertisements will focus on education and information about the benefits of functional still water beverages.

Public Relations:

A publicity campaign that will attempt to gain company owners' appearances as experts on functional still water beverages on health-related TV and radio broadcasts, and as expert sources for print publications.

Flyers:

Educational and promotional fliers will be distributed to residences within a one-mile radius.

Discounts:

Discounts will be offered to appropriate groups, such as health food cooperatives, organic gardening clubs, and cultural associations.

6.5 Feedback

When possible, HydroHut LLC's management will conduct informal interviews with its customers. Questions regarding relative enjoyment of the products, acceptance of the product's prices, and overall satisfaction with the HydroHut LLC experience will be asked. For corporate events, formal mail surveys will be sent to company coordinators, in order to receive feedback on how HydroHut LLC's products were received. In addition, analysis of the effects of any marketing or promotional campaigns on immediate revenues will be performed on a case-by-case basis.

7.0 OPERATING PLAN

HydroHut LLC will be centrally located in Austin, Texas. The retail business will have a bar and seating area, as well as a drive-through window for convenience. Equipment needed will be minimal, as most of the store's products are pre-packaged. The following sections elaborate on HydroHut LLC's operations.

7.1 Location

HydroHut LLC will be located near the intersection of Loop 1 and Enfield Road in Austin, Texas, an attractive retail location near desirable residential areas, the state Capitol complex, and the University of Texas main campus.

[Insert picture of planned location]

A second location is planned to be added in the third year of operation at a suitable site to be determined.

7.2 Facility

An existing 900-square-foot facility with seating and a drive-up window will be leased. Improvements will include additions to the seating area, a water bar, and landscaping.

-14-

Equipment purchased will be minimal, as the product line will be purchased from outside vendors. Baked goods will be pre-packaged and supplied from local producers.

7.3 Operating Equipment

Operating equipment needed by HydroHut LLC primarily consists of standard restaurant fixtures. The only specialized equipment relates to the water bar, amounting to less than $5,000 of the total capital expenditures. No future equipment is anticipated to be needed until the proposed second location is opened.

7.4 Suppliers and Vendors

HydroHut LLC's possible suppliers include Aqua Health, Water for Life, H2Ah!, Nutri-Water, Hydration Technologies, Guava Cool, Soft Beverages, and Millennium Moisture. These vendors supply a variety of beverages with features such as nutriceutical content, bacteria-free processing, and a number of natural, organic flavorings, including berries, fruits, and spices.

These suppliers are, for the most part, located in the continental United States. While they are not currently available for wholesale distribution in Austin, which partially explains the lack of local retail distribution, all operate existing distribution systems with representatives in other Texas cities, including Houston, San Antonio, and Dallas. No problems in obtaining adequate supplies of important products are anticipated.

7.5 Personnel Plan

HydroHut LLC owners, Allis Walter and Matthew Strang, will perform the majority of the duties required to operate the initial store. One part-time employee will be hired to assist with the business.

7.6 General Operations

HydroHut LLC will be open seven days a week, with the following hours of operation:

Monday - Friday, *10am - 10pm*

Saturday, *10am - 7pm*

Sunday, *12 pm - 7pm*

The current location is compliant with all local codes regarding accessibility for the disabled, environmental laws, and occupational safety regulations.

-15-

8.0 MANAGEMENT, ORGANIZATION AND OWNERSHIP

The HydroHut LLC owners are well experienced in the restaurant and bar hospitality industry. They are experienced with both customer contact tasks as well as management/operations duties. The following sections discuss the principals of HydroHut LLC and those that they will consult with.

8.1 Management/Principals

Allis Walter has five years of experience in the retail restaurant industry. He has served as Manager of the Lava Coffee Beanery and Assistant Manager of the Travis Bagel Shop. He is a 1994 graduate of the University of Texas at Austin business school.

Matthew Strang has seven years of experience in the hospitality industry. He has served as Assistant General Manager of the Hill Country Bed & Breakfast in Fredericksburg, Texas, and Manager of Bee Cave Bar & Grill.

8.2 Organizational Structure

The business will be structured as an LLC. Due to the relatively small size of the initial location, the two owners will divide the day-to-day operations of the business between themselves. One part-time employee will be hired to assist operations as needed.

8.3 Professional Consultants

Due to the size of the store and the industry experience of the partners, the need to hire outside consultants should be minimal. Professional services, primarily accounting in nature, are projected to average less than $1,500 per year.

9.0 GOALS AND STRATEGIES

HydroHut LLC will be the first of its kind in Austin, a major metropolitan area of more than 1 million people. The store's high quality products, marketed to Austin's health-conscious population, are expected to lead the partners to financial success.

-16-

9.1 Business Goals

HydroHut LLC's business goals are as follows:

- To repay initial bank loans during the first year of operation.

- To open a second retail location in the third year of operation.

- To produce net income levels of over $30,000, $45,000, and $65,000 for years one, two, and three, respectively.

9.2 Keys to Success

HydroHut LLC's success will come from educating customers about the appeal and benefits of functional still water beverages, and from providing high quality service and products not available in grocery stores. Austin has one of the highest percentages of adults possessing a college degree of any American city, and is generally regarded as a center of progressive lifestyles in the Southwest.

No other business in Austin focuses exclusively on the functional still water market. This will provide considerable flexibility in pricing and allow for the creation of a great deal of customer awareness and brand loyalty.

Customers will be reached through fliers, newspaper advertisements, publicity efforts, and special event promotions. Location will also play a crucial role in marketing and promotion. The business will be located near a high-traffic retail area in central Austin, also close to the University of Texas main campus.

9.3 Future Plans

Assuming the HydroHut LLC concept proves successful, the owners will explore possible franchising opportunities for other cities.

HydroHut LLC's future plans include:

- To expand to three additional retail locations by the end of year five.

- To explore additional expansion through the creation of more company-owned or, possibly, franchised outlets after year five.

-17-

10.0 FINANCIAL ASSUMPTIONS

This section of the business plan summarizes the financial assumptions used in creating the projected financial statements (included in the Appendix).

Follows is a summary of the assumptions used to forecast the next three years of HydroHut LLC's planned operation, including Beginning Balance Sheet, Profit & Loss, Balance Sheet, and Cash Flow data.

10.1 Beginning Balance Sheet

Beginning Balance Sheet

For year beginning January, 2008		
Assets:		
Current assets:		
Cash	1,000	
Inventory	2,278	
Total current assets	3,278	
Fixed assets (net)	5,000	
Other assets (net)	8,250	
Total assets		16,528
Liabilities:		
Current liabilities:		
Accounts payable (inventory)	2,278	
Line of credit	4,250	
Total current liabilities	6,528	
Total liabilities		6,528
Equity:		
Total equity		10,000
Total liabilities and equity		16,528
Debt-to-equity ratio		0.65

-18-

Cash - A minimum target balance of $1,000 has been set for the cash account. The owners will be infusing $10,000 into the business, and the $15,000 line of credit will be available.

Inventory - HydroHut LLC plans on having 30 days' worth of inventory on hand, due to the perishable nature of its products. Beginning inventory is calculated by looking at the total cost of sales for month 1, which is $2,278, and making sure the business has this inventory level prior to opening.

Property, Plant and Equipment (net) - This is the $5,000 of equipment HydroHut LLC needs to buy to open its store.

Other Assets (net) - This account includes mostly intangible assets that can be amortized for accounting/tax purposes. These assets include leasehold improvements of $5,000, legal and consulting fees of $1,000, permit and licenses totaling $750, and miscellaneous start-up expenses of $1,500.

Accounts Payable - HydroHut LLC will have Net 30 terms with its suppliers regarding inventory.

Line of Credit - Assumes a $15,000 line-of-credit loan is available, and $4,250 will be needed to fund initial start-up costs. The projected interest rate of this line of credit is 12 percent.

Contributed Cash - This is the $10,000 investment by the owners.

10.2 Profit and Loss

Profit & Loss Statement

For years ending December - 2008, 2009, 2010			
	Year 1	Year 2	Year 3
Income	109,600	132,000	222,400
Less COGS:			
Material	27,305	32,590	55,007
Total COGS	27,305	32,590	55,007
Gross profit	82,295	99,410	167,393
Operating expenses:			
Wages	7,500	8,256	25,500
Professional Services	1,500	1,100	1,300
Rent	19,596	19,596	39,204
Maintenance	900	900	1,500
Equipment Rental	1,200	1,800	2,400
Insurance	1,920	2,160	4,200
Utilities	2,160	2,160	3,900
Office Supplies	900	900	900
Postage	780	900	1,200
Marketing/Advertising	10,200	11,400	13,200
Travel	1,150	1,600	2,750
Entertainment	325	600	900
Amortization	1,650	1,650	3,025
Depreciation	1,000	1,000	1,833
Total operating expenses	50,781	54,022	101,812
Operating income	31,514	45,388	65,581
Interest expense	60	0	0
Net income	31,454	45,388	65,581

Sales - Assumptions are based on anticipated sales for one HydroHut LLC location, until March of the third year, when a second location is scheduled to open. Below is a breakdown summary of forecasted sales:

-20-

Income Projection

For years ending December - 2008, 2009, 2010			
Income Category	Year 1	Year 2	Year 3
Retail Walk-In	100,100	107,000	189,100
Corporate	0	8,000	13,000
Special Events	9,500	17,000	20,300
Total Income	109,600	132,000	222,400

Cost of Sales - Calculated based on industry average information. Specifically, retail walk-in sales have a 25% cost of sales, corporate sales have a 22% cost of sales, and special event sales have a 24% cost of sales.

Salaries & Wages - Based on one planned part-time employee in years 1 and 2, with two additional part-time employees in year 3.

Marketing/Advertising - HydroHut LLC will promote functional still water drinks to customers via newspaper advertisements, public relations activities, flyers, and group discounts.

Rent, Maintenance, Insurance, Utilities, and Travel - Reflects the higher expenses that will result from the second location opening in March of year 3.

-21-

10.3 Balance Sheet

Balance Sheet

For years ending December - 2008, 2009, 2010			
	Year 1	Year 2	Year 3
Assets:			
Current assets:			
Cash	30,854	78,892	136,081
Inventory	2,730	3,065	0
Total current assets	33,584	81,957	136,081
Fixed assets (net)	4,000	3,000	6,167
Other assets (net)	6,600	4,950	10,175
Total assets	44,184	89,907	152,422
Liabilities and equity:			
Current liabilities:			
Accounts payable	2,730	3,065	0
Line of credit	0	0	0
Total current liabilities	2,730	3,065	0
Total liabilities	2,730	3,065	0
Equity	41,454	86,842	152,422
Total liabilities and equity	44,184	89,907	152,422

Cash - A minimum target balance of $1,000 has been set for the cash account. The partners will be infusing $10,000 into the business, and the $15,000 line of credit will be available.

Inventory - HydroHut LLC plans on having 30 days' worth of inventory on-hand, due to the perishable nature of its products. Beginning inventory is calculated by looking at the total cost of sales for month 1, which is $2,278, and making sure the business has this inventory level prior to opening.

Property, Plant and Equipment (net) - This is the $5,000 of equipment HydroHut LLC needs to buy to open its store. A detailed equipment list can be found in the appendix.

Other Assets (net) - This account includes mostly intangible assets that can be amortized for accounting/tax purposes. These assets include leasehold improvements of $5,000, legal and consulting fees of $1,000, permit and licenses totaling $750, and miscellaneous start-up expenses of $1,500.

Accounts Payable - HydroHut LLC will have Net 30 terms with its suppliers regarding inventory.

-22-

Line of Credit - Assumes a $15,000 line-of-credit loan is available, and $4,250 will be needed to fund initial start-up costs. The projected interest rate of this line of credit is 12 percent.

Contributed Cash - This is the $10,000 investment by the owners.

10.4 Cash Plan

Cash Plan

For years ending December - 2008, 2009, 2010			
	Year 1	Year 2	Year 3
Cash receipts	109,600	132,000	222,400
Operating cash expenses:			
Inventory purchases	27,305	32,590	55,007
Other expenses	48,131	51,372	96,954
Total operating cash exp.	75,436	83,962	151,961
Cash from operations	34,164	48,038	70,439
Capital expenditures	0	0	(13,250)
Debt activities:			
Interest payments	(60)	0	0
Total debt activities	(60)	0	0
Net cash after capital			
expenditures and debt	34,104	48,038	57,189
Change in cash	34,104	48,038	57,189
Beginning cash	1,000	30,854	78,892
Cash before borrowing	35,104	78,892	136,081
Line of credit activity	(4,250)	0	0
Ending cash	30,854	78,892	136,081

Cash Receipts - Assumes sales to all customer categories will be on a cash basis. Corporate and Special Events are assumed to be collected upon completion of respective jobs, due to the limited size of HydroHut LLC's services; however, they are still treated as cash sales.

Inventory Purchases - HydroHut LLC plans on buying enough inventory for 30 days' sales. Based on HydroHut LLC research, the company assumes it will be able to secure payment terms of Net 30 with its suppliers.

Other Expenses - Below is a summary of HydroHut LLC's other expenses:

Expense Projection

For years ending December - 2008, 2009, 2010			
Expense Category	Year 1	Year 2	Year 3
Salaries & Wages	7,500	8,256	25,500
Professional Services	1,500	1,100	1,300
Rent	19,596	19,596	39,204
Maintenance	900	900	1,500
Equipment Rental	1,200	1,800	2,400
Insurance	1,920	2,160	4,200
Utilities	2,160	2,160	3,900
Office Supplies	900	900	900
Postage	780	900	1,200
Marketing/Advertising	10,200	11,400	13,200
Travel	1,150	1,600	2,750
Entertainment	325	600	900
Total Expenses	48,131	51,372	96,954

Distributions - Assumes a $1,000 distribution to each of the 2 LLC members on a monthly basis for the first 3 years. Should profitability performance meet expectations, the members may increase their monthly distribution slightly in years 2 and 3. As the LLC will elect to be taxed as a partnership, all profits (or losses) will flow through to the members at the end of each taxable year.

11. APPENDIX

This section contains the following reports and supporting documentation:

- Income Projection
- Expense Projection
- Profit & Loss
- Balance Sheet
- Cash Plan
- Ratio Analysis

Income Projection - Year 1

Income Category	Jan	Feb	Mar	Apr	May	Jun	Jul	Aug	Sep	Oct	Nov	Dec	Year 1
Retail Walk-In	8150	8150	8300	8400	8300	8350	8400	8400	8450	8400	8400	8400	100100
Corporate	0	0	0	0	0	0	0	0	0	0	0	0	0
Special Events	1000	0	1000	0	1000	1500	1000	1500	0	1500	1000	0	9500
Total Income	9150	8150	9300	8400	9300	9850	9400	9900	8450	9900	9400	8400	109600

Income Projection - Year 2

Income Category	Jan	Feb	Mar	Apr	May	Jun	Jul	Aug	Sep	Oct	Nov	Dec	Year 2
Retail Walk-In	8600	8650	8700	8700	8800	8800	8850	8900	9100	9000	9400	9500	107000
Corporate	1000	0	0	1500	0	1000	1500	0	1000	0	0	2000	8000
Special Events	1500	2000	1000	1500	2000	1000	1000	1500	1200	1600	1700	1000	17000
Total Income	11100	10650	9700	11700	10800	10800	11350	10400	11300	10600	11100	12500	132000

Income Projection - Year 3

Income Category	Jan	Feb	Mar	Apr	May	Jun	Jul	Aug	Sep	Oct	Nov	Dec	Year 3
Retail Walk-In	9500	9600	15500	16000	17000	15000	16500	16000	17750	18750	18000	19500	189100
Corporate	1500	1000	0	1000	1500	2000	0	1000	1500	1000	0	2500	13000
Special Events	1500	2000	2000	1500	2000	2000	1500	1500	1500	1600	1700	1500	20300
Total Income	12500	12600	17500	18500	20500	19000	18000	18500	20750	21350	19700	23500	222400

Expense Projection - Year 1

Expense Category	Jan	Feb	Mar	Apr	May	Jun	Jul	Aug	Sep	Oct	Nov	Dec	Year 1
Salaries & Wages	625	625	625	625	625	625	625	625	625	625	625	625	7500
Professional Services	500	0	0	350	0	0	0	0	0	0	0	650	1500
Rent	1633	1633	1633	1633	1633	1633	1633	1633	1633	1633	1633	1633	19596
Maintenance	75	75	75	75	75	75	75	75	75	75	75	75	900
Equipment Rental	100	100	100	100	100	100	100	100	100	100	100	100	1200
Insurance	160	160	160	160	160	160	160	160	160	160	160	160	1920
Utilities	180	180	180	180	180	180	180	180	180	180	180	180	2160
Office Supplies	75	75	75	75	75	75	75	75	75	75	75	75	900
Postage	65	65	65	65	65	65	65	65	65	65	65	65	780
Marketing/Advertising	850	850	850	850	850	850	850	850	850	850	850	850	10200
Travel	75	100	75	75	150	100	75	75	100	150	75	100	1150
Entertainment	25	25	25	25	25	25	25	25	25	25	25	50	325
Total Expenses	4363	3888	3863	4213	3938	3888	3863	3863	3888	3938	3863	4563	48131

Expense Projection - Year 2

Expense Category	Jan	Feb	Mar	Apr	May	Jun	Jul	Aug	Sep	Oct	Nov	Dec	Year 2
Salaries & Wages	688	688	688	688	688	688	688	688	688	688	688	688	8256
Professional Services	0	0	0	500	0	0	0	0	0	0	0	600	1100
Rent	1633	1633	1633	1633	1633	1633	1633	1633	1633	1633	1633	1633	19596
Maintenance	75	75	75	75	75	75	75	75	75	75	75	75	900
Equipment Rental	150	150	150	150	150	150	150	150	150	150	150	150	1800
Insurance	180	180	180	180	180	180	180	180	180	180	180	180	2160
Utilities	180	180	180	180	180	180	180	180	180	180	180	180	2160
Office Supplies	75	75	75	75	75	75	75	75	75	75	75	75	900
Postage	75	75	75	75	75	75	75	75	75	75	75	75	900
Marketing/Advertising	950	950	950	950	950	950	950	950	950	950	950	950	11400
Travel	150	150	200	100	75	150	150	200	100	75	100	150	1600
Entertainment	50	50	50	50	50	50	50	50	50	50	50	50	600
Total Expenses	4206	4206	4256	4656	4131	4206	4206	4256	4156	4131	4156	4806	51372

Expense Projection - Year 3

Expense Category	Jan	Feb	Mar	Apr	May	Jun	Jul	Aug	Sep	Oct	Nov	Dec	Year 3
Salaries & Wages	2125	2125	2125	2125	2125	2125	2125	2125	2125	2125	2125	2125	25500
Professional Services	0	0	0	600	0	0	0	0	0	0	0	700	1300
Rent	3267	3267	3267	3267	3267	3267	3267	3267	3267	3267	3267	3267	39204
Maintenance	125	125	125	125	125	125	125	125	125	125	125	125	1500
Equipment Rental	200	200	200	200	200	200	200	200	200	200	200	200	2400
Insurance	350	350	350	350	350	350	350	350	350	350	350	350	4200
Utilities	325	325	325	325	325	325	325	325	325	325	325	325	3900
Office Supplies	75	75	75	75	75	75	75	75	75	75	75	75	900
Postage	100	100	100	100	100	100	100	100	100	100	100	100	1200
Marketing/Advertising	1100	1100	1100	1100	1100	1100	1100	1100	1100	1100	1100	1100	13200
Travel	200	250	200	250	200	200	200	275	300	250	175	250	2750
Entertainment	75	75	75	75	75	75	75	75	75	75	75	75	900
Total Expenses	7942	7992	7942	8592	7942	7942	7942	8017	8042	7992	7917	8692	96954

Profit & Loss - Year 1

	Jan	Feb	Mar	Apr	May	Jun	Jul	Aug	Sep	Oct	Nov	Dec	Year 1
Income	9150	8150	9300	8400	9300	9850	9400	9900	8450	9900	9400	8400	109600
Less COGS:													
Material	2278	2038	2315	2100	2315	2448	2340	2460	2113	2460	2340	2100	27307
Total COGS	2278	2038	2315	2100	2315	2448	2340	2460	2113	2460	2340	2100	27307
Gross profit	6872	6112	6985	6300	6985	7402	7060	7440	6337	7440	7060	6300	82293
Operating expenses:													
Salaries & Wages	625	625	625	625	625	625	625	625	625	625	625	625	7500
Professional Services	500	0	0	350	0	0	0	0	0	0	0	650	1500
Rent	1633	1633	1633	1633	1633	1633	1633	1633	1633	1633	1633	1633	19596
Maintenance	75	75	75	75	75	75	75	75	75	75	75	75	900
Equipment Rental	100	100	100	100	100	100	100	100	100	100	100	100	1200
Insurance	160	160	160	160	160	160	160	160	160	160	160	160	1920
Utilities	180	180	180	180	180	180	180	180	180	180	180	180	2160
Office Supplies	75	75	75	75	75	75	75	75	75	75	75	75	900
Postage	65	65	65	65	65	65	65	65	65	65	65	65	780
Marketing/Advertising	850	850	850	850	850	850	850	850	850	850	850	850	10200
Travel	75	100	75	75	150	100	75	75	100	150	75	100	1150
Entertainment	25	25	25	25	25	25	25	25	25	25	25	50	325
Amortization	138	138	138	138	138	138	138	138	138	138	138	138	1656
Depreciation	83	83	83	83	83	83	83	83	83	83	83	83	996
Total operating expenses	4584	4109	4084	4434	4159	4109	4084	4084	4109	4159	4084	4784	50783
Operating income	2288	2003	2901	1866	2826	3293	2976	3356	2228	3281	2976	1516	31510
Interest expense	43	18	0	0	0	0	0	0	0	0	0	0	61
Net income	2245	1985	2901	1866	2826	3293	2976	3356	2228	3281	2976	1516	31449

Profit & Loss - Year 2

	Jan	Feb	Mar	Apr	May	Jun	Jul	Aug	Sep	Oct	Nov	Dec	Year 2
Income	11100	10650	9700	11700	10800	10800	11350	10400	11300	10600	11100	12500	132000
Less COGS:													
Material	2730	2643	2415	2865	2680	2660	2783	2585	2783	2634	2758	3055	32591
Total COGS	2730	2643	2415	2865	2680	2660	2783	2585	2783	2634	2758	3055	32591
Gross profit	8370	8007	7285	8835	8120	8140	8567	7815	8517	7966	8342	9445	99409
Operating expenses:													
Salaries & Wages	688	688	688	688	688	688	688	688	688	688	688	688	8256
Professional Services	0	0	0	500	0	0	0	0	0	0	0	600	1100
Rent	1633	1633	1633	1633	1633	1633	1633	1633	1633	1633	1633	1633	19596
Maintenance	75	75	75	75	75	75	75	75	75	75	75	75	900
Equipment Rental	150	150	150	150	150	150	150	150	150	150	150	150	1800
Insurance	180	180	180	180	180	180	180	180	180	180	180	180	2160
Utilities	180	180	180	180	180	180	180	180	180	180	180	180	2160
Office Supplies	75	75	75	75	75	75	75	75	75	75	75	75	900
Postage	75	75	75	75	75	75	75	75	75	75	75	75	900
Marketing/Advertising	950	950	950	950	950	950	950	950	950	950	950	950	11400
Travel	150	150	200	100	75	150	150	200	100	75	100	150	1600
Entertainment	50	50	50	50	50	50	50	50	50	50	50	50	600
Amortization	138	138	138	138	138	138	138	138	138	138	138	138	1656
Depreciation	83	83	83	83	83	83	83	83	83	83	83	83	996
Total operating expenses	4427	4427	4477	4877	4352	4427	4427	4477	4377	4352	4377	5027	54024
Operating income	3943	3580	2808	3958	3768	3713	4140	3338	4140	3614	3965	4418	45385
Interest expense	0	0	0	0	0	0	0	0	0	0	0	0	0
Net income	3943	3580	2808	3958	3768	3713	4140	3338	4140	3614	3965	4418	45385

Profit & Loss - Year 3

	Jan	Feb	Mar	Apr	May	Jun	Jul	Aug	Sep	Oct	Nov	Dec	Year 3
Income	12500	12600	17500	18500	20500	19000	18000	18500	20750	21350	19700	23500	222400
Less COGS:													
Material	3065	3100	4355	4580	5060	4670	4485	4580	5128	5292	4908	5785	55008
Total COGS	3065	3100	4355	4580	5060	4670	4485	4580	5128	5292	4908	5785	55008
Gross profit	9435	9500	13145	13920	15440	14330	13515	13920	15622	16058	14792	17715	167392
Operating expenses:													
Salaries & Wages	2125	2125	2125	2125	2125	2125	2125	2125	2125	2125	2125	2125	25500
Professional Services	0	0	0	600	0	0	0	0	0	0	0	700	1300
Rent	3267	3267	3267	3267	3267	3267	3267	3267	3267	3267	3267	3267	39204
Maintenance	125	125	125	125	125	125	125	125	125	125	125	125	1500
Equipment Rental	200	200	200	200	200	200	200	200	200	200	200	200	2400
Insurance	350	350	350	350	350	350	350	350	350	350	350	350	4200
Utilities	325	325	325	325	325	325	325	325	325	325	325	325	3900
Office Supplies	75	75	75	75	75	75	75	75	75	75	75	75	900
Postage	100	100	100	100	100	100	100	100	100	100	100	100	1200
Marketing/Advertising	1100	1100	1100	1100	1100	1100	1100	1100	1100	1100	1100	1100	13200
Travel	200	250	200	250	200	200	200	275	300	250	175	250	2750
Entertainment	75	75	75	75	75	75	75	75	75	75	75	75	900
Amortization	138	138	275	275	275	275	275	275	275	275	275	275	3026
Depreciation	83	83	167	167	167	167	167	167	167	167	167	167	1836
Total operating expenses	8163	8213	8384	9034	8384	8384	8384	8459	8484	8434	8359	9134	101816
Operating income	1272	1287	4761	4886	7056	5946	5131	5461	7138	7624	6433	8581	65576
Interest expense	0	0	0	0	0	0	0	0	0	0	0	0	0
Net income	1272	1287	4761	4886	7056	5946	5131	5461	7138	7624	6433	8581	65576

Balance Sheet - Year 1

	Jan	Feb	Mar	Apr	May	Jun	Jul	Aug	Sep	Oct	Nov	Dec	Year 1
Assets:													
Current assets:													
Cash	1000	1424	4546	6633	9680	13194	16391	19968	22418	25920	29117	30854	30854
Inventory	2038	2315	2100	2315	2448	2340	2460	2113	2460	2340	2100	2730	2730
Total current assets	3038	3739	6646	8943	12128	15534	18851	22081	24878	28260	31217	33584	33584
Fixed assets (net)	4917	4833	4750	4667	4583	4500	4417	4333	4250	4167	4083	4000	4000
Other assets (net)	8113	7975	7838	7700	7563	7425	7288	7150	7013	6875	6738	6600	6600
Total assets	16068	16547	19234	21315	24274	27459	30556	33564	36141	39302	42038	44184	44184
Liabilities and equity:													
Current liabilities:													
Accounts payable	2038	2315	2100	2315	2448	2340	2460	2113	2460	2340	2100	2730	2730
Line of credit	1783	0	0	0	0	0	0	0	0	0	0	0	0
Total current liabilities	3821	2315	2100	2315	2448	2340	2460	2113	2460	2340	2100	2730	2730
Total liabilities	3821	2315	2100	2315	2448	2340	2460	2113	2460	2340	2100	2730	2730
Equity	12247	14232	17134	19000	21826	25119	28096	31451	33681	36962	39938	41454	41454
Total liabilities and equity	16068	16547	19234	21315	24274	27459	30556	33564	36141	39302	42038	44184	44184

Balance Sheet - Year 2

	Jan	Feb	Mar	Apr	May	Jun	Jul	Aug	Sep	Oct	Nov	Dec	Year 2
Assets:													
Current assets:													
Cash	35018	38819	41848	46027	50016	53950	58312	61871	66232	70067	74253	78892	78892
Inventory	2643	2415	2865	2680	2660	2783	2585	2783	2634	2758	3055	3065	3065
Total current assets	37661	41234	44713	48707	52676	56733	60897	64654	68866	72825	77308	81957	81957
Fixed assets (net)	3917	3833	3750	3667	3583	3500	3417	3333	3250	3167	3083	3000	3000
Other assets (net)	6463	6325	6188	6050	5913	5775	5638	5500	5363	5225	5088	4950	4950
Total assets	48041	51392	54651	58424	62172	66008	69952	73487	77479	81217	85479	89907	89907
Liabilities and equity:													
Current liabilities:													
Accounts payable	2643	2415	2865	2680	2660	2783	2585	2783	2634	2758	3055	3065	3065
Line of credit	0	0	0	0	0	0	0	0	0	0	0	0	0
Total current liabilities	2643	2415	2865	2680	2660	2783	2585	2783	2634	2758	3055	3065	3065
Total liabilities	2643	2415	2865	2680	2660	2783	2585	2783	2634	2758	3055	3065	3065
Equity	45398	48977	51786	55744	59512	63225	67367	70704	74845	78459	82424	86842	86842
Total liabilities and equity	48041	51392	54651	58424	62172	66008	69952	73487	77479	81217	85479	89907	89907

Balance Sheet - Year 3

	Jan	Feb	Mar	Apr	May	Jun	Jul	Aug	Sep	Oct	Nov	Dec	Year 3
Assets:													
Current assets:													
Cash	80385	81893	73846	79174	86672	93060	98633	104536	112116	120183	127058	136081	136081
Inventory	3100	4355	4580	5060	4670	4485	4580	5128	5292	4908	5785	0	0
Total current assets	83485	86248	78426	84234	91342	97545	103213	109664	117408	125091	132843	136081	136081
Fixed assets (net)	2917	2833	7667	7500	7333	7167	7000	6833	6667	6500	6333	6167	6167
Other assets (net)	4813	4675	12650	12375	12100	11825	11550	11275	11000	10725	10450	10175	10175
Total assets	91215	93756	98743	104109	110775	116537	121763	127772	135075	142316	149626	152423	152423
Liabilities and equity:													
Current liabilities:													
Accounts payable	3100	4355	4580	5060	4670	4485	4580	5128	5292	4908	5785	0	0
Line of credit	0	0	0	0	0	0	0	0	0	0	0	0	0
Total current liabilities	3100	4355	4580	5060	4670	4485	4580	5128	5292	4908	5785	0	0
Total liabilities	3100	4355	4580	5060	4670	4485	4580	5128	5292	4908	5785	0	0
Equity	88115	89401	94163	99049	106105	112052	117183	122644	129783	137408	143841	152423	152423
Total liabilities and equity	91215	93756	98743	104109	110775	116537	121763	127772	135075	142316	149626	152423	152423

Cash Plan - Year 1

	Jan	Feb	Mar	Apr	May	Jun	Jul	Aug	Sep	Oct	Nov	Dec	Year 1
Cash receipts	9150	8150	9300	8400	9300	9850	9400	9900	8450	9900	9400	8400	109600
Operating cash expenses:													
Inventory purchases	2278	2038	2315	2100	2315	2448	2340	2460	2113	2460	2340	2100	27307
Other expenses	4363	3888	3863	4213	3938	3888	3863	3863	3888	3938	3863	4563	48131
Total operating cash exp.	6641	5926	6178	6313	6253	6336	6203	6323	6001	6398	6203	6663	75438
Cash from operations	2509	2224	3122	2087	3047	3514	3197	3577	2449	3502	3197	1737	34162
Capital expenditures	0	0	0	0	0	0	0	0	0	0	0	0	0
Debt activities:													
Interest payments	-43	-18	0	0	0	0	0	0	0	0	0	0	-61
Total debt activities	-43	-18	0	0	0	0	0	0	0	0	0	0	-61
Net cash after capital expenditures and debt	2466	2206	3122	2087	3047	3514	3197	3577	2449	3502	3197	1737	34101
Change in cash	2467	2207	3122	2087	3047	3515	3197	3577	2450	3502	3197	1737	34105
Beginning cash	1000	1000	1424	4546	6633	9680	13194	16391	19968	22418	25920	29117	1000
Cash before borrowing	3467	3207	4546	6633	9680	13195	16391	19968	22418	25920	29117	30854	35105
Line of credit activity	-2467	-1783	0	0	0	0	0	0	0	0	0	0	-4250
Ending cash	1000	1424	4546	6633	9680	13195	16391	19968	22418	25920	29117	30854	30854

Cash Plan - Year 2

	Jan	Feb	Mar	Apr	May	Jun	Jul	Aug	Sep	Oct	Nov	Dec	Year 2
Cash receipts	11100	10650	9700	11700	10800	10800	11350	10400	11300	10600	11100	12500	132000
Operating cash expenses:													
Inventory purchases	2730	2643	2415	2865	2680	2660	2783	2585	2783	2634	2758	3055	32591
Other expenses	4206	4206	4256	4656	4131	4206	4206	4256	4156	4131	4156	4806	51372
Total operating cash exp.	6936	6849	6671	7521	6811	6866	6989	6841	6939	6765	6914	7861	83963
Cash from operations	4164	3801	3029	4179	3989	3934	4361	3559	4361	3835	4186	4639	48037
Capital expenditures	0	0	0	0	0	0	0	0	0	0	0	0	0
Debt activities:													
Interest payments	0	0	0	0	0	0	0	0	0	0	0	0	0
Total debt activities	0	0	0	0	0	0	0	0	0	0	0	0	0
Net cash after capital													
expenditures and debt	4164	3801	3029	4179	3989	3934	4361	3559	4361	3835	4186	4639	48037
Change in cash	4164	3802	3029	4179	3989	3934	4362	3559	4361	3835	4186	4639	48039
Beginning cash	30854	35018	38819	41848	46027	50016	53950	58312	61871	66232	70067	74253	30854
Cash before borrowing	35018	38820	41848	46027	50016	53950	58312	61871	66232	70067	74253	78892	78893
Line of credit activity	0	0	0	0	0	0	0	0	0	0	0	0	0
Ending cash	35018	38820	41848	46027	50016	53950	58312	61871	66232	70067	74253	78892	78892

Cash Plan - Year 3

	Jan	Feb	Mar	Apr	May	Jun	Jul	Aug	Sep	Oct	Nov	Dec	Year 3
Cash receipts	12500	12600	17500	18500	20500	19000	18000	18500	20750	21350	19700	23500	222400
Operating cash expenses:													
Inventory purchases	3065	3100	4355	4580	5060	4670	4485	4580	5128	5292	4908	5785	55008
Other expenses	7942	7992	7942	8592	7942	7942	7942	8017	8042	7992	7917	8692	96954
Total operating cash exp.	11007	11092	12297	13172	13002	12612	12427	12597	13170	13284	12825	14477	151962
Cash from operations	1493	1508	5203	5328	7498	6388	5573	5903	7580	8066	6875	9023	70438
Capital expenditures	0	0	-13250	0	0	0	0	0	0	0	0	0	-13250
Debt activities:													
Interest payments	0	0	0	0	0	0	0	0	0	0	0	0	0
Total debt activities	0	0	0	0	0	0	0	0	0	0	0	0	0
Net cash after capital													
expenditures and debt	1493	1508	-8047	5328	7498	6388	5573	5903	7580	8066	6875	9023	57188
Change in cash	1493	1508	-8047	5328	7498	6388	5573	5903	7581	8067	6875	9023	57190
Beginning cash	78892	80385	81893	73846	79174	86672	93060	98633	104536	112116	120183	127058	78892
Cash before borrowing	80385	81893	73846	79174	86672	93060	98633	104536	112117	120183	127058	136081	136082
Line of credit activity	0	0	0	0	0	0	0	0	0	0	0	0	0
Ending cash	80385	81893	73846	79174	86672	93060	98633	104536	112117	120183	127058	136081	136081

Ratio Analysis - Year 1

	Jan	Feb	Mar	Apr	May	Jun	Jul	Aug	Sep	Oct	Nov	Dec	Year 1
Profitability ratios:													
Gross profit margin	75.11%	75.00%	75.11%	75.00%	75.11%	75.15%	75.11%	75.15%	75.00%	75.15%	75.11%	75.00%	75.09%
Operating profit margin	25.01%	24.58%	31.20%	22.22%	30.39%	33.44%	31.66%	33.90%	26.37%	33.14%	31.66%	18.05%	28.75%
Net profit margin	24.55%	24.37%	31.20%	22.22%	30.39%	33.44%	31.66%	33.90%	26.37%	33.14%	31.66%	18.05%	28.70%
Return on equity	20.19%	15.00%	18.50%	10.33%	13.85%	14.03%	11.19%	11.27%	6.84%	9.29%	7.74%	3.73%	123.59%
Return on assets	14.04%	12.29%	16.22%	9.20%	12.40%	12.73%	10.26%	10.47%	6.39%	8.70%	7.32%	3.52%	112.27%
Liquidity ratios:													
Current ratio	0.80	1.61	3.16	3.87	4.95	6.64	7.66	10.45	10.11	12.08	14.87	12.30	12.30
Quick ratio (Acid-test)	0.26	0.61	2.16	2.87	3.95	5.64	6.66	9.45	9.11	11.08	13.87	11.30	11.30
Working capital ratio	-0.09	0.17	0.49	0.79	1.04	1.34	1.74	2.02	2.65	2.62	3.10	3.67	0.28
Activity ratios:													
Accounts receivable days	0.00	0.00	0.00	0.00	0.00	0.00	0.00	0.00	0.00	0.00	0.00	0.00	0.00
Inventory days	26.84	34.09	27.21	33.07	31.72	28.68	31.54	25.76	34.93	28.54	26.92	39.00	35.99
Inventory turnover	1.06	0.94	1.05	0.95	0.97	1.02	0.98	1.08	0.92	1.03	1.05	0.87	11.90
Sales-to-assets	0.56	0.50	0.52	0.41	0.41	0.38	0.32	0.31	0.24	0.26	0.23	0.19	3.90
Leverage ratios:													
Debt-to-equity	0.31	0.16	0.12	0.12	0.11	0.09	0.09	0.07	0.07	0.06	0.05	0.07	0.07
Debt ratio	0.24	0.14	0.11	0.11	0.10	0.09	0.08	0.06	0.07	0.06	0.05	0.06	0.06
Times-interest (TI) earned:													
Operating income	2289	2004	2901	1866	2826	3294	2976	3356	2229	3281	2976	1516	31514
Interest expense (÷)	43	18	0	0	0	0	0	0	0	0	0	0	60
TI earned ratio	53.23	111.33											525.23333

Ratio Analysis - Year 2

	Jan	Feb	Mar	Apr	May	Jun	Jul	Aug	Sep	Oct	Nov	Dec	Year 2
Profitability ratios:													
Gross profit margin	75.41%	75.19%	75.10%	75.51%	75.19%	75.37%	75.48%	75.14%	75.37%	75.15%	75.15%	75.56%	75.31%
Operating profit margin	35.52%	33.62%	28.95%	33.83%	34.89%	34.38%	36.48%	32.10%	36.64%	34.10%	35.72%	35.35%	34.38%
Net profit margin	35.52%	33.62%	28.95%	33.83%	34.89%	34.38%	36.48%	32.10%	36.64%	34.10%	35.72%	35.35%	34.38%
Return on equity	9.08%	7.59%	5.57%	7.36%	6.54%	6.05%	6.34%	4.84%	5.69%	4.72%	4.93%	5.22%	71.42%
Return on assets	8.55%	7.20%	5.30%	7.00%	6.25%	5.79%	6.09%	4.65%	5.48%	4.55%	4.76%	5.04%	68.48%
Liquidity ratios:													
Current ratio	14.25	17.07	15.61	18.17	19.80	20.39	23.56	23.23	26.14	26.40	25.31	26.74	26.74
Quick ratio (Acid-test)	13.25	16.07	14.61	17.17	18.80	19.39	22.56	22.23	25.14	25.40	24.31	25.74	25.74
Working capital ratio	3.15	3.65	4.31	3.93	4.63	5.00	5.14	5.95	5.86	6.61	6.69	6.31	0.60
Activity ratios:													
Accounts receivable days	0.00	0.00	0.00	0.00	0.00	0.00	0.00	0.00	0.00	0.00	0.00	0.00	0.00
Inventory days	29.04	27.42	35.59	28.06	29.78	31.38	27.87	32.30	28.39	31.41	33.23	30.10	33.86
Inventory turnover	1.02	1.05	0.91	1.03	1.00	0.98	1.04	0.96	1.03	0.98	0.95	1.00	11.94
Sales-to-assets	0.24	0.21	0.18	0.21	0.18	0.17	0.17	0.15	0.15	0.13	0.13	0.14	1.99
Leverage ratios:													
Debt-to-equity	0.06	0.05	0.06	0.05	0.04	0.04	0.04	0.04	0.04	0.04	0.04	0.04	0.04
Debt ratio	0.06	0.05	0.05	0.05	0.04	0.04	0.04	0.04	0.03	0.03	0.04	0.03	0.03
Times-interest (TI) earned:													
Operating income	3943	3581	2808	3958	3768	3713	4141	3338	4140	3614	3965	4418	45388
Interest expense (÷)	0	0	0	0	0	0	0	0	0	0	0	0	0
TI earned ratio													

Ratio Analysis - Year 3

	Jan	Feb	Mar	Apr	May	Jun	Jul	Aug	Sep	Oct	Nov	Dec	Year 3
Profitability ratios:													
Gross profit margin	75.48%	75.40%	75.11%	75.24%	75.32%	75.42%	75.08%	75.24%	75.29%	75.22%	75.09%	75.38%	75.27%
Operating profit margin	10.18%	10.22%	27.21%	26.41%	34.42%	31.30%	28.51%	29.52%	34.40%	35.71%	32.66%	36.52%	29.49%
Net profit margin	10.18%	10.22%	27.21%	26.41%	34.42%	31.30%	28.51%	29.52%	34.40%	35.71%	32.66%	36.52%	29.49%
Return on equity	1.45%	1.45%	5.19%	5.06%	6.88%	5.45%	4.48%	4.55%	5.66%	5.71%	4.57%	5.79%	57.89%
Return on assets	1.40%	1.39%	4.95%	4.82%	6.57%	5.23%	4.31%	4.38%	5.43%	5.50%	4.41%	5.68%	55.70%
Liquidity ratios:													
Current ratio	26.93	19.80	17.12	16.65	19.56	21.75	22.54	21.39	22.19	25.49	22.96	n/a	n/a
Quick ratio (Acid-test)	25.93	18.80	16.12	15.55	18.56	20.75	21.54	20.39	21.19	24.49	21.96	n/a	n/a
Working capital ratio	6.43	6.50	4.22	4.28	4.23	4.90	5.48	5.65	5.40	5.63	6.45	5.79	0.61
Activity ratios:													
Accounts receivable days	0.00	0.00	0.00	0.00	0.00	0.00	0.00	0.00	0.00	0.00	0.00	0.00	0.00
Inventory days	30.34	42.15	31.55	33.14	27.69	28.81	30.64	33.59	30.96	27.83	35.36	0.00	0.00
Inventory turnover	0.99	0.83	0.97	0.95	1.04	1.02	0.99	0.94	0.98	1.04	0.92	2.00	12.34
Sales-to-assets	0.14	0.14	0.18	0.18	0.19	0.17	0.15	0.15	0.16	0.15	0.14	0.16	1.89
Leverage ratios:													
Debt-to-equity	0.04	0.05	0.05	0.05	0.04	0.04	0.04	0.04	0.04	0.04	0.04	0.00	0.00
Debt ratio	0.03	0.05	0.05	0.05	0.04	0.04	0.04	0.04	0.04	0.03	0.04	0.00	0.00
Times-interest (TI) earned:													
Operating income	1272	1287	4761	4886	7056	5946	5131	5461	7139	7625	6433	8581	65581
Interest expense (÷)	0	0	0	0	0	0	0	0	0	0	0	0	0
TI earned ratio													

The Business Plan for

Royal Limousine

A General Partnership

Contact Information:

Pete Olson

2006 S 127th Cir

Omaha, NE 68144

402-555-1212

polson@olson.com

Jeff Larson

1801 Hanson Dr

Bellevue, NE 68123

402-555-1313

jlarson@larson.net

Copy Number __ of Five.

Non-Disclosure and Confidentiality Agreement

The undersigned ("Recipient") hereby agrees that all financial and other information ("Information") that it has and will receive concerning Royal Limousine Company is confidential and will not be disclosed to any other individual or entity without prior written consent.

The Information shall remain the property of Royal Limousine and shall be returned to Royal Limousine promptly at its request together with all copies made thereof.

Recipient acknowledges that no remedy of law may be adequate to compensate Royal Limousine for a violation of this Agreement and Recipient hereby agrees that in addition to any legal or other rights that may be available in the event of a breach hereunder, Royal Limousine may seek equitable relief to enforce this Agreement in any Court of competent jurisdiction.

_____   _____

Date   Signature of Recipient

-2-

THE PLAN FOR ROYAL LIMOUSINE

1.0 EXECUTIVE SUMMARY

Royal Limousine is a proposed limousine rental service. It will be located in Omaha, Nebraska and will offer luxury limousine rental on an hourly basis. The company will also provide transportation for wedding parties on Saturdays, and offer round-trip transportation packages, including coupons, to the casino in Council Bluffs. In order to make this proposed service a reality, Royal Limousine will need a loan to finance initial start-up expenses.

1.1 Business Opportunity

Royal Limousine will be a full-service limousine transportation service in Omaha, Nebraska. It has partnered with the Shark Club, and will have the largest capacity limousine in the area. Offering wedding packages, casino trips, and hourly rental. Royal Limousine will fill a void in limousine transportation in Omaha by providing affordable pricing and a large capacity limousine.

1.2 Service Description

Royal Limousine will offer full-service limousine transportation to the greater Omaha, Nebraska area.

Services will include:

1. Hourly rental - The limousine will be available for hourly rental on Monday, Wednesday, and Friday nights.

2. Weddings - Royal Limousine will rent their limousine on a daily basis for Weddings.

3. Casino trips - Royal Limousine will make casino runs on Thursday and Sunday nights.

Below is a breakdown of Royal Limousine offerings and the projected revenue percentage for each:

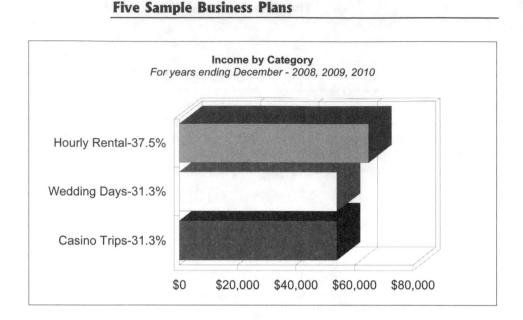

Income by Category
For years ending December - 2008, 2009, 2010

Hourly Rental-37.5%

Wedding Days-31.3%

Casino Trips-31.3%

$0 $20,000 $40,000 $60,000 $80,000

1.3 Current Business Position

Royal Limousine Co. is a new business venture. It has partnered with the Shark Club, located in the Quality Inn (West Center and 72nd Street), and will store the vehicle in their parking lot.

Royal Limousine will be built around two dedicated, hard working individuals. Pete Olson and Jeff Larson have experience as limousine drivers in the Omaha area. Pete also has business experience, working as a bookkeeper for the past 4 years. Pete and Jeff will provide exceptional value to customers and the most luxurious limousine in the greater Omaha area.

1.4 Financial Potential

Royal Limousine expects to generate $57,600 in revenues in each of its first three years of operation. Net income is projected to be $26,760 in year one, $27,508 in year two, and $28,309 in year three.

Below is Royal Limousine income projection for its first three years of operation:

-6-

Profit & Loss Statement

For years ending December - 2008, 2009, 2010			
	Year 1	Year 2	Year 3
Income	57,600	57,600	57,600
Gross profit	57,600	57,600	57,600
Operating expenses:			
Gas	4,800	4,800	4,800
Insurance	1,920	1,920	1,920
Advertising	4,440	4,440	4,440
Misc. Supplies	240	240	240
Maintenance	1,200	1,200	1,200
Apparel	400	400	400
Limo Parking Rental	600	600	600
Depreciation	13,400	13,400	13,400
Total operating expenses	27,000	27,000	27,000
Operating income	30,600	30,600	30,600
Interest expense	3,840	3,092	2,291
Net income	26,760	27,508	28,309

1.5 The Request

Royal Limousine is seeking a $61,750, 5-year loan at 6.75% A.P.R. from Omaha State Bank. These funds will help Royal Limousine purchase its limousine and begin operations.

2.0 COMPANY BACKGROUND

2.1 Business Description

Royal Limousine will be a locally owned limousine rental service. It will provide the best quality transportation and the most exciting packages at the best possible prices. In addition to the scheduled casino trips, Royal Limousine will be available for special occasions, business functions, or romantic cruises around town.

2.2 Company History

Royal Limousine is a prospective new business to be located in Omaha, Nebraska. It will rent space in the Quality Inn parking lot to house its limousine. The Quality Inn is located in central Omaha, which gives Royal Limousine access to the two main thoroughfares in Omaha (West Center and 72nd Street). In addition, Royal Limousine will be strategically located three blocks from Interstate 680, giving it access to all areas of Omaha and the casinos in Council Bluffs.

Royal Limousine is structured as a partnership between Pete Olson and Jeff Larson. Pete, with his education in accounting, will handle accounting and finance duties. Both Pete and Jeff will handle marketing opportunities. The two will split driving time, working every other night. (As the business grows the partners plan to incorporate in order to get the benefit of limited liability. In the meantime they will cover potential risk with insurance.)

2.3 Business Objectives and Mission Statement

Royal Limousine business objective is to provide the biggest and best limousine service in Omaha. With the acquisition of its new limo and the packages it will offer, Royal Limousine will attain this objective.

The Royal Limousine Mission Statement is as follows:

"Royal Limousine strives to offer the biggest limousine, the friendliest service, and the highest quality travel packages to all of its customers."

2.4 Ownership

Royal will be formed as a partnership. Each will own one-half of the operation, including its name and assets. The purpose of this business plan is to supply Omaha State Bank, 12100 West Center Road, Omaha, NE 68144, with sufficient information to warrant a $61,750, 5-year loan at 6.75% A.P.R. The amount requested will be combined with a $7,000 owner investment to purchase the limousine.

3.0 PRODUCTS

Royal Limousine will not have products initially. Branded products may be added at a later time.

-8-

4.0 SERVICES

Royal Limousine will offer limo rental, wedding packages, and casino trips in the most luxurious and largest limo available in the Omaha area.

4.1 Service Descriptions

Royal Limousine will offer three distinct services. They are as follows:

1. <u>Casino Service ($250/trip)</u> - Round trip transportation from the Shark Club to Harrah's casino in Council Bluffs on Thursday and Sunday nights. The trip will include tickets for a free dinner at the Fireside Steakhouse and a $30 certificate to be used throughout the casino.

2. <u>Wedding Packages ($500/day)</u> - Royal Limousine will provide all-day wedding packages for any size wedding. Whether transporting just the bride and groom, or the whole wedding party up to 13, Royal Limousine will offer the best service at the best price.

3. <u>Hourly Rental ($75/hour)</u> - Royal Limousine will have its giant limo available for private parties, business transportation, or any other special occasion. The limo will be available for rent on Monday, Wednesday, and Friday nights, and by special request.

Below are Royal Limousine projected annual sales:

Income Projection

For years ending December - 2008, 2009, 2010			
Income Category	Year 1	Year 2	Year 3
Hourly Rental	21,600	21,600	21,600
Wedding Days	18,000	18,000	18,000
Casino Trips	18,000	18,000	18,000
Total Income	57,600	57,600	57,600

-9-

4.2 Competitive Comparison

Currently, there are six limousine services that offer full-service limousine rental in the Omaha area, all of which offer services similar to what Royal Limousine will offer; however, Royal Limousine will bring new packages and coverage areas in comparison to the competition. Also, Royal Limousine will offer the largest and most luxurious limousine in the greater Omaha area.

4.3 Service Delivery

Royal Limousine will deliver its services in a number of ways. Hourly rentals will be picked up at designated places, most commonly at private residences. Weddings will be accommodated by pick-up and drop-off at specified locations. Casino trips will travel to and from the Shark Club, 2808 South 72nd Street, Omaha, NE 68120, which is located in the Quality Inn. Upon return to the Shark Club, Royal Limousine Co. will be available for hourly rental for customers not wanting to drive home.

5.0 THE INDUSTRY, COMPETITION & MARKET

The demand for luxury transportation is growing across the United States, and Omaha is no exception. Americans spend more time traveling than ever before, and with higher wages and an ever-growing upper-income population, luxury transportation is no longer reserved for the elite.

5.1 Industry Definition

Royal Limousine will offer the largest luxury limousine with all the amenities available. Although there are several competitors in the Omaha area, Royal Limousine will be able to compete because of its seating capacity, special packages, and pricing.

As personal disposable income continues to rise, the demand for luxury items also rises. Over the past decade, Omaha experienced a 16% increase in per capita income. This trend is expected to continue through 2012 (U.S. Census, www.census.gov).

Royal Limousine will compete in the service and entertainment industries. According to the U.S. Bureau of Labor Statistics, the service industry is the largest and fastest growing sector. It is estimated that Americans spend an average of 27% of their expendable income on services, and of that, 54% is spent on entertainment.

-10-

5.2 Primary Competitors

Royal Limousine has six primary competitors in the greater Omaha area. They are as follows:

1. A1 Shuttle Service

9642 J St, Omaha, NE 68137

Phone: (402) 555-7558

A1 Shuttle Service offers full-service limousine transportation for Omaha residents. The company has two limousines; however, both of its limousines have a capacity of only 8 people. A1 Shuttle Service only works on weekends and they charge $100 per hour.

2. Loyalty Line, Inc.

5640 Surrey Road, Elkhorn, NE 68022

Phone: (402) 555-2993

Royalty Line, Inc. offers personalized, intimate limousines. The company has two vehicles, one with seating for six, and one with seating for eight. Royalty Line, Inc. charges $80 per hour.

3. Omaha Limo Transport

6502 Grover Street, Omaha, NE 68106

Phone: (402) 555-5466

Omaha Limo Transport has been operating in Omaha for nine years. The company has four limos, and has the reputation for catering to Omaha's elite. Omaha Limo Transport's marketing efforts focus on its customers and the company runs ads naming some of its current clientele. Omaha Limo Transport's most famous client is Warren Buffet. Omaha Limousine rents by the half-day, at a price of $500.

4. Fancy Limousine

23552 N 16th St, Omaha NE 68110

Phone: (402) 555-4923

Fancy Limousine caters to the "alternative" lifestyle. From retro to pink silk, Fancy Limousine has something for everyone. The company has the largest fleet of vehicles in Omaha with eight. Fancy Limousine rents by the hour, with a two-hour minimum. Fancy Limousine charges $85 per hour.

5. Limousine Rental, Inc.

1465 N 23st St, Omaha NE 68152

Phone: (402) 555-7887

Limousine Rental, Inc. only operates during the evenings. The company offers packages for large events, and rent by the night at a price of $400.

6. Fast Limousine Service

1109 Madison St, Omaha NE 68127

Phone: (402) 555-5575

Fast Limousine Service caters to Omaha's business crowds. The company offers round-trip transportation from anywhere downtown to Eppley Airfield for $30. Fast Limousine Service does not rent by the hour, and are only open from 7:00 a.m. to 7:00 p.m.

All limousine companies accept credit cards, cash, or personal checks and advertise in the Yellow Pages.

5.3 Market Information

Omaha is a growing community with over 428,000 people (2006) located within its city limits. Omaha MSA, which includes Council Bluffs, Bellevue, and a military base, has a population of over 720,000. The area has a very diverse population, with many upper-income and wealthy families.

As a percentage, Omaha is expected to grow faster than the state is. Nebraska's population projections for the years 2010 and 2015 are 1.85 million, and 1.93 million, respectively.

Omaha has many characteristics that help service businesses:

According to the Omaha Chamber of Commerce, a recent survey of 300 U.S. cities revealed the relative price levels for consumer goods and services in Omaha are up to 13.3 percent below the national average. Utility prices are more that 12 percent lower than the national average. All of these factors contribute to the population of Omaha having larger disposable income.

5.4 Market Growth

As disposable income continues to rise across the U.S., Americans are treating themselves to more of the finer things in life. Limousine service was once reserved only for the elite; however, more and more people are using limousine services for business and pleasure. As more competitors enter the market, the price for limousine service continues to fall. The decreasing prices, in spite of rising fuel costs, are causing more individuals to take advantage of the luxury services.

5.5 Customer Profile

Royal Limousine will have a diverse clientele. Wedding parties, casino tours, and hourly rentals will be available for all residents of the greater Omaha area. Royal Limousine will serve a variety of age groups and will cater to the masses.

6.0 MARKETING PLAN

Royal Limousine has two basic marketing objectives that the owners have signified as guidelines to follow. Although these goals are instrumental at start-up, the owners will re-evaluate their marketing objectives as their needs change. They are as follows:

1. Provide the highest luxury transportation at the lowest possible price. Royal Limousine will offer the largest limousine with the most amenities in the area.

2. Royal Limousine is dedicated to becoming well known in Omaha's luxury transportation industry. When people think of luxury transportation, Royal Limousine should come to mind.

6.1 Competitive Advantage

Royal Limousine has six primary competitors in the greater Omaha area. They are as follows:

1. A1 Shuttle Service

2. Loyalty Line, Inc.

3. Omaha Limo Transport

4. Fancy Limousine

5. Limousine Rental, Inc.

6. Fast Limousine Service

Royal Limousine has a distinct advantage over its competitors in the fact that it offers the largest luxury limousine transportation in the greater Omaha area. Although all of the competition offers luxury transportation, prices vary widely depending on the provider. Royal Limousine has surveyed the prices of all of its competitors and will offer packages and hourly rates at or below the competition's prices.

6.2 Pricing

Royal Limousine will offer three pricing strategies that will cater to different clientele. These three pricing strategies will offer the best possible pricing with the highest quality service. Depending on the needs of the customer, these pricing structures are subject to negotiation in order to provide the highest value.

The pricing structure for Royal Limousine is as follows:

1. Royal Limousine will offer hourly rentals Monday, Wednesday, and Friday nights. It will charge $75 per hour with a minimum of two hours per night.

2. Royal Limousine will offer round trip transportation from the Shark Club to Harrah's casino in Council Bluffs on Thursday and Sunday nights. The trip will include tickets for a free dinner at the Fireside Steakhouse and a $30 certificate to be used in the casino. Royal Limousine Co. will sell this package for $250 for a group of four, or $60 a person for a group of six or more.

3. Royal Limousine will provide all-day wedding packages for any size wedding. Royal Limousine will charge $500 per day, max of 8 hours for its wedding package.

Follows is a breakdown of expected sales by category for Royal Limousine first three years of operation:

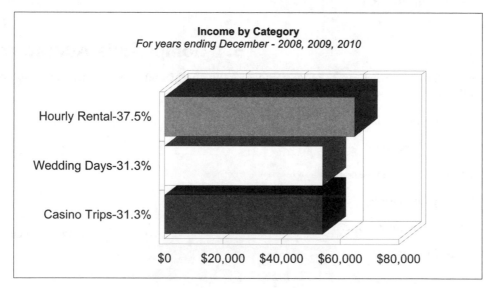

-14-

6.3 Distribution Channels

Royal Limousine will house its vehicle in the parking lot at the Quality Inn, 72nd and West Center in Omaha. This location provides immediate access to the interstate system, and fast response time to anywhere in the area.

Royal Limousine will gain exposure through its arrangement with the Quality Inn and the Shark Club. Royal Limousine will benefit from its location by the exposure it will get from the guests at the Quality Inn and the high-class clientele that frequent the Shark Club.

Pete Olson and Jeff Larson believe that they must offer a quality service in every respect. Because of this, they have allotted $400 quarterly to purchase new tuxedos. They will wear tuxedos to all of their booked functions.

6.4 Promotional Plan

Royal Limousine will be a new business in the Omaha area. Because of this, Pete and Jeff have developed the following outline for their promotional plan that takes into consideration their annual $4,440 budget:

1. Royal Limousine will have an ad in the Yellow Pages. Its ad will be placed alongside competitors'. The ad will cost $800 per year.

2. Royal Limousine will run several radio ads. Ads will be run during drive time and will feature Royal Limousine location at the Shark Club and their competitive prices. Royal Limousine has budgeted $2,400 for radio ads.

3. Royal Limousine has allotted $1,200 for print ads in the *Omaha World-Herald*. Ads will run in the classified section on select Thursdays and Saturdays, outlining the company's location and competitive prices.

This plan is subject to change depending on pricing and demand. Royal Limousine owners will actively watch for promotional ideas that will help them gain market penetration.

7.0 OPERATING PLAN

Royal Limousine has developed a partnership with the Quality Inn and the Shark Club in order to offer its service to the customers of each establishment. Royal Limousine will rent space in the parking lot at the Shark Club, 72nd Street and West Center, and will use the company's facilities as a meeting point for casino trips. The Shark Club has agreed to provide rental-booking services for Royal Limousine in exchange for being mentioned in all Royal Limousine ads.

-15-

7.1 Location

Royal Limousine will be based out of the Shark Club, located inside the Quality Inn, 2808 South 72nd Street, Omaha NE 68124. This location will give Royal Limousine Co. immediate access to all areas of Omaha through the use of the interstate system.

[Insert photo of Shark Club]

7.2 Facility

The Shark Club is a famous dance club in Omaha. It offers 12 pool tables, the largest dance floor in the area, and seating for 400. The Shark Club offers a limited menu and nightly drink specials. The owner, Angela Buscher, is a veteran of the food service/bar industry.

7.3 Operating Equipment

Royal Limousine will provide all customers with the most luxurious amenities. With a $61,750 loan from Omaha State Bank, Royal Limousine will purchase a 2008 Ford Excursion limousine. The 42-foot Ford Excursion will be the largest stretch limousine in the region. The limousine will boast two televisions, two DVDs, a CD player, custom fiber-optics, three wet bars, and room for 13 people. No matter what the occasion, Royal Limousine will get you there in style.

[Insert photo of limousine]

7.4 Personnel Plan

Royal Limousine will be owned and operated initially as a general partnership between Pete Olson and Jeff Larson. Both will share driving duties, alternating workdays.

7.5 General Operations

Royal Limousine will operate evenings, seven days a week. It will "open" for business at 5:30 p.m. weekdays and Sunday night and all day Saturday. Royal Limousine is also available by appointment.

-16-

8.0 MANAGEMENT, ORGANIZATION & OWNERSHIP

Royal Limousine consists of two individuals who have strengths in different business areas. Pete and Jeff have experience as limousine drivers, and Pete has accounting experience gained from his studies at the University of Nebraska, Omaha.

8.1 Management/Principals

Pete Olson is currently employed at John Roth Specialty Foods as its bookkeeper. He works Monday through Friday from 9:00 a.m. to 4:00 p.m. Pete went to the University of Nebraska, Omaha and studied accounting. While in college, Pete worked with his friend, Jeff Larson, at Omaha Limousine. Pete paid for his education by working part-time for Omaha Limousine, where he received all of his limousine experience.

Jeff Larson was born and raised in Omaha. Out of high school, Jeff began driving for Omaha Limousine and has driven ever since. He enjoys his job, but wants to do it on a part-time basis so he can go to college. Jeff and Pete have been friends since high school, and plan on opening their business initially as a partnership.

9.0 GOALS AND STRATEGIES

Royal Limousine realizes the opportunity to gain a large portion of the luxury transportation industry in Omaha and surrounding areas. This section will outline specific goals set forth by Pete Olson and Jeff Larson, as well as plans for the future.

9.1 Business Goals

Royal Limousine's business goals are as follows:

1. To produce sales of over $57,000 for years one through three.

2. To produce net income of over $26,000 for years one through three.

9.2 Keys to Success

Royal Limousine has outlined significant factors that are critical to its success. These include:

1. Overcoming customer loyalties - Customers that travel frequently with other carriers will be hard to convert to Royal Limousine. The conversion of these frequent travelers to Royal Limousine is crucial.

2. Gaining name recognition - Luxury travelers must think of Royal Limousine when they think of limousines. Becoming a household name for frequent limousine renters is critical.

3. Customer service and price - Although frequent limousine travelers are not typically price sensitive, new customers and infrequent limousine renters are. Royal Limousine must offer the highest quality transportation at competitive prices.

9.3 Future Plans

Pete and Jeff want to take their limousine business full-time. They plan on becoming a full-time business in four years, when Jeff graduates from the University of Nebraska, Omaha. By that time, Royal Limousine will have the majority of its limousine paid off, and will be able to acquire a second. At this point they will incorporate the business to get the limited liability benefits.

10.0 FINANCIAL ASSUMPTIONS

This section summarizes the financial assumptions used in creating the projected financials for Royal Limousine (included in the Appendix).

The enclosed financials are based on three main assumptions. They are as follows:

1. The owners will invest $7,000 of their own funds ($3,500 each).

2. Operations will begin January 1, 2008.

3. A $61,750, 5-year loan at 6.75% A.P.R. will be obtained from Omaha State Bank.

10.1 Assumptions

Below is a summary of the assumptions used to forecast the first 36 months of Royal Limousine. Detailed financial projections can be found in the Appendix.

-18-

Beginning Balance Sheet

For year beginning January, 2008		
Assets:		
Current assets:		
Cash	1,750	
Total current assets	1,750	
Fixed assets (net)	67,000	
Total assets		68,750
Liabilities:		
Current liabilities:		
Current maturities of long-term liabilities	10,746	
Total current liabilities	10,746	
Long-term liabilities (net)	51,004	
Total liabilities		61,750
Equity:		
Total equity		7,000
Total liabilities and equity		68,750
Debt-to-equity ratio		8.82

Cash - An initial investment of $7,000 by the owners will allow Royal Limousine to start operations. That along with a $61,750 loan will be used to purchase a $67,000 limousine, thus leaving $1,750 for beginning cash.

Current and long-term liabilities - The obligation owed to Omaha State Bank for the limousine.

Contributed cash - This $7,000 represents the combined total of the $3,500 cash investment made by each partner.

Profit & Loss

For years ending December - 2008, 2009, 2010			
	Year 1	Year 2	Year 3
Income	57,600	57,600	57,600
Gross profit	57,600	57,600	57,600
Operating expenses:			
Gas	4,800	4,800	4,800
Insurance	1,920	1,920	1,920
Advertising	4,440	4,440	4,440
Misc. Supplies	240	240	240
Maintenance	1,200	1,200	1,200
Apparel	400	400	400
Limo Parking Rental	600	600	600
Depreciation	13,400	13,400	13,400
Total operating expenses	27,000	27,000	27,000
Operating income	30,600	30,600	30,600
Interest expense	3,840	3,092	2,291
Net income	26,760	27,508	28,309

Sales - Assumptions are based on anticipated rentals. The forecast was computed on reasonably attainable seasonal sales estimates for a limousine company with one vehicle and two drivers working part-time. Sales remain flat due to limitations of drivers' time.

Gas - Estimated at 10 miles per gallon running at max capacity with all possible rental times being used. If fuel costs continue to escalate a fuel surcharge can be added.

Insurance - Royal Limousine was informed that an annual liability insurance policy would cost $1,920.

Advertising - Royal Limousine will appropriate $4,440 for radio, print, and the Yellow Pages advertising.

Misc. Supplies - Cups, napkins, and other miscellaneous supplies for the limousine.

Maintenance - Regular oil changes and tune-ups on the limousine.

Apparel - Royal Limousine will supply both drivers with new tuxedos quarterly.

Limo Parking Rental - Negotiated with the owner of the Shark Club.

-20-

Balance Sheet

For years ending December - 2008, 2009, 2010			
	Year 1	Year 2	Year 3
Assets:			
Current assets:			
Cash	1,165	579	500
Total current assets	1,165	579	500
Fixed assets (net)	53,600	40,200	26,800
Total assets	54,765	40,779	27,300
Liabilities and equity:			
Current liabilities:			
Line of credit	0	0	506
Notes payable	0	0	0
Current maturities	11,494	12,294	13,150
Total current liabilities	11,494	12,294	13,656
Long-term liabilities (net)	39,510	27,216	14,066
Total liabilities	51,004	39,510	27,722
Equity	3,760	1,269	(422)
Total liabilities and equity	54,765	40,779	27,300

Cash - The cash balance remains above the minimum level until the end of the third year in operation. Seasonality issues cause the cash balance to rise and fall.

PPE (net) - This is the value of the limousine net of depreciation.

Line of credit - Royal Limousine uses its line of credit very seldom because of seasonality issues. It is fully repaid by May of each year.

Cash Plan

For years ending December - 2008, 2009, 2010	Year 1	Year 2	Year 3
Cash receipts	57,600	57,600	57,600
Operating cash expenses	13,600	13,600	13,600
Cash from operations	44,000	44,000	44,000
Debt activities:			
Principal payments	(10,746)	(11,494)	(12,294)
Interest payments	(3,840)	(3,092)	(2,291)
Total debt activities	(14,585)	(14,585)	(14,585)
Net cash after debt service	29,415	29,415	29,415
Distributions	(30,000)	(30,000)	(30,000)
Change in cash	(585)	(585)	(585)
Beginning cash	1,750	1,165	579
Cash before borrowing	1,165	579	(6)
Line of credit activity	0	0	506
Ending cash	1,165	579	500
NOTE: Line of credit			
exceeded in Month 37			

Cash receipts - Sales to customers will be 100% cash.

Operating cash expenses - Outlined in the Profit & Loss summary.

Principal and Interest Payments - Repayment of the loan for the limousine.

Distributions - Owners draw of $1,250 each per month.

11. APPENDIX

This section contains the following reports and supporting documentation:

- Income Projection

- Expense Projection

- Profit & Loss

- Balance Sheet

- Cash Plan

- Ratio Analysis

Income Projection - Year 1

Income Category	Jan	Feb	Mar	Apr	May	Jun	Jul	Aug	Sep	Oct	Nov	Dec	Year 1
Hourly Rental	1800	1800	1800	1800	1800	1800	1800	1800	1800	1800	1800	1800	21600
Wedding Days	1000	2000	2000	2000	2000	2000	2000	1000	1000	1000	1000	1000	18000
Casino Trips	1500	1500	1500	1500	1500	1500	1500	1500	1500	1500	1500	1500	18000
Total Income	4300	5300	5300	5300	5300	5300	5300	4300	4300	4300	4300	4300	57600

Income Projection - Year 2

Income Category	Jan	Feb	Mar	Apr	May	Jun	Jul	Aug	Sep	Oct	Nov	Dec	Year 2
Hourly Rental	1800	1800	1800	1800	1800	1800	1800	1800	1800	1800	1800	1800	21600
Wedding Days	1000	2000	2000	2000	2000	2000	2000	1000	1000	1000	1000	1000	18000
Casino Trips	1500	1500	1500	1500	1500	1500	1500	1500	1500	1500	1500	1500	18000
Total Income	4300	5300	5300	5300	5300	5300	5300	4300	4300	4300	4300	4300	57600

Income Projection - Year 3

Income Category	Jan	Feb	Mar	Apr	May	Jun	Jul	Aug	Sep	Oct	Nov	Dec	Year 3
Hourly Rental	1800	1800	1800	1800	1800	1800	1800	1800	1800	1800	1800	1800	21600
Wedding Days	1000	2000	2000	2000	2000	2000	2000	1000	1000	1000	1000	1000	18000
Casino Trips	1500	1500	1500	1500	1500	1500	1500	1500	1500	1500	1500	1500	18000
Total Income	4300	5300	5300	5300	5300	5300	5300	4300	4300	4300	4300	4300	57600

Expense Projection - Year 1

Expense Category	Jan	Feb	Mar	Apr	May	Jun	Jul	Aug	Sep	Oct	Nov	Dec	Year 1
Gas	350	450	450	450	450	450	450	350	350	350	350	350	4800
Insurance	160	160	160	160	160	160	160	160	160	160	160	160	1920
Advertising	370	370	370	370	370	370	370	370	370	370	370	370	4440
Misc. Supplies	20	20	20	20	20	20	20	20	20	20	20	20	240
Maintenance	0	0	0	400	0	0	0	400	0	0	0	400	1200
Apparel	400	0	0	0	0	0	0	0	0	0	0	0	400
Limo Parking Rental	50	50	50	50	50	50	50	50	50	50	50	50	600
Total Expenses	1350	1050	1050	1450	1050	1050	1050	1350	950	950	950	1350	13600

Expense Projection - Year 2

Expense Category	Jan	Feb	Mar	Apr	May	Jun	Jul	Aug	Sep	Oct	Nov	Dec	Year 2
Gas	350	450	450	450	450	450	450	350	350	350	350	350	4800
Insurance	160	160	160	160	160	160	160	160	160	160	160	160	1920
Advertising	370	370	370	370	370	370	370	370	370	370	370	370	4440
Misc. Supplies	20	20	20	20	20	20	20	20	20	20	20	20	240
Maintenance	0	0	0	400	0	0	0	400	0	0	0	400	1200
Apparel	400	0	0	0	0	0	0	0	0	0	0	0	400
Limo Parking Rental	50	50	50	50	50	50	50	50	50	50	50	50	600
Total Expenses	1350	1050	1050	1450	1050	1050	1050	1350	950	950	950	1350	13600

Expense Projection - Year 3

Expense Category	Jan	Feb	Mar	Apr	May	Jun	Jul	Aug	Sep	Oct	Nov	Dec	Year 3
Gas	350	450	450	450	450	450	450	350	350	350	350	350	4800
Insurance	160	160	160	160	160	160	160	160	160	160	160	160	1920
Advertising	370	370	370	370	370	370	370	370	370	370	370	370	4440
Misc. Supplies	20	20	20	20	20	20	20	20	20	20	20	20	240
Maintenance	0	0	0	400	0	0	0	400	0	0	0	400	1200
Apparel	400	0	0	0	0	0	0	0	0	0	0	0	400
Limo Parking Rental	50	50	50	50	50	50	50	50	50	50	50	50	600
Total Expenses	1350	1050	1050	1450	1050	1050	1050	1350	950	950	950	1350	13600

Profit & Loss - Year 1

	Jan	Feb	Mar	Apr	May	Jun	Jul	Aug	Sep	Oct	Nov	Dec	Year 1
Income	4300	5300	5300	5300	5300	5300	5300	4300	4300	4300	4300	4300	57600
Gross profit	4300	5300	5300	5300	5300	5300	5300	4300	4300	4300	4300	4300	57600
Operating expenses:													
Gas	350	450	450	450	450	450	450	350	350	350	350	350	4800
Insurance	160	160	160	160	160	160	160	160	160	160	160	160	1920
Advertising	370	370	370	370	370	370	370	370	370	370	370	370	4440
Misc. Supplies	20	20	20	20	20	20	20	20	20	20	20	20	240
Maintenance	0	0	0	400	0	0	0	400	0	0	0	400	1200
Apparel	400	0	0	0	0	0	0	0	0	0	0	0	400
Limo Parking Rental	50	50	50	50	50	50	50	50	50	50	50	50	600
Depreciation	1117	1117	1117	1117	1117	1117	1117	1117	1117	1117	1117	1117	13404
Total operating expenses	2467	2167	2167	2567	2167	2167	2167	2467	2067	2067	2067	2467	27004
Operating income	1833	3133	3133	2733	3133	3133	3133	1833	2233	2233	2233	1833	30596
Interest expense	347	342	338	333	328	323	318	313	308	302	297	292	3841
Net income	1486	2791	2795	2400	2805	2810	2815	1520	1925	1931	1936	1541	26755

Profit & Loss - Year 2

	Jan	Feb	Mar	Apr	May	Jun	Jul	Aug	Sep	Oct	Nov	Dec	Year 2
Income	4300	5300	5300	5300	5300	5300	5300	4300	4300	4300	4300	4300	57600
Gross profit	4300	5300	5300	5300	5300	5300	5300	4300	4300	4300	4300	4300	57600
Operating expenses:													
Gas	350	450	450	450	450	450	450	350	350	350	350	350	4800
Insurance	160	160	160	160	160	160	160	160	160	160	160	160	1920
Advertising	370	370	370	370	370	370	370	370	370	370	370	370	4440
Misc. Supplies	20	20	20	20	20	20	20	20	20	20	20	20	240
Maintenance	0	0	0	400	0	0	0	400	0	0	0	400	1200
Apparel	400	0	0	0	0	0	0	0	0	0	0	0	400
Limo Parking Rental	50	50	50	50	50	50	50	50	50	50	50	50	600
Depreciation	1117	1117	1117	1117	1117	1117	1117	1117	1117	1117	1117	1117	13404
Total operating expenses	2467	2167	2167	2567	2167	2167	2167	2467	2067	2067	2067	2467	27004
Operating income	1833	3133	3133	2733	3133	3133	3133	1833	2233	2233	2233	1833	30596
Interest expense	287	282	276	271	266	260	255	250	244	239	233	228	3091
Net income	1546	2851	2857	2462	2867	2873	2878	1583	1989	1994	2000	1605	27505

Profit & Loss - Year 3

	Jan	Feb	Mar	Apr	May	Jun	Jul	Aug	Sep	Oct	Nov	Dec	Year 3
Income	4300	5300	5300	5300	5300	5300	5300	4300	4300	4300	4300	4300	57600
Gross profit	4300	5300	5300	5300	5300	5300	5300	4300	4300	4300	4300	4300	57600
Operating expenses:													
Gas	350	450	450	450	450	450	450	350	350	350	350	350	4800
Insurance	160	160	160	160	160	160	160	160	160	160	160	160	1920
Advertising	370	370	370	370	370	370	370	370	370	370	370	370	4440
Misc. Supplies	20	20	20	20	20	20	20	20	20	20	20	20	240
Maintenance	0	0	0	400	0	0	0	400	0	0	0	400	1200
Apparel	400	0	0	0	0	0	0	0	0	0	0	0	400
Limo Parking Rental	50	50	50	50	50	50	50	50	50	50	50	50	600
Depreciation	1117	1117	1117	1117	1117	1117	1117	1117	1117	1117	1117	1117	13404
Total operating expenses	2467	2167	2167	2567	2167	2167	2167	2467	2067	2067	2067	2467	27004
Operating income	1833	3133	3133	2733	3133	3133	3133	1833	2233	2233	2233	1833	30596
Interest expense	222	217	211	205	200	194	188	182	177	171	165	159	2291
Net income	1611	2916	2922	2528	2933	2939	2945	1651	2056	2062	2068	1674	28305

Balance Sheet - Year 1

	Jan	Feb	Mar	Apr	May	Jun	Jul	Aug	Sep	Oct	Nov	Dec	Year 1
Assets:													
Current assets:													
Cash	985	1519	2054	2188	2723	3257	3792	3026	2661	2296	1930	1165	1165
Total current assets	985	1519	2054	2188	2723	3257	3792	3026	2661	2296	1930	1165	1165
Fixed assets (net)	65883	64767	63650	62533	61417	60300	59183	58067	56950	55833	54717	53600	53600
Total assets	66868	66286	65704	64721	64140	63557	62975	61093	59611	58129	56647	54765	54765
Liabilities and equity:													
Current liabilities:													
Line of credit	0	0	0	0	0	0	0	0	0	0	0	0	0
Notes payable	0	0	0	0	0	0	0	0	0	0	0	0	0
Current maturities	10806	10867	10928	10990	11051	11113	11176	11239	11302	11366	11430	11494	11494
Total current liabilities	10806	10867	10928	10990	11051	11113	11176	11239	11302	11366	11430	11494	11494
Long-term liabilities (net)	50076	49142	48203	47259	46309	45354	44394	43428	42457	41480	40498	39510	39510
Total liabilities	60882	60009	59131	58249	57360	56467	55570	54667	53759	52846	51928	51004	51004
Equity	5986	6277	6573	6472	6780	7090	7405	6426	5852	5283	4719	3761	3761
Total liabilities and equity	66868	66286	65704	64721	64140	63557	62975	61093	59611	58129	56647	54765	54765

Balance Sheet - Year 2

	Jan	Feb	Mar	Apr	May	Jun	Jul	Aug	Sep	Oct	Nov	Dec	Year 2
Assets:													
Current assets:													
Cash	500	934	1468	1603	2137	2672	3206	2441	2076	1710	1345	579	579
Total current assets	500	934	1468	1603	2137	2672	3206	2441	2076	1710	1345	579	579
Fixed assets (net)	52483	51367	50250	49133	48017	46900	45783	44667	43550	42433	41317	40200	40200
Total assets	52983	52301	51718	50736	50154	49572	48989	47108	45626	44143	42662	40779	40779
Liabilities and equity:													
Current liabilities:													
Line of credit	101	0	0	0	0	0	0	0	0	0	0	0	0
Notes payable	0	0	0	0	0	0	0	0	0	0	0	0	0
Current maturities	11559	11624	11689	11755	11821	11887	11954	12021	12089	12157	12225	12294	12294
Total current liabilities	11660	11624	11689	11755	11821	11887	11954	12021	12089	12157	12225	12294	12294
Long-term liabilities (net)	38517	37518	36514	35504	34488	33467	32440	31407	30368	29323	28273	27216	27216
Total liabilities	50177	49142	48203	47259	46309	45354	44394	43428	42457	41480	40498	39510	39510
Equity	2806	3159	3515	3477	3845	4218	4595	3680	3169	2663	2164	1269	1269
Total liabilities and equity	52983	52301	51718	50736	50154	49572	48989	47108	45626	44143	42662	40779	40779

Balance Sheet - Year 3

	Jan	Feb	Mar	Apr	May	Jun	Jul	Aug	Sep	Oct	Nov	Dec	Year 3
Assets:													
Current assets:													
Cash	500	500	883	1017	1552	2087	2621	1856	1490	1125	759	500	500
Total current assets	500	500	883	1017	1552	2087	2621	1856	1490	1125	759	500	500
Fixed assets (net)	39083	37967	36850	35733	34617	33500	32383	31267	30150	29033	27917	26800	26800
Total assets	39583	38467	37733	36750	36169	35587	35004	33123	31640	30158	28675	27300	27300
Liabilities and equity:													
Current liabilities:													
Line of credit	686	152	0	0	0	0	0	0	0	0	0	506	506
Notes payable	0	0	0	0	0	0	0	0	0	0	0	0	0
Current maturities	12363	12433	12503	12573	12644	12715	12787	12858	12931	13003	13077	13150	13150
Total current liabilities	13049	12585	12503	12573	12644	12715	12787	12858	12931	13003	13077	13656	13656
Long-term liabilities (net)	26154	25086	24011	22931	21844	20752	19653	18548	17437	16320	15196	14066	14066
Total liabilities	39203	37671	36514	35504	34488	33467	32440	31406	30368	29323	28273	27722	27722
Equity	380	796	1219	1246	1681	2120	2564	1717	1272	835	403	-422	-422
Total liabilities and equity	39583	38467	37733	36750	36169	35587	35004	33123	31640	30158	28675	27300	27300

Cash Plan - Year 1

	Jan	Feb	Mar	Apr	May	Jun	Jul	Aug	Sep	Oct	Nov	Dec	Year 1
Cash receipts	4300	5300	5300	5300	5300	5300	5300	4300	4300	4300	4300	4300	57600
Operating cash expenses	1350	1050	1050	1450	1050	1050	1050	1350	950	950	950	1350	13600
Cash from operations	2950	4250	4250	3850	4250	4250	4250	2950	3350	3350	3350	2950	44000
Debt activities:													
Principal payments	-868	-873	-878	-883	-888	-893	-898	-903	-908	-913	-918	-923	-10746
Interest payments	-347	-342	-338	-333	-328	-323	-318	-313	-308	-302	-297	-292	-3841
Total debt activities	-1215	-1215	-1216	-1216	-1216	-1216	-1216	-1216	-1216	-1215	-1215	-1215	-14587
Net cash after debt service	1735	3035	3034	2634	3034	3034	3034	1734	2134	2135	2135	1735	29413
Distributions	-2500	-2500	-2500	-2500	-2500	-2500	-2500	-2500	-2500	-2500	-2500	-2500	-30000
Change in cash	-765	535	535	135	535	535	535	-765	-365	-365	-365	-765	-580
Beginning cash	1750	985	1519	2054	2188	2723	3257	3792	3026	2661	2296	1930	1750
Cash before borrowing	985	1520	2054	2189	2723	3258	3792	3027	2661	2296	1931	1165	1170
Line of credit activity	0	0	0	0	0	0	0	0	0	0	0	0	0
Ending cash	985	1520	2054	2189	2723	3258	3792	3027	2661	2296	1931	1165	1165
NOTE: Line of credit													
exceeded in Month 37													

Cash Plan - Year 2

	Jan	Feb	Mar	Apr	May	Jun	Jul	Aug	Sep	Oct	Nov	Dec	Year 2
Cash receipts	4300	5300	5300	5300	5300	5300	5300	4300	4300	4300	4300	4300	57600
Operating cash expenses	1350	1050	1050	1450	1050	1050	1050	1350	950	950	950	1350	13600
Cash from operations	2950	4250	4250	3850	4250	4250	4250	2950	3350	3350	3350	2950	44000
Debt activities:													
Principal payments	-929	-934	-939	-944	-950	-955	-960	-966	-971	-977	-982	-988	-11495
Interest payments	-287	-282	-276	-271	-266	-260	-255	-250	-244	-239	-233	-228	-3091
Total debt activities	-1216	-1216	-1215	-1215	-1216	-1215	-1215	-1216	-1215	-1216	-1215	-1216	-14586
Net cash after debt service	1734	3034	3035	2635	3034	3035	3035	1734	2135	2134	2135	1734	29414
Distributions	-2500	-2500	-2500	-2500	-2500	-2500	-2500	-2500	-2500	-2500	-2500	-2500	-30000
Change in cash	-765	535	535	135	535	535	535	-765	-365	-365	-365	-765	-580
Beginning cash	1165	500	934	1468	1603	2137	2672	3206	2441	2076	1710	1345	1165
Cash before borrowing	400	1035	1469	1603	2138	2672	3207	2441	2076	1711	1345	580	585
Line of credit activity	101	-101	0	0	0	0	0	0	0	0	0	0	0
Ending cash	501	934	1469	1603	2138	2672	3207	2441	2076	1711	1345	580	580
NOTE: Line of credit exceeded in Month 37													

Cash Plan - Year 3

	Jan	Feb	Mar	Apr	May	Jun	Jul	Aug	Sep	Oct	Nov	Dec	Year 3
Cash receipts	4300	5300	5300	5300	5300	5300	5300	4300	4300	4300	4300	4300	57600
Operating cash expenses	1350	1050	1050	1450	1050	1050	1050	1350	950	950	950	1350	13600
Cash from operations	2950	4250	4250	3850	4250	4250	4250	2950	3350	3350	3350	2950	44000
Debt activities:													
Principal payments	-993	-999	-1004	-1010	-1016	-1021	-1027	-1033	-1039	-1045	-1051	-1056	-12294
Interest payments	-222	-217	-211	-205	-200	-194	-188	-182	-177	-171	-165	-159	-2291
Total debt activities	-1215	-1216	-1215	-1215	-1216	-1215	-1215	-1215	-1216	-1216	-1216	-1215	-14585
Net cash after debt service	1735	3034	3035	2635	3034	3035	3035	1735	2134	2134	2134	1735	29415
Distributions	-2500	-2500	-2500	-2500	-2500	-2500	-2500	-2500	-2500	-2500	-2500	-2500	-30000
Change in cash	-765	535	535	135	535	535	535	-765	-365	-365	-365	-765	-580
Beginning cash	579	500	500	883	1017	1552	2087	2621	1856	1490	1125	759	579
Cash before borrowing	-186	1035	1035	1018	1552	2087	2622	1856	1491	1125	760	-6	-1
Line of credit activity	686	-535	-152	0	0	0	0	0	0	0	0	506	505
Ending cash	500	500	883	1018	1552	2087	2622	1856	1491	1125	760	500	500

NOTE: Line of credit
exceeded in Month 37

Ratio Analysis - Year 1

	Jan	Feb	Mar	Apr	May	Jun	Jul	Aug	Sep	Oct	Nov	Dec	Year 1
Profitability ratios:													
Gross profit margin	100.00%	100.00%	100.00%	100.00%	100.00%	100.00%	100.00%	100.00%	100.00%	100.00%	100.00%	100.00%	100.00%
Operating profit margin	42.64%	59.12%	59.12%	51.57%	59.12%	59.12%	59.12%	42.64%	51.94%	51.94%	51.94%	42.64%	53.12%
Net profit margin	34.56%	52.66%	52.75%	45.30%	52.94%	53.03%	53.13%	35.37%	44.79%	44.91%	45.05%	35.84%	46.46%
Return on equity	22.89%	45.52%	43.52%	36.80%	42.34%	40.53%	38.85%	21.99%	31.37%	34.68%	38.71%	36.35%	432.53%
Return on assets	2.70%	4.71%	4.75%	4.19%	4.86%	4.91%	4.95%	2.96%	3.70%	3.79%	3.85%	3.29%	48.86%
Liquidity ratios:													
Current ratio	0.09	0.14	0.19	0.20	0.25	0.29	0.34	0.27	0.24	0.20	0.17	0.10	0.10
Quick ratio (Acid-test)	0.09	0.14	0.19	0.20	0.25	0.29	0.34	0.27	0.24	0.20	0.17	0.10	0.10
Working capital ratio	-2.28	-1.76	-1.67	-1.66	-1.57	-1.48	-1.39	-1.91	-2.01	-2.11	-2.21	-2.40	-0.18
Activity ratios:													
Accounts receivable days	0.00	0.00	0.00	0.00	0.00	0.00	0.00	0.00	0.00	0.00	0.00	0.00	0.00
Inventory days	n/a	n/a	n/a	n/a	n/a	n/a	n/a	n/a	n/a	n/a	n/a	n/a	n/a
Inventory turnover	n/a	n/a	n/a	n/a	n/a	n/a	n/a	n/a	n/a	n/a	n/a	n/a	n/a
Sales-to-assets	0.06	0.08	0.08	0.08	0.08	0.08	0.08	0.07	0.07	0.07	0.07	0.08	0.92
Leverage ratios:													
Debt-to-equity	10.17	9.56	9.00	9.00	8.46	7.96	7.50	8.51	9.19	10.00	11.00	13.56	13.56
Debt ratio	0.91	0.91	0.90	0.90	0.89	0.89	0.88	0.89	0.90	0.91	0.92	0.93	0.93
Times-interest (TI) earned:													
Operating income	1833	3133	3133	2733	3133	3133	3133	1833	2233	2233	2233	1833	30600
Interest expense (÷)	347	342	338	333	328	323	318	313	308	302	297	292	3840
TI earned ratio	5.28	9.16	9.27	8.21	9.55	9.70	9.85	5.86	7.25	7.39	7.52	6.28	7.96875

Ratio Analysis - Year 2

	Jan	Feb	Mar	Apr	May	Jun	Jul	Aug	Sep	Oct	Nov	Dec	Year 3
Profitability ratios:													
Gross profit margin	100.00%	100.00%	100.00%	100.00%	100.00%	100.00%	100.00%	100.00%	100.00%	100.00%	100.00%	100.00%	100.00%
Operating profit margin	42.64%	59.12%	59.12%	51.57%	59.12%	59.12%	59.12%	42.64%	51.94%	51.94%	51.94%	42.64%	53.12%
Net profit margin	35.96%	53.80%	53.90%	46.46%	54.10%	54.20%	54.31%	36.83%	46.26%	46.38%	46.51%	37.34%	47.76%
Return on equity	47.10%	95.61%	85.62%	70.42%	78.32%	71.26%	65.31%	38.27%	58.09%	68.40%	82.88%	93.56%	829.28%
Return on assets	3.40%	5.95%	6.02%	5.34%	6.21%	6.28%	6.36%	3.82%	4.82%	4.98%	5.15%	4.39%	62.90%
Liquidity ratios:													
Current ratio	0.04	0.08	0.13	0.14	0.18	0.22	0.27	0.20	0.17	0.14	0.11	0.05	0.05
Quick ratio (Acid-test)	0.04	0.08	0.13	0.14	0.18	0.22	0.27	0.20	0.17	0.14	0.11	0.05	0.05
Working capital ratio	-2.60	-2.02	-1.93	-1.92	-1.83	-1.74	-1.65	-2.23	-2.33	-2.43	-2.53	-2.72	-0.20
Activity ratios:													
Accounts receivable days	0.00	0.00	0.00	0.00	0.00	0.00	0.00	0.00	0.00	0.00	0.00	0.00	0.00
Inventory days	n/a	n/a	n/a	n/a	n/a	n/a	n/a	n/a	n/a	n/a	n/a	n/a	n/a
Inventory turnover	n/a	n/a	n/a	n/a	n/a	n/a	n/a	n/a	n/a	n/a	n/a	n/a	n/a
Sales-to-assets	0.08	0.10	0.10	0.10	0.11	0.11	0.11	0.09	0.09	0.10	0.10	0.10	1.18
Leverage ratios:													
Debt-to-equity	17.88	15.56	13.71	13.59	12.04	10.75	9.66	11.80	13.40	15.58	18.72	31.14	31.14
Debt ratio	0.95	0.94	0.93	0.93	0.92	0.91	0.91	0.92	0.93	0.94	0.95	0.97	0.97
Times-interest (TI) earned:													
Operating income	1833	3133	3133	2733	3133	3133	3133	1833	2233	2233	2233	1833	30600
Interest expense ($\div$)	287	282	276	271	266	260	255	250	244	239	233	228	3092
TI earned ratio	6.39	11.11	11.35	10.08	11.78	12.05	12.29	7.33	9.15	9.34	9.58	8.04	9.8965071

Ratio Analysis - Year 3

	Jan	Feb	Mar	Apr	May	Jun	Jul	Aug	Sep	Oct	Nov	Dec	Year 3
Profitability ratios:													
Gross profit margin	100.00%	100.00%	100.00%	100.00%	100.00%	100.00%	100.00%	100.00%	100.00%	100.00%	100.00%	100.00%	100.00%
Operating profit margin	42.64%	59.12%	59.12%	51.57%	59.12%	59.12%	59.12%	42.64%	51.94%	51.94%	51.94%	42.64%	53.12%
Net profit margin	37.47%	55.03%	55.14%	47.70%	55.35%	55.46%	55.57%	38.39%	47.83%	47.97%	48.10%	38.94%	49.15%
Return on equity	195.45%	495.88%	290.01%	205.06%	200.44%	154.70%	125.74%	77.13%	137.66%	195.76%	334.13%	n/a	n/a
Return on assets	4.56%	8.03%	8.22%	7.34%	8.59%	8.73%	8.88%	5.38%	6.90%	7.23%	7.59%	6.55%	88.07%
Liquidity ratios:													
Current ratio	0.04	0.04	0.07	0.08	0.12	0.16	0.20	0.14	0.12	0.09	0.06	0.04	0.04
Quick ratio (Acid-test)	0.04	0.04	0.07	0.08	0.12	0.16	0.20	0.14	0.12	0.09	0.06	0.04	0.04
Working capital ratio	-2.92	-2.28	-2.19	-2.18	-2.09	-2.01	-1.92	-2.56	-2.66	-2.76	-2.86	-3.06	-0.23
Activity ratios:													
Accounts receivable days	0.00	0.00	0.00	0.00	0.00	0.00	0.00	0.00	0.00	0.00	0.00	0.00	0.00
Inventory days	n/a	n/a	n/a	n/a	n/a	n/a	n/a	n/a	n/a	n/a	n'/a	n/a	n/a
Inventory turnover	n/a	n/a	n/a	n/a	n/a	n/a	n/a	n/a	n/a	n/a	n'/a	n/a	n/a
Sales-to-assets	0.11	0.14	0.14	0.14	0.15	0.15	0.15	0.13	0.13	0.14	0.15	0.15	1.66
Leverage ratios:													
Debt-to-equity	103.21	47.29	29.96	28.48	20.52	15.79	12.65	18.31	23.87	35.12	70.12	-65.62	-65.62
Debt ratio	0.99	0.98	0.97	0.97	0.95	0.94	0.93	0.95	0.96	0.97	0.99	1.02	1.02
Times-interest (TI) earned:													
Operating income	1833	3133	3133	2733	3133	3133	3133	1833	2233	2233	2233	1833	30600
Interest expense (÷)	222	217	211	205	200	194	188	182	177	171	165	159	2291
TI earned ratio	8.26	14.44	14.85	13.33	15.67	16.15	16.66	10.07	12.62	13.06	13.53	11.53	13.356613

The Business Plan for
The T-Shirt Shop
A Sole Proprietorship

Contact Information:

Jan Marx

1128 Lovers Lain

Billings, Montana 59102

(406) 656-9999

jmarx@billings.marx.info

Copy Number __ of Five.

Non-Disclosure and Confidentiality Agreement

The undersigned ("Recipient") hereby agrees that all financial and other information ("Information") that it has and will receive concerning The T-Shirt Shop is confidential and will not be disclosed to any individual or entity without prior written consent.

The Information shall remain the property of The T-Shirt Shop and shall be returned to The T-Shirt Shop promptly at its request together with all copies made thereof.

Recipient acknowledges that no remedy of law may be adequate to compensate The T-Shirt Shop for a violation of this Agreement and Recipient hereby agrees that in addition to any legal or other rights that may be available in the event of a breach hereunder, The T-Shirt Shop may seek equitable relief to enforce this Agreement in any Court of competent jurisdiction.

_____   _____
Date   Signature of Recipient

-2-

THE PLAN FOR THE T-SHIRT SHOP

1.0 EXECUTIVE SUMMARY

The T-Shirt Shop is a proposed silk screening and embroidery business. It will offer custom embroidery and screen-printing, and will sell a variety of t-shirts, sweatshirts, hats, and polos. The T-Shirt Shop will be located in Billings, Montana in the Rimrock Mall. In order to start this new business opportunity, Jan Marx (owner) will need loans to pay for the start-up equipment.

1.1 Business Opportunity

Silk screening and embroidery are becoming more commonplace. Businesses are trying to get their names in front of as many potential clients as possible. Through a variety of media, businesses are purchasing many articles of clothing for their employees, customers, and as promotional items. With only one competitor in Billings that offers embroidery and screen-printing, the need for another quality provider is high.

1.2 Product/Service Description

The T-Shirt Shop will offer a wide variety of hats, t-shirts, sweatshirts, and polo shirts to their customers. The T-Shirt Shop will offer all articles of clothing for sale, with or without an emblem. Inventory will include many different styles of hats, t-shirts, sweatshirts, and polos in a variety of sizes. Also, The T-Shirt Shop will special order additional clothing styles, available from various catalogs. Sales will be split between corporate and retail customers, the majority coming from corporate customers.

The following chart shows the percentage of sales from corporate and retail customers:

Income by Category
For years ending December - 2008, 2009, 2010

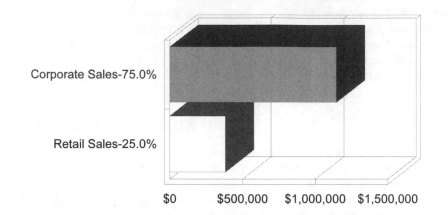

Corporate Sales-75.0%

Retail Sales-25.0%

$0 $500,000 $1,000,000 $1,500,000

1.3 Current Business Position

The T-Shirt Shop is a start-up business that will lease space upon receiving start-up loans. The T-Shirt Shop will be operated by two local champions of retail marketing: Jan Marx and Paula Nelson. Both have several years in retail and apparel marketing. The T-Shirt Shop will employ local college students to help run the equipment and cover weekends.

1.4 Financial Potential

The T-Shirt Shop expects sales of $488,000 in its first year in business. Sales are expected to grow by 4% in years two and three. Net income is expected to be $85,000 in year one, and $97,000 in year two. Year three net income is projected to be about $108,000 on sales revenue of $528,000.

Following is the T-Shirt Shop's Profit & Loss Statement for its first three years in business:

Profit & Loss Statement

For years ending December - 2008, 2009, 2010			
	Year 1	Year 2	Year 3
Income	488,800	508,352	528,684
Less COGS:			
Material	232,180	241,467	251,125
Total COGS	232,180	241,467	251,125
Gross profit	256,620	266,885	277,559
Operating expenses:			
Salaries & Wages	66,240	66,240	66,240
Lease	36,000	36,000	36,000
Advertising	15,000	15,000	15,000
Utilities	9,000	9,000	9,000
Telephone	2,400	2,400	2,400
Insurance	3,600	3,600	3,600
Repairs & Maintenance	2,100	2,100	2,100
Supplies	3,600	3,600	3,600
Bad debts	6,354	6,609	6,873
Amortization	200	200	200
Depreciation	19,914	19,914	19,914
Total operating expenses	164,409	164,663	164,927
Operating income	92,211	102,222	112,632
Interest expense	6,353	5,084	4,295
Net income	85,858	97,138	108,337

1.5 The Request

The T-Shirt Shop is interested in acquiring a $40,000 start-up loan, a $20,000 line of credit, as well as a $24,000 loan in month 24 to pay off a family obligation. The funds will be used to purchase equipment, renovate, advertise, and fund the projected negative cash flows during the first few months of operations.

2.0 COMPANY BACKGROUND

2.1 Business Description

The T-Shirt Shop will be owned and operated by members of the Billings, Montana community. It will offer the best quality apparel, and the best possible service. The shop will offer custom embroidery, and screen-printing on virtually any medium. From hats to shorts, the T-Shirt Shop will customize any apparel into a walking advertisement.

2.2 Company History

The T-Shirt Shop is a new business venture. It will lease space and will be located in the Rimrock Mall, the busiest shopping destination in Montana. The mall is the best location for The T-Shirt Shop because of the high traffic and easy accessibility for corporate customers.

The T-Shirt Shop will be run by its owner, Jan Marx, and manager, Paula Nelson, who will work the shop full-time. Together, Jan Marx and Paula Nelson will perform all duties, from administrative to janitorial. They will also have two part-time employees to help on nights, weekends, and holidays by working the equipment and assisting customers. As the business grows, Jan and Paula plan on expanding their work force; however, initially the four employees will be able to handle customer demand.

2.3 Mission & Vision

The T-Shirt Shop's Mission Statement follows:

"The T-Shirt Shop will provide the best quality products and services while promoting a friendly working environment."

The T-Shirt Shop's Vision Statement follows:

"The T-Shirt Shop will strive to supply all local merchants and businesses with custom products. The company will build sales to meet the goal of expanded operations, and will add staff to fulfill its orders. The future expansion of the T-Shirt Shop will solidify its business position, and will make the company a major contributor to the community of Billings, Montana."

2.4 Ownership

The T-Shirt Shop will be formed as sole proprietorship, owned by Jan Marx. Paula Nelson will be the general manager. Jan will provide an initial investment of $30,000 to help secure start-up financing. This is a low liability risk industry so the sole proprietor format will suffice initially. As the business grows, Jan may decide to form an LLC or a C corporation with a subchapter S election.

3.0 PRODUCTS

The T-Shirt Shop will offer a wide variety of apparel products as well as custom embroidery and silk screening. The T-Shirt Shop will have the ability to customize any of their apparel into a walking billboard for any of their customers. They will have an extensive inventory, and be able to order virtually any color, size, or style in many lines of apparel.

3.1 Products

All articles of clothing held in inventory will be available in a wide variety of colors, sizes, and styles. Additionally, special size or color requests will be filled by local distributors, or by special order. The T-Shirt Shop will offer the following manufacturers' products in inventory and via special order:

1. Anvil General Activewear

2. Fruit of the Loom Activewear

3. Gildan Activewear

4. Jerzees Activewear

Prices will vary with brand, style, quality, and size of clothing article. All articles of clothing will be available for custom embroidery and silk screening. Follows are items that will be sold at the T-Shirt Shop:

Henley Tees:

Anvil 100% Cotton Deluxe Short Sleeve Henley

Fruit of the Loom Lofteez 3-Button Short Sleeve Henley with Wood-Tone Buttons

Long Sleeve Tees:

Hanes Long Sleeve Beefy-T Cotton T-Shirts

Gildan 50/50 Ultra Blend Adult Long Sleeve T-Shirt

Gildan Ultra Cotton Adult Long Sleeve T-Shirt

Pocket Tees:

Gildan 50/50 Ultra Blend Adult Short Sleeve T-Shirt with Pocket

Gildan Ultra Cotton Adult Pocket T-Shirt

Jerzees 100% Combed Ring-Spun Cotton Short Sleeve Pocket Z-T with 3/4" Ribbed Collar

Basic Tees:

Anvil Women's Scoop-Neck All-Cotton Short Sleeve Tee

Anvil Women's V-Neck All-Cotton Short Sleeve Tee

Anvil Deluxe 100% Cotton T-Shirt

Fruit of the Loom Best Adult Short Sleeve T-Shirt

Fruit of the Loom Adult 100% Cotton T-Shirt

Fruit of the Loom Lofteez Adult T-Shirt

Gildan Adult 50/50 Ultra Blend T-Shirt

Gildan 100% Cotton Heavyweight Adult T-Shirt

Gildan Adult Ultra Cotton T-Shirt

Hanes Short Sleeve Beefy-T Cotton T-Shirt

Jerzees 100% Cotton T-Shirt

Jerzees Heavyweight T-Shirt

Jerzees 100% Cotton Short Sleeve Z-T with 3/4 Ribbed Collar

Long Sleeve Tees:

Fruit of the Loom Best Adult Long Sleeve T-Shirt with Rib-Knit Cuffs

Fruit of the Loom Lofteez Long Sleeve T-Shirt

Jerzees 100% Combed Ring-Spun Cotton Long Sleeve Z-T

3.2 Competitive Analysis

Currently, there is only one custom embroidery and silk screening business in the greater Billings, Montana area. It offers a wide variety of clothing and accessories that are comparable to those The T-Shirt Shop will offer. Although the basic product offerings will be similar, The T-Shirt Shop will have a distinct advantage provided by the vast experience of Ms. Marx and Ms. Nelson in retail marketing. They are always researching fashion trends, and will special order the newest styles or colors for display in the store.

3.3 Suppliers and Inventory

The T-Shirt Shop will maintain its inventory by ordering from local and regional vendors. Bulk purchases will be made as frequently as possible in order to take advantage of quantity discounts. Additional orders and special orders will be "shopped" in order to find the highest quality at a reasonable price.

The T-Shirt Shop will maintain $25,000 in inventory. This translates to approximately 39 days worth of inventory on hand at all times. In order to timely fulfill customer orders, this amount of inventory is necessary. Ms. Marx and Ms. Nelson will monitor inventory and fashion trends on a bi-weekly basis to keep a "fresh" look to The T-Shirt Shop's stock. The inventory will be counted on a monthly basis, and new orders will be processed accordingly. This will ensure a proper level of inventory, as well as account for any shrinkage that may occur.

3.4 Research and Fashion

Ms. Marx and Ms. Nelson are accustomed to the fashion industry. They have vast experience in retail marketing, and are on the cutting edge of local, regional, and national fashion trends. They receive many fashion magazines and frequently visit the local department stores to maintain their high level of fashion sense.

4.0 Services

No specific services are offered initially but may be added as the business expands.

5.0 THE INDUSTRY, COMPETITION AND MARKET

As attested by the myriad company-imprinted apparel, the need for quality custom embroidery and silk screening is a growing concern across the country, including Billings, Montana. More and more businesses are using employees to advertise products and services to friends, family, and the local community. From custom hats to embroidered jackets, the demand for quality products at a reasonable price is ever present.

The T-Shirt Shop will offer a wide variety of custom clothing, from the traditional polo to embroidered denim jackets. The T-Shirt Shop will capitalize on the increasing demand for embroidered corporate logos by offering a complete variety of clothing articles and having a fashion-forward, quality-concerned staff. The sections that follow will identify the T-Shirt Shop's strength in the local market, and will present the local competition.

5.1 Industry Definition

The T-Shirt Shop will offer the latest fashion trends along with customizable embroidery and screen-printing. Although the apparel industry in Billings varies greatly from store to store, The T-Shirt Shop's owner and employees have the experience to offer new and exciting things to the community.

Self-promotion by businesses has led to an increased demand for customized clothing. Because there is only one local business offering these services, there is demand for another custom embroidery store that offers new and exciting fashion ideas.

The T-Shirt Shop will compete in the retail apparel marketing industry, as well as the custom apparel market. According to the Department Store Inventory Price Index, department store retail sales are increasing at a rate of 3% annually, and the trend is expected to continue through 2010 (Source: http://www.bls.gov/cpi/#data).

5.2 Primary Competitors

The T-Shirt Shop will specialize in custom embroidery and silk screening for businesses and the general public. Although they will sell a wide variety of fashion items, the vast majority of apparel sales will be associated with some sort of customization of the apparel. With that in mind, The T-Shirt Shop only has one competitor in the greater Billings, Montana area: All Color Embroidery Service, located at 2625 Overland Avenue, Unit A. All Color Embroidery Service offers custom embroidery/silk screening, and employs 7 people. The company advertises in the local paper, the *Billings Gazette*, and has a listing in the Yellow Pages.

-12-

The T-Shirt Shop will offer many of the same products as the All Color Embroidery Service; however, The T-Shirt Shop will have cutting-edge trends for the fashion-forward citizens of Billings. This will be a distinct, competitive advantage for The T-Shirt Shop .

5.3 Market Size

Billings, nicknamed the Magic City, is located in Yellowstone County and is the county seat. It lies in south central Montana, east of Bozeman, along Interstate 90 on the banks of the Yellowstone River. The city is also near Bighorn National Recreation Area. Today, Billings, population 101,000 (est. 2008), is the state's largest city and an agricultural, retail and business center. Attractions include the downtown historic district and the J.K. Ralston Cabin on the Rocky Mountain College campus. Montana State University also has a campus in Billings

Follows is a list of the top five Montana cities that includes population, 10-year change, and size ranking in the state.

(Source: http://eire.census.gov/popest/archives/place/SC10K-T3.txt)

1. Billings, MT
Population: 92,988
Base: 81,469
Change: 11,519
Change %: 14.1

2. Missoula, MT
Population: 58,460
Base: 48,430
Change: 10,030
Change %: 20.7

3. Great Falls, MT
Population: 56,340
Base: 55,376
Change: 964
Change %: 1.7

4. Butte-Silver Bow
Population: 33,325
Base: 33,252
Change: 73
Change %: 0.2

5. Bozeman, MT
Population: 30,723
Base: 22,712
Change: 8,011
Change %: 35.3

5.4 Market Growth

With the increased need for businesses to become more efficient, advertising through apparel is becoming one of the most economical ways for businesses to get their name out. As this trend continues, and self-promotion through customization of apparel becomes even more prevalent, The T-Shirt Shop will experience rapid growth.

5.5 Customer Profile

The T-Shirt Shop's customers will vary from businesses seeking to promote themselves to average citizens who want something special to wear. The T-Shirt Shop will not segregate its marketing efforts; however, the company will concentrate on corporate customers.

Corporate customers will be targeted with bulk discounts. This will undercut the competition and will generate an immediate demand for custom apparel. The T-Shirt Shop will also target traffic in the mall with a wide variety of fashion items and customizable embroidery. The T-Shirt Shop will develop a relationship with the citizens of Billings by meeting their corporate and personal needs.

6.0 FINANCIAL PLANS

The T-Shirt Shop has two marketing objectives it will follow in its first three years of operations. As market conditions change, these objectives will be reviewed and modified accordingly. Their objectives are as follows:

1. The T-Shirt Shop will strive to become the leader in providing custom apparel for all businesses in the greater Billings, Montana area.

2. The T-Shirt Shop will strive to provide the highest quality products and the best service to all citizens in Billings. When people think of custom embroidery and silk screening, they will think of The T-Shirt Shop

6.1 Competitive Advantage

The T-Shirt Shop has two different target markets, and will use two different strategies to build their customer base. Their target markets include:

-14-

1. Corporate accounts

2. Consumer accounts (general populous)

Corporations are the major source of business for custom embroidery. They purchase hats, shirts, pants, and myriad other articles of clothing for their employees, as well as for their customers. They purchase goods during all seasons, and are a recurring source of revenue for suppliers of custom apparel.

Consumers purchase custom apparel for many reasons—hats with local team names, softball uniforms with numbers and lettering, shirts with family names on them, and so on. The T-Shirt Shop will supply the community with a source of custom apparel for all occasions.

The annual retail clothing market in Billings is $306 million dollars. Of that, it is estimated that $3.2 million is spent on custom apparel for businesses and consumers. Approximately fifty percent (50%) of that is paid to non-local suppliers. The T-Shirt Shop has a distinct opportunity to acquire many of the consumers who have been purchasing from outside vendors. These statistics were provided by the Association of Retail Marketers.

6.2 Pricing

The T-Shirt Shop will use a market penetration pricing strategy. Because there is only one local competitor, The T-Shirt Shop will begin business with prices lower than the competition. This initial pricing strategy will provide immediate results and will provide the catalyst to acquire many corporate accounts. This pricing strategy is sound because of the ability to receive discounts on bulk orders. Rather than maintaining basic pricing for corporate customers and pocketing the extra profits, The T-Shirt Shop will pass on these savings to their corporate customers. This will build a solid relationship between The T-Shirt Shop and their newly acquired corporate clients. As The T-Shirt Shop builds its business, prices will be adjusted according to demand and the environment.

The T-Shirt Shop will also offer discounts for bulk purchases to their walk-in traffic; however, these discounts will not completely reflect the discounts received by The T-Shirt Shop from its suppliers. The consumers will get quality products at competitive prices.

The T-Shirt Shop will receive a fifty percent (50%) mark-up on its corporate sales, and a sixty percent (60%) mark-up on its retail sales to walk-in traffic. These margins are very competitive in the retail industry, and are the most competitive in the custom embroidery market in Billings.

6.3 Distribution Channels

All distribution will be via a direct channel. All products and services will be purchased by The T-Shirt Shop from its suppliers and will be passed through to the customers.

-15-

6.4 Promotional Plan

The T-Shirt Shop will market itself and its products to the community of Billings in a variety of ways:

Newspaper advertisements: Introductory ads that identify location and type of business services will run weekly in the *Billings Gazette*.

Radio advertising: Ms. Marx has developed several radio spots that will air on the local radio stations during drive time and the local news.

Direct mail: The T-Shirt Shop will direct mail local businesses in order to identify themselves, convey products and services they provide, and offer the special pass-through pricing available to business customers.

Signage: The T-Shirt Shop will be provided with a sign at their location in the Rimrock Mall that will direct customers to their business.

The annual advertising budget for the T-Shirt Shop is as follows:

Print Media: $5,000

Radio: $6,250

Direct Mail: $3,750

6.5 Feedback

The T-Shirt Shop will measure success in many ways; specifically, sales by item type, gross sales, and customer satisfaction. They will monitor inventory to ensure proper stock is always maintained, and by doing so, will identify key items that need to be expanded. This will ensure complete customer satisfaction. Sales will measure their advertising success. Ms. Marx will stay abreast of sales trends and will increase marketing efforts as trends develop. Customer satisfaction will be measured through customer service surveys. Surveys, with questions about customer satisfaction, will be provided with all delivered goods. Returned surveys will be used to measure overall satisfaction, price sensitivity, and product quality. In addition, surveys will be used to identify customer concerns and product focus.

7.0 OPERATING PLAN

The T-Shirt Shop will lease space in the Rimrock Mall, Montana's largest shopping destination. The mall is located at 300 S. 24th St. West, Billings, MT 59102. The space will be 1,140 square feet, with 400 square feet being used for machinery. The location within the mall is one spot from center court. The space leases for $30,000 per year, plus $5.25 per square foot for maintenance, insurance, and promotional fees. The lease will be signed for three years at a cost of $3,000 per month.

7.1 Location

The location in the Rimrock Mall will deliver daily traffic from passers-by. Also, the mall is centrally located and convenient for all businesses. The mall is Montana's largest shopping destination, with over 85 specialty shops and three anchor stores: Dillard's, JCPenney, and Herberger's. The mall receives an average of 24,000 shoppers daily.

[Insert photograph of location]

7.2 Facility

The T-Shirt Shop needs a location that is central to all of their business customers, provides enough space for their equipment, and allows enough room for a sales floor. The area identified in the Rimrock Mall fits all of these requirements. The facility has been sectioned by a previous renter in the proportions necessary for The T-Shirt Shop to begin business. Minor repairs, maintenance, and decorating will provide the finishing touches on the establishment. The location will be leased for an initial three-year term.

7.3 Operating Equipment

In order for the T-Shirt Shop to begin business, Ms. Marx needs to secure multiple items that will allow them to perform their business objectives. Follows is a list, with prices, of the initial start-up equipment:

1. Press $25,000

2. Silk Screening Equipment $45,000

3. Cash Register $5,000

4. Furniture and Fixtures $5,000

5. Office Supplies $1,000

6. Delivery Van $18,000

7. Sewing Machine $3,000

The delivery van and minor equipment will be purchased in Billings from local businesses. The press and silk screening equipment will be purchased from a national distributor. Ms. Marx and Ms. Nelson will complete all minor repairs and decorating.

7.4 Suppliers and Vendors

The T-Shirt Shop will acquire their entire inventory through national distributors. By buying in bulk, Ms. Marx will negotiate the best pricing for all of her purchases. Follows is a list of nationally recognized distributors that the T-Shirt Shop will utilize:

- American Apparel - http://americanapparel.net/products.html

- EZ Shirt: - http://www.ezshirt.com/T-Shirts/t-shirts.html

- Corporate Apparel Wholesale - http://www.cawholesale.com/home/products

7.5 Personnel Plan

The T-Shirt Shop will be owned and operated by Jan Marx. She will employ Paula Nelson, a veteran of retail and fashion marketing in Billings, and two part-time college students. Ms. Marx will handle all administrative tasks, including payroll and bookkeeping. Ms. Nelson and Ms. Marx will share in the ordering and displaying of products. All four employees will act as sales staff and will share in the duties of operating the machinery and fulfilling orders.

7.6 General Operations

The T-Shirt Shop will maintain a regular work schedule with the exception of holidays as dictated by the mall hours. The store will be open from 10 a.m. to 9 p.m. Monday through Friday, 10 a.m. to 7 p.m. Saturdays, and 12 p.m. to 6 p.m. on Sundays. As the need arises, Ms. Marx will work additional hours to fulfill orders.

The T-Shirt Shop will follow all federal, state, and local regulations regarding OSHA standards and employee-related rules. No employee under the age of 18 will be allowed to operate the heavy equipment.

8.0 MANAGEMENT, ORGANIZATION & OWNERSHIP

The T-Shirt Shop will be owned and operated by Jan Marx. Paula Nelson will be the manager. Both have many years experience in retail marketing and bring different points of view to the business. They each have superior visual merchandising skills, as well as a vast knowledge of leading-edge fashion sense. Ms. Marx has extensive training in retail management, and Ms. Nelson has a degree in visual merchandising.

8.1 Management/Principals

Jan Marx has been working in retail marketing for 16 years. She studied business management at the University of Montana, Billings, and joined the Management Training Program at JCPenney immediately after graduation. After two years of training in the Children's and Home departments, Ms. Marx was appointed Merchandising Manager for the Junior's department at the JCPenney in Columbus, Montana. She worked there for eight years, exceeding all goals and expectations, and was offered a promotion to Merchandising Manager of the Women's department at the JCPenney in the Rimrock Mall, Billings, MT. She has been employed there for the last six years.

Paula Nelson received her undergraduate degree in Visual Merchandising from August and Lowes College in Big Horn, Montana. She moved with her husband to Billings four years ago and began her career as the Visual Merchandising Manager at the Dillard's store in the Rimrock Mall.

8.2 Organizational Structure

The T-Shirt Shop will be owned and operated as a sole proprietorship by Jan Marx. She will handle all administrative tasks, including payroll and bookkeeping. Ms. Nelson and Ms. Marx will share in the ordering and displaying of products. All four employees will act as sales staff and will share in the duties of operating the machinery and fulfilling orders.

9.0 GOALS AND STRATEGIES

The T-Shirt Shop has the opportunity, through its pricing strategy, to gain a large market share in the greater Billings area. The following sections will identify the specific goals of the business, as well as future goals.

9.1 Business Goals

The T-Shirt Shop has the following sales and income goals for its first three years in operation:

1. Net sales of at least $488,000 in year one, $500,000 in year two, and $525,000 in year three.

2. Net income of at least $85,000 in its first year, $95,000 in year two, and $105,000 in year three.

The following report shows the projected sales and income for the T-Shirt Shop in its first three years in operation:

Profit & Loss Statement

For years ending December - 2008, 2009, 2010			
	Year 1	Year 2	Year 3
Income	488,800	508,352	528,684
Less COGS:			
Material	232,180	241,467	251,125
Total COGS	232,180	241,467	251,125
Gross profit	256,620	266,885	277,559
Operating expenses:			
Salaries & Wages	66,240	66,240	66,240
Lease	36,000	36,000	36,000
Advertising	15,000	15,000	15,000
Utilities	9,000	9,000	9,000
Telephone	2,400	2,400	2,400
Insurance	3,600	3,600	3,600
Repairs & Maintenance	2,100	2,100	2,100
Supplies	3,600	3,600	3,600
Bad debts	6,354	6,609	6,873
Amortization	200	200	200
Depreciation	19,914	19,914	19,914
Total operating expenses	164,409	164,663	164,927
Operating income	92,211	102,222	112,632
Interest expense	6,353	5,084	4,295
Net income	85,858	97,138	108,337

-20-

9.2 Keys to Success

The T-Shirt Shop has identified two critical keys to the success of the business. The company must develop a strong relationship with area businesses, capturing major accounts rapidly. The other key is developing awareness within the city.

The T-Shirt Shop must acquire major accounts rapidly. Through the use of direct mail, The T-Shirt Shop will get its name in front of decision makers and purchasers throughout the community. These direct mail pieces will bring awareness to the business, and will inform potential customers about the savings they will receive by shopping at The T-Shirt Shop.

The T-Shirt Shop will bring awareness to the business through radio and print advertising. It will utilize these mediums in order to identify the business as a major player in the Billings area. Local customers will think of The T-Shirt Shop when they think of silk screening and embroidery.

9.3 Future Plans

The T-Shirt Shop will establish itself as the leader in screen-printing and embroidery in the greater Billings, Montana, area. As demand increases, Ms. Marx plans on expanding to additional product lines, and possibly a larger location.

10.0 FINANCIAL ASSUMPTIONS

This section summarizes the financial assumptions used in creating the projected financials. The financials are based on 3 main assumptions. They are:

1. Jan Marx will initially invest $30,000 of her own funds

2. The business will open its doors for business on January 1, 2008

3. A $40,000 start-up loan and a $20,000 line-of-credit are established with a local bank

11.0 APPENDIX

This section contains the following reports and supporting documentation:

- Income Projection
- Expense Projection
- Profit & Loss
- Balance Sheet
- Cash Plan
- Ratio Analysis

-22-

Income Projection - Year 1

Income Category	Jan	Feb	Mar	Apr	May	Jun	Jul	Aug	Sep	Oct	Nov	Dec	Year 1
Corporate Sales	30000	30100	30200	30300	30400	30500	30600	30700	30800	30900	31000	31100	366600
Retail Sales	10000	10033	10067	10100	10133	10167	10200	10233	10267	10300	10333	10367	122200
Total Income	40000	40133	40267	40400	40533	40667	40800	40933	41067	41200	41333	41467	488800

Income Projection - Year 2

Income Category	Jan	Feb	Mar	Apr	May	Jun	Jul	Aug	Sep	Oct	Nov	Dec	Year 2
Corporate Sales	31200	31304	31408	31512	31616	31720	31824	31928	32032	32136	32240	32344	381264
Retail Sales	10400	10435	10469	10504	10539	10573	10608	10643	10677	10712	10747	10781	127088
Total Income	41600	41739	41877	42016	42155	42293	42432	42571	42709	42848	42987	43125	508352

Income Projection - Year 3

Income Category	Jan	Feb	Mar	Apr	May	Jun	Jul	Aug	Sep	Oct	Nov	Dec	Year 3
Corporate Sales	32448	32556	32664	32772	32881	32989	33097	33205	33313	33421	33530	33638	396514
Retail Sales	10816	10852	10888	10924	10960	10996	11032	11068	11104	11140	11177	11213	132170
Total Income	43264	43408	43552	43696	43841	43985	44129	44273	44417	44561	44707	44851	528684

Expense Projection - Year 1

Expense Category	Jan	Feb	Mar	Apr	May	Jun	Jul	Aug	Sep	Oct	Nov	Dec	Year 1
Salaries & Wages	5520	5520	5520	5520	5520	5520	5520	5520	5520	5520	5520	5520	66240
Lease	3000	3000	3000	3000	3000	3000	3000	3000	3000	3000	3000	3000	36000
Advertising	1250	1250	1250	1250	1250	1250	1250	1250	1250	1250	1250	1250	15000
Utilities	750	750	750	750	750	750	750	750	750	750	750	750	9000
Telephone	200	200	200	200	200	200	200	200	200	200	200	200	2400
Insurance	300	300	300	300	300	300	300	300	300	300	300	300	3600
Repairs & Maintenance	175	175	175	175	175	175	175	175	175	175	175	175	2100
Supplies	300	300	300	300	300	300	300	300	300	300	300	300	3600
Total Expenses	11495	11495	11495	11495	11495	11495	11495	11495	11495	11495	11495	11495	137940

Expense Projection - Year 2

Expense Category	Jan	Feb	Mar	Apr	May	Jun	Jul	Aug	Sep	Oct	Nov	Dec	Year 2
Salaries & Wages	5520	5520	5520	5520	5520	5520	5520	5520	5520	5520	5520	5520	66240
Lease	3000	3000	3000	3000	3000	3000	3000	3000	3000	3000	3000	3000	36000
Advertising	1250	1250	1250	1250	1250	1250	1250	1250	1250	1250	1250	1250	15000
Utilities	750	750	750	750	750	750	750	750	750	750	750	750	9000
Telephone	200	200	200	200	200	200	200	200	200	200	200	200	2400
Insurance	300	300	300	300	300	300	300	300	300	300	300	300	3600
Repairs & Maintenance	175	175	175	175	175	175	175	175	175	175	175	175	2100
Supplies	300	300	300	300	300	300	300	300	300	300	300	300	3600
Total Expenses	11495	11495	11495	11495	11495	11495	11495	11495	11495	11495	11495	11495	137940

Expense Projection - Year 3

Expense Category	Jan	Feb	Mar	Apr	May	Jun	Jul	Aug	Sep	Oct	Nov	Dec	Year 3
Salaries & Wages	5520	5520	5520	5520	5520	5520	5520	5520	5520	5520	5520	5520	66240
Lease	3000	3000	3000	3000	3000	3000	3000	3000	3000	3000	3000	3000	36000
Advertising	1250	1250	1250	1250	1250	1250	1250	1250	1250	1250	1250	1250	15000
Utilities	750	750	750	750	750	750	750	750	750	750	750	750	9000
Telephone	200	200	200	200	200	200	200	200	200	200	200	200	2400
Insurance	300	300	300	300	300	300	300	300	300	300	300	300	3600
Repairs & Maintenance	175	175	175	175	175	175	175	175	175	175	175	175	2100
Supplies	300	300	300	300	300	300	300	300	300	300	300	300	3600
Total Expenses	11495	11495	11495	11495	11495	11495	11495	11495	11495	11495	11495	11495	137940

Profit & Loss - Year 1

	Jan	Feb	Mar	Apr	May	Jun	Jul	Aug	Sep	Oct	Nov	Dec	Year 1
Income	40000	40133	40267	40400	40533	40667	40800	40933	41067	41200	41333	41467	488800
Less COGS:													
Material	19000	19063	19127	19190	19253	19317	19380	19443	19507	19570	19633	19697	232180
Total COGS	19000	19063	19127	19190	19253	19317	19380	19443	19507	19570	19633	19697	232180
Gross profit	21000	21070	21140	21210	21280	21350	21420	21490	21560	21630	21700	21770	256620
Operating expenses:													
Salaries & Wages	5520	5520	5520	5520	5520	5520	5520	5520	5520	5520	5520	5520	66240
Lease	3000	3000	3000	3000	3000	3000	3000	3000	3000	3000	3000	3000	36000
Advertising	1250	1250	1250	1250	1250	1250	1250	1250	1250	1250	1250	1250	15000
Utilities	750	750	750	750	750	750	750	750	750	750	750	750	9000
Telephone	200	200	200	200	200	200	200	200	200	200	200	200	2400
Insurance	300	300	300	300	300	300	300	300	300	300	300	300	3600
Repairs & Maintenance	175	175	175	175	175	175	175	175	175	175	175	175	2100
Supplies	300	300	300	300	300	300	300	300	300	300	300	300	3600
Bad debts	520	522	523	525	527	529	530	532	534	536	537	539	6354
Amortization	17	17	17	17	17	17	17	17	17	17	17	17	204
Depreciation	1660	1660	1660	1660	1660	1660	1660	1660	1660	1660	1660	1660	19920
Total operating expenses	13692	13694	13695	13697	13699	13701	13702	13704	13706	13708	13709	13711	164418
Operating income	7308	7376	7445	7513	7581	7649	7718	7786	7854	7922	7991	8059	92202
Interest expense	521	640	618	594	570	545	520	494	472	466	459	453	6352
Net income	6787	6736	6827	6919	7011	7104	7198	7292	7382	7456	7532	7606	85850

Profit & Loss - Year 2

	Jan	Feb	Mar	Apr	May	Jun	Jul	Aug	Sep	Oct	Nov	Dec	Year 2
Income	41600	41739	41877	42016	42155	42293	42432	42571	42709	42848	42987	43125	508352
Less COGS:													
Material	19760	19826	19892	19958	20024	20089	20155	20221	20287	20353	20419	20484	241468
Total COGS	19760	19826	19892	19958	20024	20089	20155	20221	20287	20353	20419	20484	241468
Gross profit	21840	21913	21985	22058	22131	22204	22277	22350	22422	22495	22568	22641	266884
Operating expenses:													
Salaries & Wages	5520	5520	5520	5520	5520	5520	5520	5520	5520	5520	5520	5520	66240
Lease	3000	3000	3000	3000	3000	3000	3000	3000	3000	3000	3000	3000	36000
Advertising	1250	1250	1250	1250	1250	1250	1250	1250	1250	1250	1250	1250	15000
Utilities	750	750	750	750	750	750	750	750	750	750	750	750	9000
Telephone	200	200	200	200	200	200	200	200	200	200	200	200	2400
Insurance	300	300	300	300	300	300	300	300	300	300	300	300	3600
Repairs & Maintenance	175	175	175	175	175	175	175	175	175	175	175	175	2100
Supplies	300	300	300	300	300	300	300	300	300	300	300	300	3600
Bad debts	541	543	544	546	548	550	552	553	555	557	559	561	6609
Amortization	17	17	17	17	17	17	17	17	17	17	17	17	204
Depreciation	1660	1660	1660	1660	1660	1660	1660	1660	1660	1660	1660	1660	19920
Total operating expenses	13713	13715	13716	13718	13720	13722	13724	13725	13727	13729	13731	13733	164673
Operating income	8127	8198	8269	8340	8411	8482	8553	8625	8695	8766	8837	8908	102211
Interest expense	447	440	434	427	421	414	407	401	394	387	380	533	5085
Net income	7680	7758	7835	7913	7990	8068	8146	8224	8301	8379	8457	8375	97126

Profit & Loss - Year 3

	Jan	Feb	Mar	Apr	May	Jun	Jul	Aug	Sep	Oct	Nov	Dec	Year 3
Income	43264	43408	43552	43696	43841	43985	44129	44273	44417	44561	44707	44851	528684
Less COGS:													
Material	20550	20619	20687	20756	20825	20893	20961	21030	21098	21167	21236	21304	251126
Total COGS	20550	20619	20687	20756	20825	20893	20961	21030	21098	21167	21236	21304	251126
Gross profit	22714	22789	22865	22940	23016	23092	23168	23243	23319	23394	23471	23547	277558
Operating expenses:													
Salaries & Wages	5520	5520	5520	5520	5520	5520	5520	5520	5520	5520	5520	5520	66240
Lease	3000	3000	3000	3000	3000	3000	3000	3000	3000	3000	3000	3000	36000
Advertising	1250	1250	1250	1250	1250	1250	1250	1250	1250	1250	1250	1250	15000
Utilities	750	750	750	750	750	750	750	750	750	750	750	750	9000
Telephone	200	200	200	200	200	200	200	200	200	200	200	200	2400
Insurance	300	300	300	300	300	300	300	300	300	300	300	300	3600
Repairs & Maintenance	175	175	175	175	175	175	175	175	175	175	175	175	2100
Supplies	300	300	300	300	300	300	300	300	300	300	300	300	3600
Bad debts	562	564	566	568	570	572	574	576	577	579	581	583	6872
Amortization	17	17	17	17	17	17	17	17	17	17	17	17	204
Depreciation	1660	1660	1660	1660	1660	1660	1660	1660	1660	1660	1660	1660	19920
Total operating expenses	13734	13736	13738	13740	13742	13744	13746	13748	13749	13751	13753	13755	164936
Operating income	8980	9053	9127	9200	9274	9348	9422	9495	9570	9643	9718	9792	112622
Interest expense	420	409	398	387	375	364	353	341	330	318	306	294	4295
Net income	8560	8644	8729	8813	8899	8984	9069	9154	9240	9325	9412	9498	108327

Balance Sheet - Year 1

	Jan	Feb	Mar	Apr	May	Jun	Jul	Aug	Sep	Oct	Nov	Dec	Year 1
Assets:													
Current assets:													
Cash	500	500	500	500	500	500	500	1179	4317	7523	10797	14139	14139
Accounts receivable (net)	25480	25565	25650	25735	25820	25905	25990	26074	26160	26244	26329	26414	26414
Inventory	25000	25000	25000	25000	25000	25000	25000	25000	25000	25000	25000	25000	25000
Total current assets	50980	51065	51150	51235	51320	51405	51490	52253	55477	58767	62126	65553	65553
Fixed assets (net)	99340	97681	96021	94362	92702	91043	89383	87724	86064	84405	82745	81086	81086
Other assets (net)	983	967	950	933	917	900	883	867	850	833	817	800	800
Total assets	151303	149713	148121	146530	144939	143348	141756	140844	142391	144005	145688	147439	147439
Liabilities and equity:													
Current liabilities:													
Accounts payable	19000	19063	19127	19190	19253	19317	19380	19443	19507	19570	19633	19697	19697
Line of credit	18867	16333	13714	11009	8218	5340	2374	0	0	0	0	0	0
Notes payable	0	0	0	0	0	0	0	0	0	0	0	24500	24500
Current maturities	10690	10764	10839	10915	10991	11067	11145	11222	11301	11380	11459	11539	11539
Total current liabilities	48557	46160	43680	41114	38462	35724	32899	30665	30808	30950	31092	55736	55736
Long-term liabilities (net)	70959	70027	69089	68144	67193	66235	65270	64299	63321	62336	61344	35845	35845
Total liabilities	119516	116187	112769	109258	105655	101959	98169	94964	94129	93286	92436	91581	91581
Equity	31787	33526	35352	37272	39284	41389	43587	45880	48262	50719	53252	55858	55858
Total liabilities and equity	151303	149713	148121	146530	144939	143348	141756	140844	142391	144005	145688	147439	147439

Balance Sheet - Year 2

	Jan	Feb	Mar	Apr	May	Jun	Jul	Aug	Sep	Oct	Nov	Dec	Year 2
Assets:													
Current assets:													
Cash	17550	21031	24583	28205	31899	35664	39500	43407	47385	51433	55553	58492	58492
Accounts receivable (net)	26499	26588	26676	26764	26853	26941	27029	27118	27206	27294	27383	27471	27471
Inventory	25000	25000	25000	25000	25000	25000	25000	25000	25000	25000	25000	25000	25000
Total current assets	69049	72619	76259	79969	83752	87605	91529	95525	99591	103727	107936	110963	110963
Fixed assets (net)	79426	77767	76107	74448	72788	71129	69469	67810	66150	64490	62831	61171	61171
Other assets (net)	783	767	750	733	717	700	683	667	650	633	617	600	600
Total assets	149258	151153	153116	155150	157257	159434	161681	164002	166391	168850	171384	172734	172734
Liabilities and equity:													
Current liabilities:													
Accounts payable	19760	19826	19892	19958	20024	20089	20155	20221	20287	20353	20419	20484	20484
Line of credit	0	0	0	0	0	0	0	0	0	0	0	0	0
Notes payable	24500	24500	24500	24500	24500	24500	24500	24500	24500	24500	24500	0	0
Current maturities	11620	11701	11783	11865	11948	12032	12116	12201	12287	12373	12460	19968	19968
Total current liabilities	55880	56027	56175	56323	56472	56621	56771	56922	57074	57226	57379	40452	40452
Long-term liabilities (net)	34839	33826	32806	31779	30745	29703	28654	27598	26534	25463	24384	39285	39285
Total liabilities	90719	89853	88981	88102	87217	86324	85425	84520	83608	82689	81763	79737	79737
Equity	58539	61300	64135	67048	70040	73110	76256	79482	82783	86161	89621	92997	92997
Total liabilities and equity	149258	151153	153116	155150	157257	159434	161681	164002	166391	168850	171384	172734	172734

Balance Sheet - Year 3

	Jan	Feb	Mar	Apr	May	Jun	Jul	Aug	Sep	Oct	Nov	Dec	Year 3
Assets:													
Current assets:													
Cash	62104	65788	69547	73379	77285	81265	85319	89446	93648	97923	102272	106696	106696
Accounts receivable (net)	27559	27651	27743	27834	27927	28018	28110	28202	28294	28385	28478	28570	28570
Inventory	25000	25000	25000	25000	25000	25000	25000	25000	25000	25000	25000	25000	25000
Total current assets	114663	118439	122290	126213	130212	134283	138429	142648	146942	151308	155750	160266	160266
Fixed assets (net)	59512	57852	56193	54533	52874	51214	49555	47895	46236	44576	42917	41257	41257
Other assets (net)	583	567	550	533	517	500	483	467	450	433	417	400	400
Total assets	174758	176858	179033	181279	183603	185997	188467	191010	193628	196317	199084	201923	201923
Liabilities and equity:													
Current liabilities:													
Accounts payable	20550	20619	20687	20756	20825	20893	20961	21030	21098	21167	21235	21304	21304
Line of credit	0	0	0	0	0	0	0	0	0	0	0	0	0
Notes payable	0	0	0	0	0	0	0	0	0	0	0	4905	4905
Current maturities	20105	20244	20383	20524	20665	20808	20951	21096	21242	21388	21535	16780	16780
Total current liabilities	40655	40863	41070	41280	41490	41701	41912	42126	42340	42555	42772	42989	42989
Long-term liabilities (net)	37546	35794	34031	32255	30467	28667	26854	25029	23191	21340	19477	17601	17601
Total liabilities	78201	76657	75101	73535	71957	70368	68766	67155	65531	63895	62249	60590	60590
Equity	96557	100201	103932	107744	111646	115629	119701	123855	128097	132422	136835	141333	141333
Total liabilities and equity	174758	176858	179033	181279	183603	185997	188467	191010	193628	196317	199084	201923	201923

Cash Plan - Year 1

	Jan	Feb	Mar	Apr	May	Jun	Jul	Aug	Sep	Oct	Nov	Dec	Year 1
Cash receipts	14000	39527	39658	39790	39921	40053	40185	40316	40448	40580	40711	40843	456032
Operating cash expenses:													
Inventory purchases	25000	19000	19063	19127	19190	19253	19317	19380	19443	19507	19570	19633	237483
Other expenses	11495	11495	11495	11495	11495	11495	11495	11495	11495	11495	11495	11495	137940
Total operating cash exp.	36495	30495	30558	30622	30685	30748	30812	30875	30938	31002	31065	31128	375423
Cash from operations	-22495	9032	9100	9168	9236	9305	9373	9441	9510	9578	9646	9715	80609
Debt activities:													
Issuance of debt	0	0	0	0	0	0	0	0	0	0	0	0	0
Principal payments	-851	-857	-863	-869	-875	-881	-887	-894	-900	-906	-912	-919	-10614
Interest payments	-521	-640	-618	-594	-570	-545	-520	-494	-472	-466	-459	-453	-6352
Total debt activities	-1372	-1497	-1481	-1463	-1445	-1426	-1407	-1388	-1372	-1372	-1371	-1372	-16966
Net cash after debt service	-23867	7535	7619	7705	7791	7879	7966	8053	8138	8206	8275	8343	63643
Distributions	-5000	-5000	-5000	-5000	-5000	-5000	-5000	-5000	-5000	-5000	-5000	-5000	-60000
Change in cash	-28867	2534	2619	2705	2791	2878	2966	3053	3138	3206	3274	3342	3639
Beginning cash	10500	500	500	500	500	500	500	500	1179	4317	7523	10797	10500
Cash before borrowing	-18367	3034	3119	3205	3291	3378	3466	3553	4317	7523	10797	14139	14139
Line of credit activity	18867	-2534	-2619	-2705	-2791	-2878	-2966	-2374	0	0	0	0	0
Ending cash	500	500	500	500	500	500	500	1179	4317	7523	10797	14139	14139

NOTE: Line of credit
exceeded in Month 56

Cash Plan - Year 2

	Jan	Feb	Mar	Apr	May	Jun	Jul	Aug	Sep	Oct	Nov	Dec	Year 2
Cash receipts	40974	41108	41245	41381	41518	41655	41792	41929	42066	42202	42340	42476	500686
Operating cash expenses:													
Inventory purchases	19697	19760	19826	19892	19958	20024	20089	20155	20221	20287	20353	20419	240681
Other expenses	11495	11495	11495	11495	11495	11495	11495	11495	11495	11495	11495	11495	137940
Total operating cash exp.	31192	31255	31321	31387	31453	31519	31584	31650	31716	31782	31848	31914	378621
Cash from operations	9782	9853	9924	9994	10065	10136	10208	10279	10350	10420	10492	10562	122065
Debt activities:													
Issuance of debt	0	0	0	0	0	0	0	0	0	0	0	24000	24000
Principal payments	-925	-932	-938	-945	-951	-958	-965	-971	-978	-985	-992	-26091	-36631
Interest payments	-447	-440	-434	-427	-421	-414	-407	-401	-394	-387	-380	-533	-5085
Total debt activities	-1372	-1372	-1372	-1372	-1372	-1372	-1372	-1372	-1372	-1372	-1372	-2624	-17716
Net cash after debt service	8410	8481	8552	8622	8693	8764	8836	8907	8978	9048	9120	7938	104349
Distributions	-5000	-5000	-5000	-5000	-5000	-5000	-5000	-5000	-5000	-5000	-5000	-5000	-60000
Change in cash	3411	3481	3552	3623	3694	3765	3836	3907	3978	4049	4120	2939	44355
Beginning cash	14139	17550	21031	24583	28205	31899	35664	39500	43407	47385	51433	55553	14139
Cash before borrowing	17550	21031	24583	28206	31899	35664	39500	43407	47385	51434	55553	58492	58494
Line of credit activity	0	0	0	0	0	0	0	0	0	0	0	0	0
Ending cash	17550	21031	24583	28206	31899	35664	39500	43407	47385	51434	55553	58492	58492

NOTE: Line of credit exceeded in Month 56

Cash Plan - Year 3

	Jan	Feb	Mar	Apr	May	Jun	Jul	Aug	Sep	Oct	Nov	Dec	Year 3
Cash receipts	42613	42752	42894	43036	43179	43321	43464	43606	43748	43890	44033	44176	520712
Operating cash expenses:													
Inventory purchases	20484	20550	20619	20687	20756	20825	20893	20961	21030	21098	21167	21236	250306
Other expenses	11495	11495	11495	11495	11495	11495	11495	11495	11495	11495	11495	11495	137940
Total operating cash exp.	31979	32045	32114	32182	32251	32320	32388	32456	32525	32593	32662	32731	388246
Cash from operations	10634	10707	10780	10854	10928	11001	11076	11150	11223	11297	11371	11445	132466
Debt activities:													
Issuance of debt	0	0	0	0	0	0	0	0	0	0	0	0	0
Principal payments	-1602	-1613	-1624	-1635	-1646	-1658	-1669	-1681	-1692	-1704	-1716	-1728	-19968
Interest payments	-420	-409	-398	-387	-375	-364	-353	-341	-330	-318	-306	-294	-4295
Total debt activities	-2022	-2022	-2022	-2022	-2021	-2022	-2022	-2022	-2022	-2022	-2022	-2022	-24263
Net cash after debt service	8612	8685	8758	8832	8907	8979	9054	9128	9201	9275	9349	9423	108203
Distributions	-5000	-5000	-5000	-5000	-5000	-5000	-5000	-5000	-5000	-5000	-5000	-5000	-60000
Change in cash	3612	3685	3758	3832	3906	3980	4054	4128	4201	4275	4349	4424	48204
Beginning cash	58492	62104	65788	69547	73379	77285	81265	85319	89446	93648	97923	102272	58492
Cash before borrowing	62104	65789	69546	73379	77285	81265	85319	89447	93647	97923	102272	106696	106696
Line of credit activity	0	0	0	0	0	0	0	0	0	0	0	0	0
Ending cash	62104	65789	69546	73379	77285	81265	85319	89447	93647	97923	102272	106696	106696
NOTE: Line of credit													
exceeded in Month 56													

Ratio Analysis - Year 1

	Jan	Feb	Mar	Apr	May	Jun	Jul	Aug	Sep	Oct	Nov	Dec	Year 1
Profitability ratios:													
Gross profit margin	52.50%	52.50%	52.50%	52.50%	52.50%	52.50%	52.50%	52.50%	52.50%	52.50%	52.50%	52.50%	52.50%
Operating profit margin	18.27%	18.38%	18.49%	18.60%	18.70%	18.81%	18.92%	19.02%	19.13%	19.23%	19.33%	19.44%	18.86%
Net profit margin	16.97%	16.79%	16.96%	17.13%	17.30%	17.47%	17.64%	17.82%	17.98%	18.10%	18.22%	18.34%	17.57%
Return on equity	21.97%	20.63%	19.83%	19.06%	18.32%	17.61%	16.94%	16.30%	15.69%	15.07%	14.49%	13.94%	204.73%
Return on assets	5.06%	4.90%	5.00%	5.10%	5.20%	5.31%	5.41%	5.51%	5.55%	5.53%	5.52%	5.50%	63.55%
Liquidity ratios:													
Current ratio	1.05	1.11	1.17	1.25	1.33	1.44	1.57	1.70	1.80	1.90	2.00	1.18	1.18
Quick ratio (Acid-test)	0.54	0.56	0.60	0.64	0.68	0.74	0.81	0.89	0.99	1.09	1.19	0.73	0.73
Working capital ratio	0.06	0.12	0.19	0.25	0.32	0.39	0.46	0.53	0.60	0.68	0.75	0.24	0.02
Activity ratios:													
Accounts receivable days	29.40	29.40	29.40	29.40	29.40	29.40	29.40	29.40	29.40	29.40	29.40	29.40	29.93
Inventory days	39.47	39.34	39.21	39.08	38.95	38.83	38.70	38.57	38.45	38.32	38.20	38.08	38.76
Inventory turnover	0.76	0.76	0.77	0.77	0.77	0.77	0.78	0.78	0.78	0.78	0.79	0.79	9.29
Sales-to-assets	0.28	0.27	0.27	0.27	0.28	0.28	0.29	0.29	0.29	0.29	0.29	0.28	3.37
Leverage ratios:													
Debt-to-equity	3.76	3.47	3.19	2.93	2.69	2.46	2.25	2.07	1.95	1.84	1.74	1.64	1.64
Debt ratio	0.79	0.78	0.76	0.75	0.73	0.71	0.69	0.67	0.66	0.65	0.63	0.62	0.62
Times-interest (TI) earned:													
Operating income	7309	7377	7446	7514	7582	7650	7718	7786	7855	7923	7991	8060	92211
Interest expense (÷)	521	640	618	594	570	545	520	494	472	466	459	453	6353
TI earned ratio	14.03	11.53	12.05	12.65	13.30	14.04	14.84	15.76	16.64	17.00	17.41	17.79	14.51456

Ratio Analysis - Year 2

	Jan	Feb	Mar	Apr	May	Jun	Jul	Aug	Sep	Oct	Nov	Dec	Year 2
Profitability ratios:													
Gross profit margin	52.50%	52.50%	52.50%	52.50%	52.50%	52.50%	52.50%	52.50%	52.50%	52.50%	52.50%	52.50%	52.50%
Operating profit margin	19.54%	19.64%	19.75%	19.85%	19.96%	20.06%	20.16%	20.26%	20.36%	20.46%	20.56%	20.66%	20.11%
Net profit margin	18.46%	18.59%	18.71%	18.84%	18.96%	19.08%	19.20%	19.32%	19.44%	19.56%	19.68%	19.42%	19.11%
Return on equity	13.43%	12.95%	12.49%	12.07%	11.66%	11.27%	10.91%	10.56%	10.23%	9.92%	9.62%	9.17%	132.03%
Return on assets	5.48%	5.46%	5.44%	5.41%	5.39%	5.36%	5.33%	5.30%	5.26%	5.23%	5.20%	5.18%	63.96%
Liquidity ratios:													
Current ratio	1.24	1.30	1.36	1.42	1.48	1.55	1.61	1.68	1.74	1.81	1.88	2.74	2.74
Quick ratio (Acid-test)	0.79	0.85	0.91	0.98	1.04	1.11	1.17	1.24	1.31	1.38	1.45	2.13	2.13
Working capital ratio	0.32	0.40	0.48	0.56	0.65	0.73	0.82	0.91	1.00	1.09	1.18	1.64	0.14
Activity ratios:													
Accounts receivable days	29.40	29.40	29.40	29.40	29.40	29.40	29.40	29.40	29.40	29.40	29.40	29.40	29.93
Inventory days	37.96	37.83	37.70	37.58	37.46	37.33	37.21	37.09	36.97	36.85	36.73	36.61	37.27
Inventory turnover	0.79	0.79	0.80	0.80	0.80	0.80	0.81	0.81	0.81	0.81	0.82	0.82	9.66
Sales-to-assets	0.28	0.28	0.28	0.27	0.27	0.27	0.26	0.26	0.26	0.26	0.25	0.25	3.18
Leverage ratios:													
Debt-to-equity	1.55	1.47	1.39	1.31	1.25	1.18	1.12	1.06	1.01	0.96	0.91	0.86	0.86
Debt ratio	0.61	0.59	0.58	0.57	0.55	0.54	0.53	0.52	0.50	0.49	0.48	0.46	0.46
Times-interest (TI) earned:													
Operating income	8128	8199	8270	8341	8412	8483	8554	8625	8696	8767	8838	8909	102222
Interest expense $(\div)$	447	440	434	427	421	414	407	401	394	387	380	533	5084
TI earned ratio	18.18	18.63	19.06	19.53	19.98	20.49	21.02	21.51	22.07	22.65	23.26	16.71	20.106609

Ratio Analysis - Year 3

	Jan	Feb	Mar	Apr	May	Jun	Jul	Aug	Sep	Oct	Nov	Dec	Year 3
Profitability ratios:													
Gross profit margin	52.50%	52.50%	52.50%	52.50%	52.50%	52.50%	52.50%	52.50%	52.50%	52.50%	52.50%	52.50%	52.50%
Operating profit margin	20.76%	20.86%	20.96%	21.06%	21.16%	21.26%	21.35%	21.45%	21.55%	21.64%	21.74%	21.83%	21.30%
Net profit margin	19.79%	19.92%	20.04%	20.17%	20.30%	20.43%	20.55%	20.68%	20.80%	20.93%	21.05%	21.18%	20.49%
Return on equity	9.03%	8.79%	8.55%	8.33%	8.11%	7.91%	7.71%	7.52%	7.34%	7.16%	6.99%	6.83%	93.27%
Return on assets	5.17%	5.15%	5.13%	5.11%	5.08%	5.06%	5.03%	5.01%	4.98%	4.95%	4.92%	4.88%	60.41%
Liquidity ratios:													
Current ratio	2.82	2.90	2.98	3.06	3.14	3.22	3.30	3.39	3.47	3.56	3.64	3.73	3.73
Quick ratio (Acid-test)	2.21	2.29	2.37	2.45	2.54	2.62	2.71	2.79	2.88	2.97	3.06	3.15	3.15
Working capital ratio	1.71	1.79	1.86	1.94	2.02	2.10	2.19	2.27	2.36	2.44	2.53	2.61	0.22
Activity ratios:													
Accounts receivable days	29.40	29.40	29.40	29.40	29.40	29.40	29.40	29.40	29.40	29.40	29.40	29.40	29.93
Inventory days	36.50	36.37	36.25	36.13	36.02	35.90	35.78	35.66	35.55	35.43	35.32	35.20	35.84
Inventory turnover	0.82	0.82	0.83	0.83	0.83	0.84	0.84	0.84	0.84	0.85	0.85	0.85	10.05
Sales-to-assets	0.25	0.25	0.24	0.24	0.24	0.24	0.24	0.23	0.23	0.23	0.23	0.22	2.84
Leverage ratios:													
Debt-to-equity	0.81	0.77	0.72	0.68	0.64	0.61	0.57	0.54	0.51	0.48	0.45	0.43	0.43
Debt ratio	0.45	0.43	0.42	0.41	0.39	0.38	0.36	0.35	0.34	0.33	0.31	0.30	0.30
Times-interest (TI) earned:													
Operating income	8980	9054	9127	9201	9275	9349	9423	9497	9570	9644	9719	9793	112632
Interest expense ($\div$)	420	409	398	387	375	364	353	341	330	318	306	294	4295
TI earned ratio	21.38	22.14	22.93	23.78	24.73	25.68	26.69	27.85	29.00	30.33	31.76	33.31	26.223981

Index

W

BizFilings ℠

Whether you are just starting your business or you've been operating a business as a sole proprietorship or general partnership, you may be missing the benefits of forming your business as a limited liability company (LLC) or corporation. Often business owners think that forming a business as an LLC or corporation is too costly or too time-consuming. However, BizFilings makes the process easy.

BizFilings professionally forms LLCs, corporations, and nonprofits faster than anyone else, nationwide. Our rush service makes it possible to file a corporation or LLC in as little as 24 hours.

PROTECT YOUR ASSETS
LLCs and corporations are business entities that offer limited liability protection. They exist as a separate entity from their owners. Therefore, the owners cannot typically be held personally responsible for the debts and liabilities of the company.

GAIN TAX ADVANTAGES
Depending on the nature of your business, forming an LLC, standard corporation, or s corporation can provide tax advantages to a business owner and make it easier to track business-related, tax-deductible expenses.

GET IMMEDIATE SAVINGS
Save $20 off any basic formation package; $40 off any standard formation package; and $60 off any complete formation package.

When placing your order online, use the link below. Your discount will be applied automatically in BizFilings' order form. If you prefer to order by phone, please call 800-981-7183. Please remember to mention the 'Toolkit Tax Guide' when ordering to receive your discount.

WWW.BIZFILINGS.COM/TOOLKIT

BUSINESS OWNER'S TOOLKIT
Total Know-How For Small Business

FREE TOOLS
With an emphasis on problem solving, Business Owner's Toolkit™ offers more than 5,000 pages of free cost-cutting tips, step-by-step checklists, real life case studies, startup advice, and business templates.

FREE MEMBERSHIP
Get immediate access to helpful content, webinars, templates, and checklists; receive important news and information that will help you keep up-to-date; and receive special discounts and rewards.

FREE LAPTOP
Members are automatically entered into monthly drawings for a laptop computer .

The New York Times:
"When it comes to sorting through financial information... Business Owner's Toolkit has templates to help examine financial issues as well as other model business documents, checklists and government forms."

PC Computing:
"... a Top Five Small Business Site."

Entrepreneur Magazine:
"... a Top 100 Supersite for Entrepreneurs."

The Wall Street Journal:
"... and Business Tools, a nicely organized library, provides business forms, checklists, and best of all, financial worksheets that can be downloaded."

SIGN UP TODAY! ▶ ▶ ▶ WWW.TOOLKIT.COM